WELCOME TO SOYLANDIA

A volume in the series

Cornell Series on Land: New Perspectives on Territory, Development, and Environment

Edited by Wendy Wolford, Nancy Lee Peluso, and Michael Goldman

A list of titles in this series is available at cornellpress.cornell.edu.

WELCOME TO SOYLANDIA

Transnational Farmers in the
Brazilian Cerrado

Andrew Ofstehage

CORNELL UNIVERSITY PRESS   **ITHACA AND LONDON**

First published 2025 by Cornell University Press

Library of Congress Cataloging-in-Publication Data

Names: Ofstehage, Andrew, 1984– author.
Title: Welcome to Soylandia : transnational farmers in the Brazilian Cerrado /
    Andrew Ofstehage.
Description: Ithaca : Cornell University Press, 2025. | Series: Cornell series
    on land: new perspectives on territory, development, and environment |
    Includes bibliographical references and index.
Identifiers: LCCN 2024029691 (print) | LCCN 2024029692 (ebook) |
    ISBN 9781501780240 (hardcover) | ISBN 9781501780233 (paperback) |
    ISBN 9781501780226 (epub) | ISBN 9781501780257 (pdf)
Subjects: LCSH: Soybean farmers—Brazil. | Agriculture—Social aspects—Brazil. |
    Agriculture—Economic aspects—Brazil. | Americans—Agriculture—Brazil.
Classification: LCC HD8039.F32 B62 2025 (print) | LCC HD8039.F32 (ebook) |
    DDC 338.10981—dc23/eng/20240906
LC record available at https://lccn.loc.gov/2024029691
LC ebook record available at https://lccn.loc.gov/2024029692

Contents

Preface

THE FARMER'S PROBLEM

As a young adult I thumbed through my father's farmer magazines like *Successful Farming* and *Progressive Farmer* and came across stories about young midwestern farmers in Brazil. I read them curiously. Years later, conversations with my mentor Rudi Colloredo-Mansfeld encouraged me to think of these migrant farmers as a viable and interesting research subject. I had recently completed a study of quinoa farmers and middlewomen in Bolivia where I found that soil, altitude, reciprocal relations, and social values of work played important roles in how the quinoa boom unfolded. To me, the soy boom of South America, particularly large-scale foreign farmers, posed a challenge. I wanted to know how these large-scale, industrial, transnational farmers adjusted to different soils, pests, and climates in Brazil; how they created community there; and whether they did all of this for profit or for something else. But mostly I was driven by curiosity. How can we make sense of this movement of farmers from the US Midwest to Brazil? Is there something wrong with rural America that made farmers look for land elsewhere?

For the rural sociologist Michael Bell, the 1980s farm crisis never really ended but rather is part of a perpetual farm crisis of a decreasing number of farms and farm consolidation. This "farmer's problem" places farmers in direct competition with each other for the most basic unit of agricultural production: land. Common solutions to the farmer's problem include buying, renting, and controlling more land; scaling up; and reducing costs per productive unit. Scaling up industrialized, monocultural, and simplified agricultural landscapes has transformed integrated crop and livestock farms into fencerow-to-fencerow corn and soybeans and concentrated animal feeding operations (CAFOs). There is too much land for a few and not enough land for many.

The farmer and activist George Naylor (2017) succinctly describes the state of twenty-first-century farming in the United States:

> The typical farmer in the Midwest owns probably only ten percent of the land they farm; the rest is cash rented. Landlords often take the highest rent bid from the biggest, most industrialized farmer. Through the years, farmers have invested in bigger and bigger livestock facilities, only to lose money, watch their facilities become "obsolete," and abandon their beneficial crop rotations. Today, almost all the pigs, chickens,

and even market cattle in the United States are owned by corporations and fed in giant feedlots and concentrated animal feeding operations (CAFOs). The millions of gallons of CAFO manure, along with the remaining farmers' fencerow-to-fencerow corn and soybeans rotation, pollute our lakes and waterways. Getting bigger is clearly not the answer to our problems. (xviii)

This research stems from a similar interest and curiosity about rural America. While preparing for fieldwork, I read the classic *Debt and Dispossession* (Dudley 2002). I introduced Dudley's tragic story of loss, blame, and suicide in rural America to my father, a recently retired farmer, and he found the story familiar. My mother and father began farming in 1980 and endured the farm crisis. My father had neighbors who lost their lives to suicide after losing their farms. For him, Dudley's ethnography reflected our family and community's experience, yet he expressed discomfort about the book's apparent critique of capitalism. He knew from experience that something was wrong.

In many US farmers' view, the farm crisis was deeply unfortunate but ultimately tied to individuals' work ethic—not to class, structure, or capital. At the same time, scholars have recognized a general shift away from the so-called traditional farming values of environmental stewardship, family-centered work, and community life and toward individualized and market-centered rural life. This rupture of rural America seems to stem from three interconnected changes happening in US agriculture: oppositional relations between farmers; increasing ambiguity around who is a farmer with the cultural politics of who counts; and an increasing disconnection of the individual farmer from collective, social worlds centered on the farm as an economic unit. In the following examples I will not answer but rather illuminate these questions to demonstrate the emerging tensions within farming today.

The Gorilla and the Iowa Renter or What Is a Farm Community?

Growing up on our South Dakota farm, my family and neighbors directed our ire at an Iowa farmer who outbid any local farmers for rental contracts, hired contract workers to drive his tractors, and had gone bankrupt several times. He was well-known for outbidding any local farmers for scarce farmland and for not spending money locally besides his rental payment. His workers, inputs, and machinery were brought over from Iowa. Worse than occupying scarce farmland, most area farmers believed he implemented poor soil management practices and had little regard for land stewardship. While we complained about the Iowa farmer, we resented our neighbors who rented to outsiders and reduced the local land base. Social conflict in rural communities stems from the defense of the community from outsiders but also from internal strife.

Later in my youth, rumors circulated in the community about a mysterious investor who appeared to be making land deal offers to local farmers for large tracts of land at above-market prices. Soon the project had a name—Project Gorilla—named as much for its size and strength as its strangeness. Some neighbors optioned out land and others held out. The politics around this became a dominant topic of conversation and clouded over social relations in the area. Local opposition to Project Gorilla—later formally announced as a planned oil refinery project—decried the company and project as unsustainable, destructive, and a catalyst for crime, violence, and unwanted social change. Personal attacks were directed at those farmers who had optioned out land rather than at the venture itself. Neighbors directed their most passionate vitriol at neighbors who had agreed to option out their land.

Thank the Farmer or Thank the Farmworker?

During Super Bowl XLVII, Ram Trucks ran a commercial featuring images of pensive farmers praying at their dinner tables and driving tractors and pickups. Paul Harvey's speech, "Thank a Farmer," played in the background. The ad transitioned between images of mostly white male farmers working in fields, standing against working landscapes, and hands held in prayer. Like Eastern North Carolina billboards that remind drivers "If you ate today, thank a farmer," the Dodge Super Bowl ad suggested that farmers are forgotten members of society whose contributions are underappreciated. Farmers widely supported the advertisement, thanked Dodge for honoring their work, and celebrated the ad on social media. The speech itself is frequently hung on kitchen walls across the Heartland. At the same time, the advertisement sparked backlash from advocacy groups who noted that the ad and speech placed an undue focus on farmers (especially white male farmers) over farmworkers. The Coalition of Immokalee Workers noted that "the vast majority of physical labor done on the vast majority of commercial fruit and vegetable farms in this country is done by farmworkers—the vast, vast majority of whom are not white" (North Carolina Council of Churches 2013). The homogenized, gendered, and racialized images of the US farmer portrayed by Ram Trucks make other ways of farming invisible but also fit into long histories of marginalizing Black, Latinx, women, and queer farmers. The conflict between advocates of farmers and farmworkers challenges the legitimacy and authority of claims of producing food, working hard, and demanding gratitude for farmwork and production.

From Bean Buggies to Roundup or What Is Farmwork?

My brothers and I spent much of our childhood working on the farm. Our work included watering the pigs on sweltering days; keeping feed troughs and watering tanks full; collecting chicken eggs; corralling escaped pigs, which inevitably destroyed Mom's flowers; and collecting and husking sweet corn from the field before the raccoons and our sweet corn–loving dog got to it. The most grueling and rewarding work was the bean walking and bean barring. For each task we would wake up early, so as to get into the field before the sun was at its highest. For a day of bean walking we would fill a jug of ice water, collect a grocery bag of snacks, throw a few machetes into the pickup—and we would be off. Each of us would take a number of rows and walk from one end of the field to the other, cutting every cocklebur, buttonweed, sunflower, and cornstalk we saw. The days were tough—our backs sore from bending down, our hands raw from pulling weeds and blistering where the machete rubbed our skin, and our feet often wet and cold from walking in the mud. Yet I enjoyed those days. We talked, played, and roamed free. It was rewarding to play a part in the farm tasks; it also gave us a feeling of independence and importance. Alone in the field, we knew what to do and were contributing.

Bean barring provided a similar feeling of hard work and responsibility. Again, leaving early in the morning, we would set out. Our job was to sit on seats on a bar, called a "bean buggy," at the front of the tractor. Each of us held a spray gun in our gloved hands connected to a tank of herbicide. As Dad drove the tractor slowly through the field, we squirted any weeds we saw, being careful not to hit any soybeans, which the herbicide would also kill. We were learning the importance of paying close attention and being extra careful. Riding through the field, strapped to a tractor, and shooting weeds with an oversized squirt gun was also a lot of fun. When Dad was looking, we were careful not to miss a weed and to avoid killing any crops. When we thought Dad was not looking, we sprayed each other's feet, turning old gym shoes pink. Farmwork for me as a child was social. We got to work together, and with neighbor kids and older brothers' friends—all under Dad's watchful eye.

Weed control in the post-Monsanto world is different. In 1996 Roundup-Ready soybean seeds were sold commercially in the United States. Monsanto had genetically engineered soybeans to resist the effects of Roundup (tradename for glyphosate). This allowed farmers to spray a soybean field with Roundup to kill weeds but leave the crop intact, thus reducing the need for cutting weeds by hand and bean barring. There is a common saying in corn-and-bean country that "Roundup makes a good farmer lazy and a lazy farmer good." Technology has a leveling effect on hard work and skill. In our experience it also had the effect of dividing the farm into separate spheres—one of social reproduction of the family and the other as an economic unit of production. After the introduction of Roundup, my Dad simply sprayed the fields with glyphosate and a few other chemicals, assigning us other jobs on the farm, but those too dwindled. Our free-range chickens fell victim to hungry foxes and coyotes, and we sold our hogs when we could not compete with local CAFOs.

Community, Farmers, and Work in Soylandia and Beyond

So what is this book about? What about Soylandia? On its face this book is an ethnography of a transnational farming community in Brazil—a group of midwestern farmers seeking adventure, land, and profit who had purchased large tracts of land and adopted Brazilian farming practices. More generally, it is about the trajectory and possibilities of industrial farming. It is about what happens to farmwork, farmer identity, farm community, and farm ecologies when we leave behind assumptions of connectedness with the land, tight-knit communities, and the agrarian work ethic. This story is also about connections and disconnections: how farmers disconnect from land, plants, and work, and how they generate new relationships with those basic units of agriculture. The changes I saw on my childhood farm and in the farming community are so patently obvious and extreme in the story I tell here as to seem like a complete rupture of farming life. Yet, where old connections are severed, new ones are forged. Farmers in a foreign land give their land names, improve the soil, and defend their right to own it. Farmers who come to depend on farmworkers redefine a good farmer as a good businessperson, and those farmers who are seemingly without community build new relationships amid rumors, rivalries, and antagonism. While the destructiveness of large-scale transnational farming is easy to see, the generativity of transnational farming is less obvious. I argue that such generativity is both more sinister and more hopeful than it appears on the surface. It is hopeful in that these farmers do not just do as they please. Regardless of their nationality, capital, or race, they contend with the Brazilian state, workers, the land itself, and pests as small as the miniscule whitefly. This multispecies opposition generates new practices, discourses, and even origin narratives. This opposition is what Anna Tsing (2011) calls "friction"—the local flavor that development must contend with to entrench itself and that needs to be resolved. The takeaway of this story is about the other side of that friction: generativity. The discourses, new skills, business and farming practices, and flows of capital that emerge out of this local friction grease the wheels of development and create a readily exported model that can be practiced elsewhere in Brazil, Mozambique, and even the United States.

The Brazilian geographer Milton Santos wondered about "what remains of the process of suppression, accumulation, and superposition with which things accumulate everywhere" and called these material and ideological remains "roughness" (2012, 140). This is the new world of Soylandia and all the roughness it leaves behind.

Acknowledgments

When I was already several weeks behind my deadline, I informed the editors of the Cornell Series on Land that I did not have a revised manuscript ready, but that it would be ready soon (it would not be). Michael Goldman, the series coeditor, responded by saying "Writing is like wrestling a bear; the fun is only if you survive! Keep it up." A book manuscript calls for a seemingly endless cycle of writing, critique, revision, critique, and revision again so much so that a book is made not by fingers tapping a keyboard but by the community of voices that say, "Keep going, you're doing alright." This book came into being thanks to those many voices.

My academic career is a story of finding the right people and more often the right people finding me. I struggled at South Dakota State University until Zeno Wicks pulled me aside and told me I had promise as a writer and that I needed to go to West Africa with him and experience something besides corn and soybeans. Zeno's early encouragement reminded me to be curious and to put in the effort necessary to make something worthwhile.

At Wageningen University, Alberto Arce sat down with me for meeting after meeting in which I listened in awe to the way his mind worked. Alberto would never answer my questions; he would just give me leads to follow up on. He taught me the value of patience and figuring things out over time. He introduced me to Pablo Laguna, "el Viejo," who always missed our lunch plans in La Paz, but who I count as one of my greatest influences in leading with the empirical. He is still a great friend.

Before I even started at the University of North Carolina at Chapel Hill, Rudi Colloredo-Mansfeld was guiding me through the peer review process for my first publication and inviting me to conferences. It was our first conversation after I had arrived on campus that pushed me to consider conducting entirely new research in Brazil with a few US farmers. He gave a tremendous amount of attention to my project, entertained my son when I had to bring him to meetings, and engaged deeply with my research and writing. He provided sage and creative advice at every step. My mentors included some of most incredible scholars in anthropology and geography and who were arguably also the kindest. The late Dottie Holland asked the tactful questions that always made me nervous. They pinpointed my project's inconsistencies with surgical precision, which she would then think through with me. I will remember her questions and her laughter.

Gabriela Valdivia introduced me to political ecology and deepened my understanding of class, power, and struggle; she never let me get away with simple explanations of why I was doing what I was doing. Peter Redfield and Hannah Gil dove into the project without hesitation. I owe extensive debts to friends and colleagues in Chapel Hill. Arturo Escobar's enthusiasm and curiosity reminded me to have fun with my work. Elizabeth Havice's constant encouragement and openness modeled for me the very kindest of academic relationships. Colin West showed me how to be a parent in academia. My friends—Pavithra Abhirami, Liz Berger, Lindsay Bloch, Paolo Bocci, Orisanmi Burton, Tomas Gallareta Cervera, David Cranford, Maia Dedrick, Achsah Dorsey, Laura Gutierrez-Escobar, Taylor Livingston, Maggie Morgan-Smith, Erin Nelson, Claire Novotny, Caela O'Connell, Ashley Peles, Seana Monley Rodriguez, Anna Semon, Eric Thomas, Bill Westermeyer, Justine Williams, and Joe Wiltberger—made my time in Chapel Hill fun and always interesting.

At Cornell University, the incredible Wendy Wolford offered me the job of a lifetime. She gave me opportunities to focus on my writing and research, to work with an incredible group of colleagues, and to gain from her critical, thoughtful, supportive feedback. This book might never have been completed without my time at Cornell and would have been a shadow of itself without Wendy's feedback. Wendy's writing lab, the Wolfpack, served as a safe and thoughtful space to discuss writing, research, and academia. The Wolfpack—including at various times Mike Cary, Hilary Faxon, Delilah Griswold, Kendra Kintzi, Juliet Lu, Ryan Nehring, Liz Packard, Karla Peña, Ewan Robinson, Fernando Galeana Rodriguez, and Jarvis Tilton—was my community in Ithaca.

This research received generous funding from both small and large grants. I was able to begin this research in 2012 thanks to small grants from the Latino Migration Fund, the Tinker Foundation, and the Halperin Memorial Fund Travel Grant; these small grants funded research and gave a young academic enough encouragement to keep going. Grants from the Wenner-Gren Foundation, the Fulbright Institute of International Education, and the University of North Carolina Graduate School funded my primary research, and writing grants from the UNC Graduate School allowed me to focus on writing for my last two years in Chapel Hill.

The participants in this research gave me their precious time and energy. Many of these farmers showed me kindness and vulnerability. I enjoyed conversations about our shared experiences of farming and living abroad. Throughout this book I am critical of the impact these farmers have had on the land and people of Western Bahia, but I admire their courage and initiative to take on both the known and unknown risks of starting a farm in another country. I began this research doubting that these farmers were either the swashbuckling frontiersmen or the harbingers of destruction I had heard about; spending time with them showed me that they do enact a certain power over the people and the land, but that they too are victims of crisis.

At Cornell University Press, the editors of the Cornell Series on Land—Wendy Wolford, Nancy Lee Peluso, and Michael Goldman—have been ever-encouraging and patient with my manuscript. They have worked tirelessly to bring this book to publication. Jim Lance, Clare Jones, and Mahinder Kingra have worked to move the manuscript from step to step with clear communication all along the way. My book conference participants—Sarah Besky, Jeremy Campbell, Jenny Goldstein, Julie Guthman, Nick Kawa, Pablo Lapegna, and Paul Nadasdy—gave me one of the most brutal experiences that I have survived. In so doing, they remade this book as a more nuanced, clear, and respectful work. James Welch and Gabriela Russo Lopes provided feedback on advanced drafts of the manuscript with incredible insight and encouragement. Finally, I thank the external reviewers who provided kind and critical feedback.

My Mom and Dad, Glenda and Bernard, have encouraged me at every step along the way, tactfully asking about the progress of my writing. Mom's editing of earlier drafts was a gift and Dad's printing off of my articles to place on his desk is the highest praise I can ask for. They also, along with my mother-in-law Michelle Johnson and father-in-law Duane Johnson, cared for our children for hours at a time while my family lived in South Dakota for eight months of the COVID-19 pandemic. The love and support of my sister, Ellen, and brothers Steve, Dan, James, and Pete keep me going when things get difficult. My brother Dan passed away unexpectedly during the writing of this manuscript. Dan was a constant source of encouragement and praise. He was one of the kindest and most compassionate people I have ever known, and he was also funny as hell. The world is a worse place without him.

To my eldest son, Arlo, I owe appreciation for his sense of wonder and surprise every time I told him I was writing a book. The cycle of him forgetting that I was writing a book, me mentioning it in conversation, and him exclaiming "You're writing a book!?" never got old. I owe my youngest son, Henry, for modeling how to advocate for oneself with vigor. And to my wife Amanda, where to start? Amanda has been behind every good decision I have ever made and had nothing to do with all the bad ones. She encouraged me to travel internationally while I was in college, to be curious about the world, and to pursue the crazy idea of going to a college in the Netherlands that I could not even pronounce. She moved to North Carolina with me to follow my studies, then made a life for us in the Carolina Piedmont. The sacrifices she has made for this book are too many to list. She took care of the kids when I needed to focus, listened to me talk about "my book" for years on end, and reminded me to take a break to focus on the things that really matter.

Abbreviations

ABAPA Associação Baiana dos Produtores de Algadão (Bahian Association of Cotton Producers)

AIBA Associação de Agricultures e Irrigantes da Bahia (Bahian Association of Farmers and Irrigators)

CAFO concentrated animal feeding operation

CSA community-supported agriculture

Emater Empresa de Assistência Técnica e Extensão Rural (Rural Institute of Technical Assistance of the Brazilian state of Paraná)

Embrapa Empresa Brasileira de Pesquisa Agropecuária (Brazilian Agricultural Research Corporation)

FAS Foreign Agricultural Service

FHA Farmers Home Administration

GFI Global Farmland Investments

GMO genetically modified organism

GPS global positioning system

IBAMA Instituto Brasileiro do Meio Ambiente e dos Recursos Naturais Renováveis (Brazilian Institute of the Environment and Renewable Natural Resources)

INCRA Instituto Nacional de Colonização e Reforma Agrária (National Institute of Land Colonization and Reform)

IUCN International Union for Conservation of Nature

JICA Japan International Cooperative Agency

LLC limited liability company

Mapitoba Brazilian states of Maranhão, Piauí, Tocantins, and Bahia

MST Movimento dos Trabalhadores Rurais Sem Terra (landless workers' movement)

NPK the macronutrients nitrogen, phosphorous, potassium

POLOCENTRO Programa de Desenvolvimento dos Cerrados (Development Program for the Cerrado)

PRODECER   Programa de Cooperação Nipo–Brasileiro para o
            Desenvolvimento Agrícola dos Cerrados (Progam of
            Japanese–Brazilian Cooperation for the Agricultural
            Development of the Cerrado)
PROTERRA   Programa de Redistribuição da Terra (Land Redistribution
            Program)
USDA   United States Department of Agriculture
YBP   Years Before Present

WELCOME TO SOYLANDIA

INTRODUCTION

What Was a Dream Will Become a Reality

The town of Luís Eduardo Magalhães (hereafter Luís Eduardo) in the state of Bahia, Brazil is not beautiful, but it is spectacular. Traveling from Brasilia to Luís Eduardo, our bus passed through the woody savanna of the Brazilian Cerrado, punctuated by small towns with bus stops, *lanchonetes* (diners), mechanic shops, and children playing in the streets. Entering Western Bahia from Goiás, the landscape transitioned from scattered vibrant towns, grasslands, shrubs, and short trees of the Cerrado to a flat uniform landscape of seemingly dead, monocultural soy fields. The soy commodity frontier seemed to divide what I call Soylandia from the rest of the world like a bold line on a map—diverse, unpredictable life on one side and controlled, tamed commodities on the other. As we neared Luís Eduardo, semitrucks flashed their lights before quickly overtaking our plodding bus. The semitrucks overflowing with cotton seeds were on their way to regional chicken farms and those brimming with soy were on their way to the port at Salvador and eventually to China or Europe. We passed billboards advertising fertilizer inputs, soybean seed dealers, and farming implements. The recent harvest had left fields nearly bare. Red clay soil stretched from the highway to the horizon, broken up only by neat bales of cotton stacked in rows along the edges of fields and the short stubble of left-behind plants in harvested soy fields. We passed Fazenda Illinois, a smattering of Chinese-owned farms, and several Brazilian farms.[1] At the outskirts of town, the number of agricultural input advertisements marketing seeds, agrochemicals, and machinery increased. The traffic of semitrucks picked up. Upon arriving at the bus stop I alighted along with my fellow passengers into a dusty, busy, and poorly lit street.

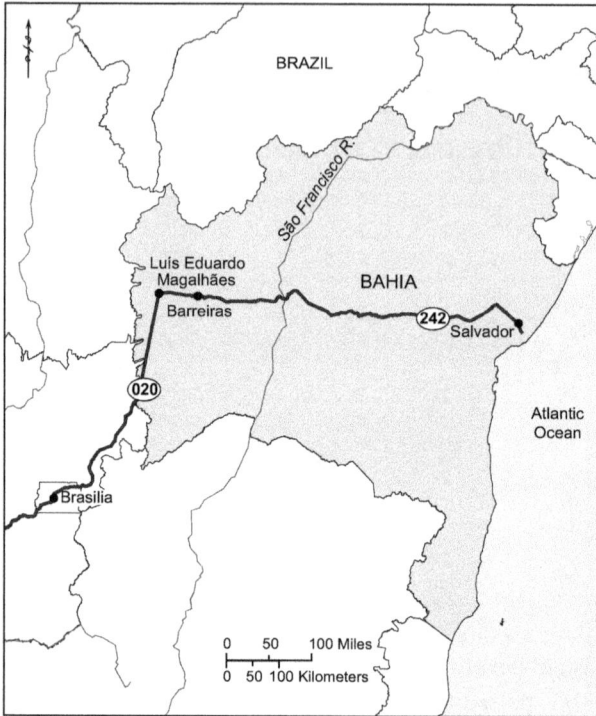

FIGURE 1. Map of Luís Eduardo Magalhães, created by Gordon Thompson.

Luís Eduardo is a town constructed by and for agribusiness. In twenty years it has grown from a small outpost for travelers to a bustling, dusty, concrete city of seventy thousand people, all of whom seem to be involved in some facet of agricultural production. Many agronomists and farm owners migrated from the South of Brazil, seeking cheaper land or work; others from the United States or Europe are there for the same reason; and laborers from the surrounding region migrated there to work in the fields or in the service sector. The town shows signs of its fast growth. Wide, paved roads pass through shiny neighborhoods and abruptly end at the edge of the savanna of the Brazilian Cerrado. Concrete buildings seem to be dropped in from above. The town itself feels artificial, but its markets, restaurants, and bars hum with activity. Yet ecological and social life interfere with this dream. Red dust, blown in from cleared fields, follows one everywhere. Everything smells of red dust. The sight and feel of dust on one's skin is perpetual—a visceral reminder of the rapid aeolian erosion of the Cerrado.

A twenty-minute stroll connects the wealthy neighborhood of Jardim Paraiso (Paradise Garden) with its manicured lawns, parks, and grand hotels to the Santa Cruz neighborhood that US farmers and their Brazilian neighbors in Jardim

FIGURE 2. The dusty streets of Luís Eduardo Magalhães.

FIGURE 3. Road's end at the edge of Luís Eduardo Magalhães and the Cerrado.

Paraiso call Iraq, named in reference to violence that the neighborhood has faced since it was founded. The city is highly segregated by social class, cultural background, and occupation (Filho 2016).[2] Jardim Paraiso—as a billboard with a faded image of a happily married white couple attests—is a place where dreams become reality. The dusty roads are busy with old donkey carts alongside expensive BMWs. *Churrascarias* (Brazilian barbecues) cater to wealthy farm owners, young agronomists on their first job, and input and implement sales managers; tabletops hold placard ads for Bunge, John Deere, and fertilizer suppliers, reminding diners again that this is not just another agricultural town, it is indeed the "capital of agribusiness." It is an emerald city that is held up as a beacon to agribusiness by some and as a dystopia by others. In this book, it embodies the rise of flexible farming and a dream called Soylandia.

Soylandia is both a territory and an imagined near-future, sometimes framed as a dystopian nightmare, sometimes as a utopian dream. The phrase was coined by Susanna Hecht and Charles C. Mann in a *Fortune Magazine* article about the expansion and consolidation of soy production in a territory stretching from "the Andes and the Atlantic forest and from northern Argentina to the southern flanks of the Amazon basin" (Hecht and Mann 2008). A later article by Hecht

FIGURE 4. A billboard in Luís Eduardo Magalhães: "What was a dream will become a reality."

FIGURE 5.   Seemingly perpetual road construction in Luís Eduardo.

and Gustavo Oliveira engages further with the concept of Soylandia as an imagined space of social and ecological sameness, saying that the concept implied a homogenization of "production technologies/techniques, domination of input markets and commodity trading by transnational corporations, increasing involvement of international finance, privatization of research and infrastructure, and deregulation across South America" (G. Oliveira and Hecht 2016, 271).[3] Soylandia represents both the territory occupied by soybeans and the imagined dream/nightmare of an agricultural future dominated by homogenous production practices, transnational corporations, and finance unhindered by societal resistance, ecological diversity, or governmental interference.

Like those who coined it, I work with and against the term "Soylandia." It captures the dominance of the soy plant across the landscapes, communities, and economies of Brazil, Bolivia, Argentina, Paraguay, and Uruguay and also obscures the vibrant differences within that territory. For US farmers in Brazil, as much as for Brazilians in Bolivia or Paraguay, Mennonites in Bolivia and Brazil, or Japanese settlers in Brazil and Bolivia, life in Soylandia takes practice. It is not a simple matter of taking ownership of land but rather a long process that unfolds in relation to plants, soils, workers, governments, capital, and investors. Soylandia itself cannot be simplified in a description of a landscape, a graph of expanding soy acres, or a map of where soy is grown. However, it is one possible pathway for the future of farming. For the purpose of this book, Soylandia is both the territory of Argentina, Bolivia, Brazil, Paraguay, and Uruguay in which soy production is the dominant economic activity and a utopian/dystopian dream of achieving modernized and financialized agricultural development.[4] That dream/nightmare aspires to tame and neutralize nature—including weeds, pests, and plant diseases; strip social values and noneconomic human relations from agricultural work; reimagine agricultural land as a strictly economic asset without social, community, or ecological value; select crops based primarily on market demand and other economic considerations; and limit legitimate government intervention to the opening of markets and support for export agriculture but not the protection for workers, the environment, or traditional communities. Soylandia as a territory is bounded by its relation to the planting of soy within a demarcated border; Soylandia as a way of doing agriculture can be implemented nearly anywhere with nearly any crop.

The Creation of Soylandia

Luís Eduardo is the utopian dream of Soylandia. The city houses workers, farmers, agronomists, and lenders, while the countryside is home to extensive soy, cotton, and corn fields that demonstrate productivity and growth for some, and death and loss for others. Outside of the city/country duality, there is what remains of the Cerrado, a tropical savanna that is a barren wasteland for farmers and agribusiness interests and a vibrant home for people (both local dwellers and activists), plants, and animals. Luís Eduardo is the nerve center (Styles 2019) of Soylandia where the dreams, aspirations, and desperation of farmers and farmworkers collide.

Luís Eduardo, at the soy frontier of Western Bahia, has experienced rapid demographic and agricultural change after soybean production began in the region in 1979. Luís Eduardo appears to be a place of dominance by capital and science over people, plants, and place. Yet it is more than that. It encompasses a set of practices of farming and business and emerging values of what is good and what is wrong, and it is a place where new ecologies emerge from the ruins and rubble (Gordillo 2014; Kirksey 2015; Tsing 2015). For many, this is what is happening or should be happening everywhere. We see the same logics of control, development, and loss across the global agricultural landscape. Mirroring what many call the Plantationocene (Wolford 2021), the logic of Soylandia entails dependence on and exploitation of farmworkers; control of land, landscapes, and soil as productive and speculative assets; and intensive monocultural farm practices designed to maximize crop yields and kill everything else in the field.

Soybean production in South America is inseparable from the increased global market for soy, and the increased global market for soy is largely due to rising demand in China where imported soy is processed and incorporated as soybean meal to add cheap protein to animal feed; a small portion of soybean oil is mixed with other cooking oils (Gale, Valdes, and Ash 2019). Rising demand for soy in China has increased overall exports from Brazil and dramatically shifted trade routes. In 1990 the European Union received 68 percent of Brazilian soy exports and China received 4 percent; by 2015 China received 67 percent of Brazilian soy exports compared to the European Union's share of 20 percent (Peine 2021). While soybean trade routes have shifted toward China, the buying, selling, and processing of soybeans has been controlled by the so-called ABCD companies (ADM, Bunge Ltd., Cargill, and Louis Dreyfus) who powerfully "flex" soy by maintaining direct access to suppliers and buyers in Brazil and abroad (G. de L. T. Oliveira and Schneider 2016). In Western Bahia, Bunge (in Luís Eduardo) and Cargill (in nearby Barreiras) are the most visible and active of the ABCDs.

The soybean boom of South America—the rapid expansion of soybean production into Brazilian Amazonia, the Argentinian and Uruguayan Pampas, the Chaco of Paraguay and Bolivia, and the Brazilian Cerrado—has transformed the region. In the Brazilian Cerrado, savanna land accounted for 73 percent of land cover in 1986 and only 40 percent of land cover in 2002 (Brannstrom et al. 2008). As of 2014 soy covered more than fifty-five million hectares of South American farmland, and South American farmers and agribusinesses accounted for 51 percent of global soy production (FAOSTAT 2020). The expansion of soy production has extended and consolidated capital and industrial agricultural practices across savanna, woodlands, and pastures. As industrial agriculture produced an agro-industrial landscape dominated by large farms, the general public and local interests have raised the alarm over agrochemical risks, waged farm labor has replaced smallholder agriculture, and communities have dispersed and disintegrated. Governments have restructured policy, social life, and ecological life around the production, transport, and processing of soy—violently reshaping the territory and those who reside within it (see J. E. Correia 2019).

For many, the soy boom is a triumph of Green Revolution technologies over underutilized land and inefficient farming systems—a model for increasing yield, transforming marginal agricultural land to breadbasket, and feeding a growing global population. Still, detractors of the soy boom are numerous. Soy production contributes to deforestation and habitat loss, soil nutrient depletion, and increased risks associated with high rates of pesticide use (Altieri 2009). Community destruction and land loss has accelerated with the expansion of soy production. The selective application of existing environmental protections increases competition for resources in the margins of the soy commodity frontier, thus increasing competition between soy farmers and local Indigenous populations and forcing confrontations around existence and resistance. Cases of agrochemical exposure have risen with soybean production and disproportionally affected local communities (Lapegna 2016), while direct confrontations have led to assassinations, confirming that, indeed, *la soja mata* (soy kills) (Hetherington 2020). Indigenous groups throughout the Cerrado continue to engage in acts of resistance, making themselves visible in a land where some claim nothing existed prior to soy production.

Soy production in the Brazilian Cerrado has exacerbated processes of land dispossession (Polizel et al. 2021) that began in the colonial era. Present-day *grileiros* (land-grabbers), follow in the footsteps of colonial *bandeirantes*. Bandeirantes, literally "flag carriers," claimed land, enslaved Indigenous people, and expanded the extent of colonial power as well as their own fortunes and power (Franco 1940). Likewise, present-day grileiros claim Indigenous and traditional community land for themselves, often violently, and later sell the land to agribusinesses. This enclosure and dispossession of land has had the continued support of the Brazilian state.

In his proposed "March to the West," the Brazilian president Getulio Vargas hoped to populate and modernize the Cerrado by funding agricultural research and incentivizing agricultural production in 1937. Later, in 1955, the Brazilian president Juscelino Kubitschek built on this; he was determined to "rationalize agriculture" and extend the presence and visibility of the Brazilian state into the interior of Brazil (including the Cerrado and Amazonia, which the Brazilian military called "A land without men for men without land"). In the late 1960s the military government enacted an agrarian development project, POLOCENTRO (Programa de Desenvolvimento dos Cerrados), to incorporate the Cerrado into the national economy and to support rural producers through funding for infrastructure development and agricultural research. Concurrently, the government provided loans for land purchases on generous terms through the PROTERRA (Programa de Redistribuição da Terra) program. In the 1970s the Japan International Cooperative Agency (JICA) cooperated with the newly formed Embrapa (Empresa Brasileira de Pesquisa Agropecuária) to implement PRODECER (Programa de Cooperação Nipo–Brasileiro para o Desenvolvimento dos Cerrado), providing financing and technical agronomy research and training to induce southern Brazilian farmers to migrate and settle the Cerrado. Both financial and research inducements drew farmers to what a former minister of agriculture for Brazil called a "barren land where nothing can grow without neutralizing the soil with a large amount of lime and fertilizer" (Rodrigues 2016, 221). Already in 1969, government researchers had claimed that within three years they could conquer the *vazio agricola* (agricultural abyss) of the Cerrado and incorporate the region into the productive life of the country (*Folha de S.Paulo* 2019).

PRODECER had the goal of "settling" the Cerrado with farmers from the South and making the Cerrado a sacrifice zone to buffer deforestation in the Amazon.[5] In 2015 the federal government passed Decreto No. 8.447, the Agricultural Development Plan for Matopiba (referring to the Brazilian states of Maranhão, Tocantins, Piauí, and Bahia) to support the expansion of soybean production in the Cerrado. The plan committed the government to developing infrastructure, supporting agricultural research, and strengthening the rural middle class in the region. Agricultural development and modernization in the Brazilian Cerrado is a long-held dream of the right-wing *ruralista* (rural caucus) political faction. During his presidency, former president Jair Bolsonaro emphatically deepened this long-held interest in agricultural development and disdain for environmentalism and traditional land claims in both policy and practice (Russo Lopes and Bastos Lima 2020; Gortázar 2021).

Government support for agricultural development in the Cerrado is moderately offset by environmental, worker, and land protections, though these have been weakened under the administrations of Michel Temer (2016–2019) and Jair Bolsonaro (2019–2022). The *Codigo Florestal* (Forest Law) (LEI No. 12.651) places land near waterways under permanent protection from agricultural development and requires farmland owners to purchase a legal reserve (uncleared land) of 20 percent of owned land in Western Bahia. NR (*Norma Regulatoria*) is a labor regulation that imposes minimum worker housing quality standards, maximum working hours, access to facilities, and access to personal protective equipment. The foreign land law (LEI No. 5.709) restricts foreign farmland ownership in Brazil, including Brazilian corporations with majority foreign control as of 2010. These protections are hated by the ruralistas and were loosened by the Temer and Bolsonaro administrations. Under the Bolsonaro administration, fifty-seven acts in the Brazilian legislature weakened environmental protections (Vale et al. 2021). Bolsonaro came to power with enthusiastic support from wealthy Brazilian landowners (Pompeia 2024) and he quickly rewarded them after the election of 2018 by picking a ruralista leader for agricultural and environmental minister (Mano and Boadle 2018). Bolsonaro, with the support of the ruralistas, has reduced regulatory surveillance and issued fewer fines for illegal deforestation. From August 2019 to July 2020, Brazil experienced its fastest rate of deforestation in twelve years. Further, farmers and loggers became increasingly bold and violent in their encroachments on indigenous lands (Boadle 2019). Bolsonaro's "policy of confrontation" (Sauer, Leite, and Tubino 2020) implemented an ultraneoliberal agenda and culture war.

Budget cuts and limits paralyzed INCRA (Instituto Nacional de Colonização e Reforma Agrária), the foreign land law came under threat, and the administration offered unconditional support for agribusiness (Araujo 2020). Soylandia and Luís Eduardo itself were produced and are now sustained by this ruralista agenda for agribusiness.

When I stepped off the bus from Brasilia, my first impressions of Luís Eduardo were that it was entirely constructed by and for agribusiness. As such, it is a case of deterritoriality in which no one can claim it as their rightful territory—a constructed, liminal place.[6] My further research reminded me that the Emerald City is an imperfect illusion—here too, there were places where the Cerrado made itself apparent as red dust, where local inhabitants reminded outsiders that this place had a past and an alternate present and future. This book tells these two stories: of the indomitability of Soylandia and its porosity. New possibilities emerge out of Soylandia, whether the stuff of dreams or nightmares. This is the figure of Soylandia—a twinned process of destruction and creation; of death and regeneration; of rows of combines marching through a field with rheas, pequi trees, and Indigenous people standing in their path.[7]

The Arrival of US Farmers in Soylandia

If Luís Eduardo, with its red dust and concrete, "Iraq" and Garden Paradise neighborhoods, and community of farmworkers and farmer-capitalists, is the exemplar of Soylandia, then perhaps the exemplar of the soy farmer looks something like a transnational soy farmer. After all, Soylandia is populated with all sorts of transnational farmers—Brazilian farmers in Paraguay and Bolivia; US-born Mennonite farmers in Brazil, Bolivia, and Paraguay; and Europeans, Australians, and New Zealanders mostly centered in Brazil. Soy farming represents a new rural reality of South America ruled by MBAs, managers, and capital. Eduardo Gudynas calls this a "great transformation" of rural life in which rural life is commodified and decoupled from the social and cultural lives of farming (2008, 514). However, industrial soy production in South America is neither homogenous nor settled. Differences in scale, capital-intensiveness, work, and even production systems of Brazilian soybean farms complicate broad analyses of rural life.

This ethnography is centered on the story of US farmers who have migrated to Brazil to become large-scale soybean farmers. They come mostly from family farms in the US Midwest. Mostly young white men, they had little opportunity to start their own farms in the Midwest where farmland prices regularly exceed $10,000/acre, but with investment capital from neighboring farmers they could purchase far cheaper farmland in the Brazilian Cerrado. They now operate farms that range between 3,000 and 30,000 hectares in the Brazilian Cerrado (primarily in Western Bahia). Their farms employ 30–160 workers, including manual laborers, agronomists, accountants, and sometimes public relations teams. Their migration to Brazil is facilitated by their privilege (i.e., access to financial capital) and driven by their precarity (i.e., inability to access expensive US farmland).[8] These farmers were not elite landowners in their home communities; they had to migrate to Brazil to become elite. The community of transnational farmers is small, numbering a few dozen, and their impact on Brazilian agriculture and economics is negligible compared to Brazilian farmers, though they operate together over 100,000 hectares of farmland. US farmers in Western Bahia tell a story of movement from a region of land scarcity to a frontier with cheap land, cheaply paid workers, and seemingly perfect growing conditions. Other large-scale landowners in the area tell a similar story (Gracia 2017; Lopez 2014).

Neighboring farmers hail primarily from southern Brazil (*sulistas* from the South and *gauchos* from the far South). Sulistas migrated first to the soybean frontiers of Goiás and Mato Grosso, until that frontier became the center of soy production and land prices skyrocketed. Many then sold their farmland and converged with US, Dutch, Belgian, Australian, and New Zealand farmers in Western Bahia, where land was cheaper. Like Brazilian farmers in the area, US farmers had difficulty accessing farmland at home, so they followed capital, seeds, and agrarian dreams to the soybean commodity frontier in Luís Eduardo. While ostensibly continuing family farming legacies as well as migration and settler colonial legacies, they built farms that would be unrecognizable as family farms in the US Midwest and the Brazilian South alike in their scale and dependence on farmworkers. The community is made up mostly of young, white men, though a few brought wives and fewer brought children. For the most part, they are university-educated, born on family farms in the US Midwest, and had access to capital but not to land.

I first learned of the migrant US farmers in American newspaper articles and producer magazines. With headlines like "American Farmers Try Their Luck in Brazil," "U.S. Farmers Scramble to Buy Brazil's Farmland," and "U.S. Farmers Put Roots Down in Brazilian Soil," the arrival of US farmers in Brazil has been greeted with a blend of pity, curiosity, triumphalism, and doom. The headlines provide an insight into this migration—the search for opportunity and a second chance in Brazil. The articles told a story of farmers fulfilling agrarian dreams outside of the US heartland, on farms named Fazenda Illinois and Iowegian Farms, and in fields named Iowa 1, Iowa 2, and Iowa 3 at the ends of dirt lanes. These farmers faced an unforgiving environment with poor soils as well as piranhas, vipers, and dengue fever. They faced a government that was unfriendly and inefficient in the best of cases, and xenophobic and corrupt in the worst. In interviews, farmers spoke of barren landscapes, favorable agronomic conditions (a paradox of inhospitable environment and an aptness for agribusiness that I return to in chapter 2), and cheap land in Brazil as well as the strangeness of their endeavor. "We aren't in Kansas anymore" said one farmer from Missouri. Magazine articles painted these farmers as rugged, adventure-seeking, independent, and grounded, akin to Raymond Craib's "adventure capitalist" on the prowl for adventure and profit and on the run from regulation and rule (Craib 2022).

My curiosity, piqued by these representations, led me to wonder whether the transnational farming community in Luís Eduardo had common meeting places; whether they went to church and the farmers' cooperative to visit; or if they had red barns, grain silos, and farmhouses with broad porches. These images were quickly dispelled upon my arrival. A US farm in Brazil is not simply a land title, a financialized asset, or a business entity, though it is all of these to be sure, as my first farm visit, to Fazenda Illinois demonstrated.

Ian Illinois's farm is just off highway BR-242. The entrance is impressive. The long driveway splits massive fields; the last hundred yards are lined with coconut trees. At the end of the out-of-place row of trees is a heavy metal gate with an armed guard dressed in black. A ten-foot barbed-wire fence surrounds the farm, built after a series of robberies of chemicals. Inside the heavy gates, the farm has several rows of farmworkers' quarters, a machinery workshop, a row of offices, a mess hall, and a soccer field. There is also a small vegetable garden for the farmworkers—mostly to save money but also to provide greens that are otherwise difficult to procure. Finally, there is a small airfield with a plane undergoing repair and a working, rented plane. The guard, barbed-wire fence, and strong gate separated space into dualities of inside:outside, farm:field, tamed:wild, secure:dangerous, and it widened the already considerable distance that separated farmer from farm.

This separation of the farmer from work, from farm, and from crops is different from what I had expected, recalling for me the plantation and its alienation and reconstitutions of workers, crops, and land—owned but not lived on by family, and entirely dependent on farmworkers. These workers are invisible in the celebratory newspaper articles of the pioneers of Brazil. Invisible too are their struggles to control pests such as the tiny whitefly, their dependence on speculative land deals for their business model, and the capital flows that depend on midwestern capital investments from farmers' retirement plans.

At Ian's farm, and those of his US and Brazilian peers (see Gracia 2017), women are generally excluded from the fields and have limited roles in the farm offices in town. Most US-owned farms are operated by unmarried heterosexual men who may have a romantic partner who is not involved in the farm. Further, there is significant value attributed to the masculinity expressed on these farms (in terms of farmwork and farm management) and off the farms (expressed in the management of investors) as I will discuss in later chapters. This gender-based separation on family farms continues decades-long trends of minimizing and devalorizing women's work on farms in the United States (Barlett 1993; Keller 2014; Barlett and Conger 2004; Anderson 2020; Rosenberg 2015) and in Brazil (Brumer 2004; Waltz 2016).

As I discuss in chapter 3, the population of transnational farm owners resembles an oil rig crew more than a farm in its extreme gender imbalance and heightened focus on masculinity. For this reason, women's voices are lacking in this research. Any proper study of movement and migration must have a gender component to document the gendered dimensions of the migration experience (Kosminsky 2007), and this ethnography contributes to this study by showing how masculinity shapes migration and farming experiences. Masculinity provides these farmers privileged access and freedom that are not available to women migrants in agriculture. For example, upriver from Western Bahia on the São Francisco River, young women migrate to Pernambuco for work in the fruit-growing industry. Mirroring the movement of US farmers to Western Bahia, they migrate in search of a little more freedom and flexibility, but unlike the male US migrants, they face constant frustration—sensing that they moved out of patriarchal family homes only to become imprisoned by new figures of authority in the homes of relatives and in their workplaces (Scott and Santos 2014). Female workers in the region face gender-based discrimination in the workplace and a diminished role in male-dominated labor unions (C. de A. Silva, Menezes, and Oliveira 2018). The US farmers face their own gilded imprisonment in their struggle to demonstrate their masculinity both on and off the farm (Ofstehage 2022). While Keisha-Khan Perry's analysis of Black Brazilian women fighting against land grabs in Salvador do Bahia explores their intersectional struggle for land and community (Perry 2013), this ethnography demonstrates the intersectional privileges afforded to whiteness, masculinity, and nationality.

Perhaps this story conjures up images of Henry Ford's dream of Fordlândia, where he created a rubber supply chain and built a US-style worker town in Amazonia in which workers were expected to adopt ascetic lifestyles, diets, and dwellings (Grandin 2010). But while the transnational farm owners I interviewed spoke of bringing "American agriculture" to Brazil, few of them espoused an interest in the lifestyle of the farmworkers. Or perhaps this story calls forth comparisons to the infamous *confederados* who, facing Reconstruction after defeat in the American Civil War, chose to migrate to Brazil to continue their slave-dependent livelihoods (Kawa 2016). Many of these transnational farm owners did say that their migration was a way to continue their family farm livelihoods and traditions. Or, if we follow the lead of my informants in Brazil, we can trace their narratives back to the Northern European migrants who occupied the American Prairie in the nineteenth century. Yet this group has little concern for long-term settlement. A more apt comparison is the gentlemen farmers who settled the American Prairie of Iowa and Kansas (Harnack 2011). These British aristocrats had uncertain futures in England as second sons with no claim to family estates and they were bored with the other available options at home. Drawn by the dreamlike landscapes and conquering narratives of the American West, they migrated to the Prairie to form small communities. After a few years, finding the work distasteful and the climate unbearable, they went back to England.

The story of Soylandia, from the perspective of farmer-migrants, is a story of migration, movement, crisis, and hope. Early migrations of Italian (Pereira 2002), German (Willems 1946), and Japanese (Lone 2001) farmers created farming communities that would later engage in soy production in the South of Brazil. Their descendants migrated from the South of Brazil to Santarém in the North bringing with them know-how, capital, and the legacies of farming and migration. They now occupy privileged positions as "missionaries of modernity" and drivers of cultural and economic progress (Adams 2010). Gaucho migrants to the soy frontier link their movement to land inaccessibility in southern Brazil and to their dreams of continuing farming traditions (Haesbaert 1998; Botelho and Andrade 2012; J. V. T. dos Santos 1991). Unfortunately, they created the same conditions of land inequality and barriers to farming they had escaped from (D. H. Costa and Mondardo 2013) in addition to the social and ecological violence they perpetrated on people and land.

Japanese colonists also have a rich history with soy production in both Brazil and Bolivia (Suzuki 2006) and JICA-supported agricultural research in the Brazilian Cerrado alongside the work of the US-based Rockefeller Foundation (Nehring 2016; J. E. S. de Oliveira 2022). Mennonites from Canada and the United States dominate soybean production in Paraguay, play a significant role in Bolivia, and claim to have brought agronomic practices from Georgia to Goiás to make the Cerrado productive (Ofstehage 2019; 2018c). In Bolivia, Brazilians tell a story of bringing technology, know-how, and capital and playing a large role in the development of the soy agroindustry (Valdivia 2010; Soruco, Plata, and Medeiros 2008). In Paraguay, primarily poor, landless sulista (Brazilians from the southern states of Paraná, Santa Catarina, and Rio Grande do Sul) farmers settled in the Gran Chaco; their circumstances are precarious relative to that of the large-scale, highly capitalized Mennonite farmers of the region (Blanc 2015). More recently, Brazilian farmers, capitalists, and agronomists have relocated to Mozambique to capitalize on cheap farmland and introduce the Brazil Model of industrial soy farming to the Nacala Corridor in that sister country of Portuguese colonialism. These "fugitive strategies" of moving frontiers creates short-term resource depletion and long-term ecological devastation but can also create lasting settlements, as in the case of the creation of the city of Londrina out of the agricultural colonization of Paraná in the twentieth century (Margolis 1977, 1973).[9] Life at the agricultural frontier is perilous and it is also generative. Despite the destructive nature of expansion and conversion, life persists in the face of capitalist destruction (Tsing 2015; Lacerda 2021) whether in the form of a nonnative cash crop legume or a maned wolf capering through a field.

The movement of people to the soy frontier and the expansion of soy production (pushing that frontier's boundaries) are driven by lucrative commodity markets, supportive government programs, and capital, but farmers in Soylandia authorize and celebrate soy expansion as something more than markets and capital. Large-scale farmers throughout Latin America balance both agrarian and industrial regimes of value and defy portrayals of them as disinterested economic actors. Mirroring changes in US agriculture, soy farming in Brazil has undergone a shift from poor farmers planting diversified crops in the South of Brazil to MBA-holding farm managers directing the cultivation of bioengineered monocultures. However, the role of large-scale farmers in general—be it as harbingers of oppression and destruction, as improvisational entrepreneurs, or as refugees of crisis—remains undefined, as does the specific role of US farmers. This is a story of an emblematic site in Luís Eduardo in Western Bahia, and an emblematic group of transnational farmers. They alone did not make Soylandia what it is, but their story is the story of Soylandia.

As Arturo Escobar (2008) states, difference matters. Soylandia has been shaped by capital, state policies, and colonialism along with local contours of landscape topographies, soil profiles, and emergent ecologies. It has also been shaped by the dreams, actions, and memories of those who have resisted soy and those who have planted it. Capital is parasitic on social (Braun 2015; Paredes, Sherwood, and Arce 2015; Ofstehage 2017a) and ecological life, but it is also generative of practices and ideas that reproduce it over different sociomaterial landscapes yet also undermine it. This book, *Welcome to Soylandia*, is thus three welcomes.

First, it describes how US farmers entered Soylandia to become dwellers, extractors, villains, and heroes of that world. These farmers were newcomers not only to Brazil but to Soylandia and had to learn how to become Soylanders. Ethnographic research, including semistructured interviews in English and Portuguese, participant observation, and other methodologies—delineated in the appendix—provided detailed data on how US farmers came to consider migration to Brazil, how they arranged the purchase and establishment of farms in

Brazil, and how they made sense of the cultural, agronomic, and business aspects of farming in Soylandia. Ethnography provides a grounded, situated perspective. Inspired by ethnographies of Wall Street traders (Ho 2009), elite farmers (Bobrow-Strain 2007), rural activists (Wolford 2010), I document the processes and meaning-making that make transnational farming possible. Second, it is an invitation to the reader to hear how this process of soybean cultivation expansion, foreignization, and exploitation happens on the ground. Ethnography produces data, but ethnographic writing tells a story; this is a story of Soylandia. And third, this book, rather gloomily, is an invitation to the rest of the world to see what agriculture as flexible farming might look like if—as suggested by the *Economist*, the UN, and the Bill and Melinda Gates Foundation—everyone follows the pathway to Soylandia. Soylandia is a dystopian vision of replaceable parts, alienation, and capital, but to many this kind of agriculture has the potential to reduce global famine and accelerate rural development. This ethnography serves as a case study of flexible farming to show the extent to which the dream of Soylandia is really possible.

Flexible Farming: Making Agriculture Work for Finance

Transnational farmers practice a method of capitalist agriculture designed to be unmoored from social and ecological connections.[10] Soylandia as a territory includes a diversity of farming styles (Mier y Terán Giménez Cacho 2016; Vennet, Schneider, and Dessein 2016), economic relations (Wesz Junior 2016), and values (Ofstehage 2016), reflecting the inherent diversity of the land, the people on the land, and the markets, economies, and climates that shape agricultural realities. Soylandia as a dream, however, has a relatively consistent appearance. The conceptual side of Soylandia provides a model for how agriculture should be done (Ofstehage 2018c). It is not so much a technological package—though in this case it would include no-till, genetically engineered seeds, and agrochemicals—but rather an approach that favors capital-intensive solutions over labor-intensive solutions, simplicity over complexity, consistency and sameness over diversity, control over wonder, short-term profit and action over long-term investment and patience. Technological advancement in agriculture has been ongoing for ten thousand years—from selective seed saving accelerating plant breeding to the steel plow digging through deep soils and later to self-driving combines harvesting two hundred bushels per acre of corn. Soylandia is more than technological advancement; it is a change in the frame of reference for agriculture from an agrarian endeavor toward a business endeavor. I call this strategy flexible farming (Ofstehage 2018a).

Flexible farming requires cutting loose the rooted and grounded aspects of farming. Land, work, and plants are made into flexible, fungible, and replicable commodities that are planted, hired, fired, bought, and sold according to market prices, farmland values, changing government policies, and fluctuating exchange rates. It is not the flexibility afforded through diversified crops, intercropped fields, and the use of diverse agroecologies and landscapes, or achieved through dependence on collective forms of resilience. Rather, it is a flexibility of the farm as a business entity, afforded by treating both land and workers as interchangeable and replaceable cogs in a machine. This way of farming is exemplified by US farmers in Western Bahia as well as by sulista farmers in Mato Grosso (Mier y Terán Giménez Cacho 2014), contract poultry operations in Bolivia (Kollnig 2019), and hog operations in North America (Blanchette 2020).

Flexible farming depends on alienated forms of land, labor, and crops. Fungibility first requires alienation from physical and social relations, meaning a reduction of material differences (e.g., in soil profiles, fieldwork skills, or seed phenotypes) and a concomitant severing of social relations. This renders the farm fungible like a machine with replaceable parts; the farmer is the mechanic on the lookout for cheaper and more reliable parts. An injured, combative, or unneeded farmworker can be fired or replaced; crop rotations are determined by market prices; and a plot of ground is not a permanent part of the farm but rather a replaceable asset. This turning away from connection and relational existence allows for the second aspect of fungibility: exchangeability. Work, land, and crops must be made exchangeable by becoming commodified (expressible in market terms) and replaceable (added or removed from a farm's repertoire with little cost); they must be broken down into replaceable parts to become flexible.

Flexible Land

Flexible land is flat, homogenous, and amenable to industrial agriculture. This topographically and agronomically simplified landscape allows for a simplification of production. Flat topographies allow large farm machinery to easily pass through a field; large swaths of agroecologically consistent land encourage monocultural practices; and amenability of the land to Green Revolution technology allows for both the implementation of industrial farming practices and a programatization of farming tasks. My questions about differences in farming practices in Brazil were often greeted with disinterested answers as farmers explained that they farmed the same way their Brazilian neighbors did. Farming was easy, they argued, especially after you hire managers, agronomists, and farmworkers. Developing the land, which entailed clearing it of native vegetation, adding lime and other fertilizers, and implementing a crop rotation, took time, energy, and capital, but after that it was simple; it was the business side they worried about.

In addition to the physical characteristics of the soil, land value, liquidity, and speculative prospects ensure that farmers reap at least a speculative profit if not a productive one. Further, contiguous tracts of cheap but marketable land with access to infrastructure enable access to agricultural commodity markets as well as farm real estate markets. Ideally for flexible farmers, land can be bought at commodity frontiers where land is cheap and infrastructure is improving. As commodity frontiers advance and the region around their farm becomes incorporated into the national economy, land value rises and farmers can sell land for speculative profit (Fairbairn 2020). As noted by Madeleine Fairbairn, investors may see farmland as a cut-and-dried financial asset and forget about the "unruly materiality of agricultural land" (105). The flexible farmer's task is to minimize this unruliness as much as possible.

Flexible land must be commodified, but it must also be liquid to enable quick and easy entry to and exit from the region. Also necessary for this turn is a social disconnection from the land and the farm. Farmland value often refers to the monetary exchange value, or perhaps the use-value of the land, but farmland is

FIGURE 6. A barbed-wire fence separating a US-owned farm from the countryside.

also valued for its noneconomic uses, its political significance, and family connection.[11] Flexible farms are units of economic production, not social production. They are centralized, sterile, and protected by guards and fences. Farmworkers live there but without their families.

Flexible Crops

Flexible crops require few long-term investments, have little nonmarket value, and can be easily replaced depending on commodity market swings. These crops are materially flexible in terms of uses and products and discursively flexible in terms of narratives of progress and development. As commodities, flex crops "have multiple uses (food, feed, fuel, fiber, industrial material, etc.) that can be flexibly interchanged while some consequent supply gaps can be filled by other flex crops" (Borras et al. 2016, 94). The flexibility and multiplicity of flex crops allows producers and corporations to quickly respond to changes in market prices, public policies, and production possibilities by redirecting economic production. Soy is as close to being perfectly commodified as any other crop. US farmers in Brazil do not eat their soy, do not boast about their soy fields, and do not tie their identity or politics to soy. For comparison, the pseudocereal quinoa has recently emerged as a globally commercialized commodity; *quinueros* in Bolivia produce quinoa for market reasons, yet they also maintain strong social connections with the crop through shared histories, work, and political life (Ofstehage 2010; 2011; 2012). Even soy holds value for some farmers. Kregg Hetherington writes of a soy farmer in Paraguay who did indeed have an intimate connection with soy: "'Why don't you plant something else?' the policeman asked him, innocently. 'Why don't you plant corn?' The soy farmer, beside himself with frustration, threw a tantrum. With his face twisted in rage, he yelled, 'I only want to plant soy! I want to plant soy!' before jumping in his truck and careening off down the road" (Hetherington 2013, 80).

This passionate defense of soy did not arise from soy farmers in Bahia. Farmers noted repeatedly that their crop rotation decisions were based primarily on market prices and trends and only secondarily on agroecological dynamics (such as pest management, soil fertility, and restrictions of the growing season).

Soy is the ideal flexible crop. It is an annual crop that fixes its own nitrogen (though it still requires other types of fertilizers); requires less pesticide treatment (though still high); and is suitable for a wide range of agroecological environments. Incorporating glyphosate-resistant GMO seeds along with no-tillage further simplifies soy production—reducing both the need for integrated pest management and labor requirements. A flexible crop requires little long-term commitment, simplifies farming with monocultures and Green Revolution technology, and is subject to minimal social value outside of market value.

This enables a farmer to switch crops quickly, simplify farm management, and respond quickly to market prices and climatic changes.

Flexible Work

Farmwork and farmworkers are also made flexible. Typically, farmers visit the farm a few times a week to meet with managers, check on progress in the fields, and ensure that things are in working order. Otherwise they can be found in their offices completing paperwork, communicating with investors in the United States or with workers on their farm, and managing their office staff.[12] According to the soy ethnographer Ane Gracia, large-scale soy production in Bahia produces monotonous work for tractor drivers and manual laborers alike. One tractor driver, Tonho, told her that his labor could be replaced by a computer. Gracia describes this as the temporality of soy. "The hours of the day are slow, every day is the same day, every day has the same routine" (Gracia 2017, 90; my translation). The monotony is only broken up by machinery breakdowns and burst tires.

Farmers operate farms from nearby urban centers or from as far away as the United States. Farming can be done by email as farmers embrace the Brazil Model of farming and outsource the work to local laborers. Work is alienated from the farmer by hiring out farm labor and by a bureaucratization of worker relations; these relations are governed more by minimal work requirements determined by Brazilian law than by reciprocal worker-capitalist relations common to plantation economies. Several farmers described losing interest in the well-being of workers because of the strength of the farmworkers' federation; they suggested that if the Brazilian government was taking care of the workers, the farmers did not need to. Workers were regarded as low-skilled positions and as easily replaced by other workers or machinery. Turnover is high on these farms. Rumors centered on management of the farm and the farmworkers, sometimes about poor or unsafe working conditions for workers, other times about farmers treating their workers too well.

Through flexible farming, US farmers in Brazil have embarked on a new pathway based not on groundedness, family, and community but rather on movement, capital, and business savvy. These transnational farmers' pattern of crisis, decoupling, reencounter, and reengagement with the temporalities and subjectivities of farming mirror the migration of southern Brazilians to the Cerrado or Bolivia as well as the trajectories of Soylandia and the US Midwest.

Flexible farming is distinct from the related processes of settler colonialism/imperialism, plantation agriculture, and neoliberal agriculture. Despite occupying and controlling large tracts of land, farmers are not interested in settling or colonizing that land. Despite simplifying agriculture to vast monocultures, it lacks the static and social connections of plantations. Despite reducing land, labor, and crops to exchange values, the embodied memories, legacies, and temporal frames endure and new material assemblages of land, labor, and crops emerge.[13] Still, it is a colonial practice enacted with a colonial mindset that, in the case of the Brazilian Cerrado, leaves an area colonized and incorporated into the soy commodity frontier regardless of which farmer remains on the farm. Flexible farming is out of place within reified notions of farming, and out of physical place as "farming" becomes detached from place and attached to subjective agricultural careers and legacies (Ofstehage 2018a). Flexibility becomes the corollary to fixity (Besky 2017) in that it avoids persistent associations between work, workers, and place while eschewing a sense of stability, belonging, and rootedness of place and people.

Flexible farming is not devoid of social values, ecologies, and practices; it is generative of values, ecologies, and practices suited for extraction. Flexible farmers alienate themselves from labor, land, and crop; yet rural life cannot be totally alienated from social and material relations, nor can it be fully commodified. Even in an industrial, stripped-down world where capital seemingly drives action and the rest is waste, life emerges unexpectedly from the ruins (Tsing 2015).

Flexible farmers use flexible work, land, and crops, but they still have to engage with the soil, workers, and plants and assemble them as productive units of the farm. This engagement entails learning to be a manager of workers, learning about pests and soils of the Cerrado, and learning how to grow soy and cotton in the tropics. It also involves a social engagement by which farmers give meaning to their work in Brazil. As Tania Li argues, the mechanisms of capital do not operate alone but rather "combine with the character of crops, habits and desires, local and global prices, droughts, diseases, and other elements" (2014a, 128). At this conjuncture of habits and habitats, farmers make changes to the landscape while the landscape makes changes to the farmers.

In the Brazilian Cerrado, farmers shaped and were shaped by the soil, climate, and biodiversity of the land. Friction (Tsing 2011) is often held up as a barrier to development, but as Anna Tsing notes, friction also gives development the traction it needs to establish itself in place. Friction is generative not only of resistance but of new and efficient methods of extractivism and the expansion of extractive models. The Brazilian Cerrado has long been held up as a laboratory for the expansion of capitalist agriculture. Transnational farmers learned to implement minimum tillage practices to conserve soil moisture content in dry Cerrado soils; they changed fertilization practices to make the acidic, ancient Cerrado soils fertile; and they increased pesticide use to replace tillage as a weed killer and to combat vibrant insect and fungi populations. As noted by ecologists, the Brazilian Cerrado is both a fragile ecosystem with many endemic species and a resilient landscape with a tendency to reclaim lost land. Farmers work with and against the Cerrado to create new material assemblages of soy, soil, and other life held together through farmers' work and the Cerrado's constant resistance to development. In this ongoing battle, the Cerrado and farmers create emergent ecologies marked by geological histories of soil formation, scientific research by Brazilian agronomists, the labor of Bahian farmworkers, capital of farmer financiers, and entrepreneurship of transnational farmers.

Out of this industrial transformation new practices, landscapes, soil profiles, and life emerge. Farmers frame the Cerrado as a redeemed wasteland, rescued from obscurity by soy farming. To take discourses of development, redemption, and improvement seriously allows us to connect this movement back to long legacies of farming and migration, and to connect it forward to imagined futures of agricultural modernity. Instead of abandoning the label of farmer in favor of the label of capitalist, entrepreneur, or businessman, they frame their work as the natural and progressive next step in legacies of farming and migration. Despite the radical transformation of rural life, subjectivities and materialities endure, even if changed. They place themselves within the legacies of farming, migration, and improvement yet claim to further this trajectory of change—connecting the past and future through their separation from the romantic ideals of farming. They dominate the land, but they adjust their farming methods to suit the soil, climate, and pests of the Brazilian Cerrado—resulting not simply in destruction but in the emergence of new material relations.

Traditional, Indigenous, and *quilombola* (Afro-Brazilian) communities of the Cerrado, including the Canela people, generate life through regenerative practices of care. Perhaps counterintuitively, I turn to frameworks of care to understand how transnational farmers engage with Brazilian farmworkers, the Cerrado, and soy. Care is how we maintain our world; it is a hands-on, speculative, open-ended ethics (de la Bellacasa 2017). We often equate care with love, purpose, and shared meaning, but care is also repair work, and a transnational farm requires constant repair work. Farmers need to maintain the soil and soy plants enough to produce sufficient yields; maintain their workers enough that they complete their jobs at minimal legal and financial liability; and maintain their relationships with investors so that they will keep investing. Beyond this minimal maintenance or care, farmers perform roles as caregivers, even if only partially. They claim to build up the soil, not despoil it; they claim to be job creators and offer good working conditions, not exploitation; they claim that the pests of Brazil call for expert agronomic hands to protect the plants. Even their work in Brazil is sometimes held up as care for the family farm which, unable to thrive in the United States, continues in Brazil away from the farm and the family. My attention to these narratives and practices of care are not meant to claim that these farmers are improving the Cerrado, as many of them might argue, but rather to show that a transnational farm does require maintenance and repair. Capital and power are enough to occupy land but not enough to manage a farm. Tinkering is the care that makes technology work (Mol, Moser, and Pols 2010).

The flexibility and alienation of extractivist soy production, surprisingly, is made possible by generative processes and care. Care—as tinkering and maintenance but not love—makes a soy farm work. Workers require attention and concern to keep them productive without inducing them to quit or attracting the attention of the labor ministry. Plants, soils, and pests call for constant attention to be at least minimally placed under control. Even finance calls for attention. A farmer who harms their workers or comes under pressure for environmental regulation infractions may lose investments; so will one who underperforms relative to other farmers. This constant adjustment is deeply generative of work regimes, farming practices, relationships to the land, and even the land itself.

Midwestern farmers in Brazil possess highly technified machinery, operate within market-driven institutions (be they farmer cooperatives or family corporations), and engage in a global commodity market of soy. It may be tempting, then, to view them as "capital personified," their souls being the soul of capital (Marx 2008, 257). However, research on large-scale farmers throughout Latin America (Valdivia 2010; Adams 2010; Bobrow-Strain 2007; Hoelle 2015) indicates that elite farmers hold ethical and social values of work aloft as they defend their own work, often balancing agrarian and industrial regimes of value. US farmers' migration and work in Brazil support new meanings of action that can be tied to both agrarian and capitalist regimes of value.

Value is both a foundation and a product of the material and social relations that underpin transnational soy farming. Action, specifically work, is the subject of value realization and contestation; it is also a product of that negotiation (Elson 1979; Gidwani 2008; Graeber 2001; 2013), Value, as the importance of action, is subject to legitimation as actors defend their know-how and their work, thus entailing a process of "people-making" (Graeber 2013). Actions are people-making in two senses. On the one hand, they establish one's status as a legitimate social actor, be it a good farmer, a risk-taking adventurer, or a savvy businessperson. On the other, actions remake farmers as they tie emerging actions, such as managing labor or speaking Portuguese, to articulations of the self and community.

As told in the stories that follow, flexible farmers create new models, practices, values, and relationships. Large fauna and flora suffer in the emergent ecologies of industrial soy production, but plant diseases like soybean rust and insects like the tiny whitefly thrive. Farmers are trained in the conversion of grasslands to farmland, in making a farm and farmland into investments, and in becoming managers of labor. Transnational soybean farmers are participating in a process of disconnection, exploitation, and extraction in Soylandia and then bringing it back to the United States; but their attempts to make flexible, to exploit, and to extract face sociomaterial obstacles on the ground. They try to manage and control the soil, plants, pests, workers, and investors, but the sociomaterial reality is a hard-fought compromise that leaves all parties changed and generates new (but not necessarily improved) practices, values, communities, and ecologies.

Soil, Land, Work, and Value

The remainder of this book is divided into six substantive chapters and a conclusion. Chapter 1 begins with crisis. I point to farmland access in the midwestern United States as a critical factor along with market opportunities, dreams of adventures, and hopes of saving Christian souls as reasons for farmer migration. More important than these motivations, and the factor that separates flexible farmers from exfarmers, is access to capital. This access in most cases is dependent on the support of investors.

In chapter 2, I explore the reasons why these flexible farmers chose the Cerrado in particular. They echo rhetorics of value and waste, and cast their role as transforming wasteland to productive farmland, though not without the aid of Brazilian agronomists. Flexible farming is impeded by environmental protections and conservation; discourses of waste and improvement, along with government support, open up land for development.

Chapter 3 is about the work involved in maintaining a flexible farm with an increasing distance from soil, work, and plants. Flexible farmers adopt managerial practices and learn to manage workers, paperwork, and investors. At the same time—like their agribusiness counterparts elsewhere (Chung 2024)—they work to reshape both the agricultural economy and the mindset of farmworkers to focus on growth and modernization.[14]

In chapter 4, I consider the soil, along with the plants and root nodules that make this all possible. I tackle the problems of farming, so I engage with soil, crops, fungi, weeds, pests, and the land assemblage as an encounter that changes both farmer and land. Farming practices in Brazil emerge out of scientific research, farmer knowledge, the material reality of soil and plants, and improvisation. In turn these practices generate meanings for land and models for farming. The farmers do not impose on but rather encounter soil and plants and mycorrhizae to "build soil" and "make it productive." In so doing they become different farmers themselves. Flexible farming does not require fertile productive land but rather land that can be managed and made to be productive.

Chapter 5 explores value on the flexible farm, how farmers redefine value, and what it means to be a farmer when the farmer does not belong in a field but in an office. We follow these changes in work and value on the way to community transformation. A community built on exploited work and capitalist values becomes antagonistic, but it is still a community in that it is held together through shared practices, values, and relationships. This is a community of antagonism more than of cooperation—a community built around competition, rivalry, and rumors. These farmers create a community with a shared set of values and practices, but unfortunately these practices involve undermining one another at every turn.

Chapter 6 takes a look at what is coming next for Soylandia and its residents. The aftermath of this Brazilian adventure features endings as well as continuing trajectories in the form of learned farm and business practices, continued land ownership in Brazil, and expanding the frontiers of Soylandia.

Finally, in the conclusion, we see how this experiment is playing out for the farmers, and how it may play out for the rest of us. Flexible farming is about creating a model, without kin or reciprocity, that contains reimagined relationships with the land, work, plants, and with models themselves. The members of this community are becoming flexible farmers and detaching from everything, including community as we usually see it. These farmers have also had to engage with fixity in several ways. One way is making a model for the future of farming. They are generating forms of relating to the world, models, and antagonistic relationships. In the conclusion, I ask "What does this say about the future of agriculture?" In the process we see how Soylandia is both on the march and fragile because as these transnational farmers' dreams fail, they pass the baton on to better-capitalized, better-managed, and more-financialized farms.

BRAZIL IS "THE BIG ANSWER TO A LOT OF QUESTIONS"

We set out early from Luís Eduardo Magalhães to get to Ian Illinois's farm atop the escarpment. The escarpment marks the political border of Bahia and Tocantins states; it is also a natural boundary that separates native Cerrado from the soybean production frontier.[1] Ian, in his work boots, clean jeans, button-down work shirt, and John Deere hat, was dressed like a midwestern farmer, if only a little tidier. He, as most US farmers in Bahia, was used to conducting interviews after having hosted the BBC, NPR, the *Los Angeles Times*, the *New York Times*, the *Chicago Tribune*, *Forbes Magazine*, *Progressive Farmer*, and others for interviews. While we drove past endless fields of soybeans and cotton, we discussed the difficulties of managing farmworkers, "inefficient" and "backward" environmental and worker protections, and even his theories on race and morality. After more than an hour driving on a busy highway, we passed one of his family's fields. At 11,450 acres it stretched to the horizon. Ian's family bought 4,400 acres of Brazilian farmland in 2003 when they first arrived from black-soiled Illinois.[2] By 2009 the Brazilian farm had grown to 30,000 acres. Their farm was owned and managed by Ian and his father John: one of them at the Illinois farm and one at the Bahian farm, and both in perpetual transit. Together they managed the Brazilian farm, employing more than one hundred farmworkers, several farm managers, agronomists, a legal team, an accounting department, and a human resources department.

The Illinois family is one of dozens of migrant US soy farm families in Western Bahia, Tocantins, Roraima, Goiás, and Mato Grosso, Brazil. Most US farmers came to Brazil between 2000 and 2004. Today the number of US-owned farms is

FIGURE 7.   Cotton fields present a new challenge to farmers from the US Midwest.

decreasing as many sell Brazilian land and farms, either on their own initiative or as determined by their investors. The end of their Brazilian adventure comes about in spectacular fashion in some cases but more often as a calculated decision built into their business. They are situated at the frontier in order to buy cheap land but also to sell developed, titled land for a speculative profit.

They are not unique in seeing a business and farming opportunity in Mapitoba (the emergent soy-producing states of Maranhão, Piauí, Tocantins, and Bahia). Gauchos in southern Brazil, unable to further divide family landholdings among family members, migrated to Mato Grosso in the 1980s in search of large, cheap tracts of land (Peine 2010). José Santos (1993) describes these Mato Grosso colonists as previous beneficiaries of colonization projects in Santa Catarina and Paraná in the 1950s and 1960s who had familiarity with mechanized agriculture but had come to experience land inaccessibility in the South. For them, Mato Grosso offered an opportunity to continue both farming and colonization histories. By the early 2000s, farmland values had increased, and accessibility had decreased in Mato Grosso. Farmland consolidation, along with drought and pest outbreaks, led farmers to look elsewhere for the next soybean frontier; many migrated to the Mapitoba region. The migration of farmers and farmworkers to agricultural hubs at the commodity frontier are not linear. They include permanent and temporary migration, short- and long-distance migration, and one-off and periodic migrations (Palmeira and Heredia 2009) as people crisscross territory and commodities to create and re-create livelihoods, communities, and families. Migrant farmers are differentiated by farm size, community of origin, and role in the rural economy; soy farmers in nearby Maranhão are identified as *gauchos*, *pioneiros*, and *soldados rasos* (crazy soldiers) (Gaspar and Andrade 2014).[3]

According to one US farmer, local oral histories remember early pioneers who struggled to produce on unfamiliar soils in the 1950s and 1960s. They had small tractors, little infrastructure, and very little agronomic knowledge of Cerrado soils; accordingly "they had huge amounts of land, but they just couldn't develop it." Beginning in the 1970s and 1980s, southern Brazilian farmer migration to Western Bahia accelerated (Mondardo 2010). In accounts of gaucho and sulista migration to the soy frontier, southern Brazilians expressed an interest in settling new land and establishing themselves on cheap farmland. Gaucho and sulista migrants to Western Bahia described themselves as *pioneiros* (pioneers), *desbravadores* (trailblazers), and *novo bandeirantes* (lit. new bandeirantes; bandeirantes are groups of early Portuguese land invaders who were and are celebrated as heroically expanding national boundaries despite their role in enslavement and violence).

Southern Brazilians claimed a role in "modernizing" the interior of Brazil even as local Bahians called them *invasores* (invaders) (Haesbaert 1998). In Marcos Mondardo's study of sulista migration to Western Bahia, an early colonist claimed, "The main motivation that brought me here was to teach Bahians how to plant soybeans, because they didn't know how." The idealistic (and perhaps disingenuous) farmer continued to reflect that when he arrived locals had said "'Get out grileiros' and now they understand that [southern farmers] came to give them jobs" (Mondardo 2010). While few of the US farmers espoused such paternalistic goals, their migration closely aligns with the motivations and concerns of their Brazilian counterparts. They experienced land inaccessibility at home and saw an opportunity to access cheap land in the Cerrado; they spoke of continuing migratory and agricultural traditions; and they repeated similar ideas and narratives of progress and backwardness. The farmer who told me about the early farmers' struggles with land development also told a story of success. After those early struggles, Brazilian farmers built dirt roads to haul grain to town, established and grew their farms, and passed their farms down to their sons. Their sons bought bigger tractors with more horsepower and developed more land. Then, in the 1990s, farming in Luís Eduardo "just started to boom." Now this second generation of farmers were millionaires with "beautiful farms" who had to pay little besides the "price of calcium to put on there."

Brazilian and US farmers were both drawn to cheap lands, seemingly boundless opportunity, and heroic narratives of the Cerrado; they were also drawn to strong government support for agricultural development in the region. Land privatization and "modernization" began in the 1970s and is defined by local communities as a process of exclusion, as an enclosure of common land and traditional territories driven by manifestations of crises of soybean production in Brazil and capital accumulation at the commodity frontier (Alves 2006). Governmental and intergovernmental programs such as POLOCENTRO, PRO-DECER, and PROTERRA provided rural credit; Embrapa (the Brazilian Agricultural Research Corporation) developed industrial agricultural practices suited for tropical climates and acidic soils; Emater (the federal agricultural extension service) introduced those practices to farmers from elsewhere; and the ruralista agenda supported the loosening of regulations and incentivization for the "conquest of the agricultural frontier of the Cerrado" (Pires and Pires 2020).[4] The Mapitoba region as a whole has experienced an acceleration of foreign land-ownership due to institutional and economic incentives (Sauer and Pereira Leite 2012; Brandão 2015; Cunha 2016).

The creation of Soylandia is made possible by repeated agricultural crises defined by land inaccessibility and government support for migration and farmland expansion; the migration of US farmers to Brazil have followed the same path from crisis to frontier expansion (Ofstehage 2017b). Arturo Escobar writes that "economic crises are ecological crises are cultural crises" (2008, 14). Likewise, this chapter connects the consolidation of the US farm economy, the transformation of the Cerrado into farmland, and the perceived threat to the US family farm. Experiences of crisis coupled with access to capital lead farmers to pursue flexible farming. I provide the collective and personal narratives of migration to understand the economic and social rationale for migration and the affective significance of Brazil, farming, and soy.

Soylandia, and the Cerrado in particular, is an attractive site for land investment due to low farmland prices, highly productive yields, speculative potential, and strong government support. It is also a place that inspires hope in migratory farmers. Farmers speak of the potential profits of farming in the Cerrado but more often of experiences of crisis in the United States and of moments of improvisation. Farming crises demand that farmers respond by changing their agronomic or business strategies or leave farming altogether. In moments of improvisation they act. In this chapter I explore the roots of their migration in crises of different shapes at different times, the process of acquiring land, and their early encounters with the Cerrado. I find that while their migration and flexible farming are rooted in crisis and vulnerability, their improvisation is made possible by their access to capital. These farmers are not elites in the

United States, but in assembling capital in the United States and land in Brazil, they become elites through migration.

Cheap Farmland, High Margins, and a Little Adventure

US farmers have been in Western Bahia for decades. A *Forbes* article, "Deadwood, Brazil," likens the town of Luís Eduardo Magalhães to a Wild West town before US farmers arrived:

> American farmers were among the first to spot the region's reliable sun and rain and the flatness of its plateau. They knew lime could correct the poor soil quality of the savannah that Brazilians call *Cerrado*. When their crops flourished in the "worthless" land they had claimed through a Brazilian homestead act, well-connected bandits called *grileiros*—named after the desiccated crickets the bandits used to "age" forged property deeds—murdered three of the four pioneering American farmers. Clay Earl—a son of one of the murdered farmers, who, as a boy, repeatedly helped defend the family farm during shoot-outs—says 'it was just like the far West 150 years ago.' (Morais 2005)

News clippings from the 1960s claim that US-owned farms employed armed gunmen to expel small producers from their land, and that a third of the Bahian Cerrado was illegally in the hands of US and Brazilian *grileiros* (land-grabbers). Sometimes these conflicts led to "death by land problems." A current farmer once told me that this early generation was far more interested in escaping the United States than in producing soy or making money in Brazil. Among them, he joked, he had met twelve different people who claimed to be the first person to plant soy in Bahia—"people do this kind of thing to make money or to have a good living or to stay alive." Now "each one of them claims that they were the very first one to plant soybeans here." They arrived before agronomic techniques were developed to produce row crops on a large scale and before seeds were bred for the climate in the Cerrado. So, he explained, "when you meet someone who came here in '68, '74, '78—they didn't come here to farm. They were getting away from something." However, they found that the lands they had purchased—one had bought 500,000 hectares—were not occupied by "squatters" but by legitimate landholders. Lawsuits among themselves and between them and local landowners led to the nullification of US-held land titles and many of them returned to the United States.

Midwestern farmers' more recent migration to Brazil is an extension of the long decline of the family farm in the United States. The 1980s farm crisis was defined by low commodity prices, heavy debt loads, and falling farmland values. The debt load of the US farm sector nearly doubled from 1972 to 1982, and debt/asset ratios skyrocketed in the mid-1980s as debt increased and farm assets such as land and machinery lost value (Buttel 1989). Financial stress led to bank foreclosures on farms throughout the Midwest. The liberal lending policies of the 1970s Farmers Home Administration (FHA) abruptly ended in the 1980s as the Reagan administration tightened lending and substantially raised interest rates. Faced with low crop prices and high interest rates in the early 1980s, many farmers took out mortgages on their farms through FHA, the lender of last resort. Farm foreclosures became the sites not only of economic insolvency but also of personal and community trauma. Farm sales auctioned away farmers' means of production alongside relics of family farming traditions. Communities fractured as foreclosed farmers blamed predatory banks, and surviving farmers blamed their neighbors' lack of frugality. In the worst of cases, farmers died by suicide (Dudley 2002).

"Farm loss" meant the loss of a desired occupation, farm property, a steady income, and even a home. While the farm crisis did not force a mass exodus of farmers, it did redefine the work, values, and relations of farm families as farmers changed management styles, became part-time workers, and engaged with government farm support (Barlett 1993). Many farm women also left farmwork and household work behind in favor of part-time or full-time wage labor, which provided a stable income and health insurance; they joked about supporting their husbands' "farming habits."[5]

The 1980s farm crisis is over, but many US farmers experience a perpetual farm crisis of a decreasing number of farms and farm consolidation. At the time of this research (2012–2014), the farm crisis, characterized by financialization, similarly deepened the role of the market in rural life.[6] The farm crisis of the 1980s accelerated processes of farm consolidation and corporatization that have led to narrower profit margins, increased dependency on finance markets, and a shift in expertise from agroecological knowledge to understanding high finance. Midwestern farmers confront high land prices and unpredictable weather patterns linked to global climate change. Together the structural barriers of farmland access and remembered, collective experiences of trauma have forestalled any hope of farming in the United States.

Meanwhile, farmer trade magazines of the late 1990s and early 2000s steadily increased coverage of soybean production in Brazil—sometimes celebrating phenomenal production gains there and sometimes stoking fear of US farmers being outcompeted by their Brazilian counterparts. A 2003 agricultural extension report presents an auspicious outlook for soybean production in Brazil, where soybean acreage and production were growing faster than in the United States and were only limited by infrastructure. Costs of production were "considerably lower", and soybean production was "considerably more profitable" (Flaskerud 2003, 14). The success and, more importantly, the potential of Brazil gave impetus to the ongoing crisis of farming in the United States. Warned for years that they ought to "get big or get out," US farmers saw boundless opportunities in Brazilian agriculture and chose first to get out *and then* get big.[7]

A now-defunct website for Bender Farms, a US-owned farm in Brazil, frames their interest in South American agriculture against the perceived limitations of US agriculture. They cited a shrinking land base in the United States due to urban sprawl and "hobbyist" farms, loss of control over farmland to meet "unrealistic environmental concerns," concern for continued farm consolidation, and an interest in profiting from improved global living standards that may lead to a higher demand for grain. They concluded by saying:

> The increased world demand for food will come from a global supply that will grow by putting new land into production and improving yields through biotechnology, fertility, irrigation, and so forth. As the true global business of production agriculture becomes controlled by ever fewer entities (people, families, companies), we believe we cannot confine our thinking to tradition or locale. We must responsibly plan for growth. All these and more have led us to production in Brazil.

Bender Farms identified two problems that justified their farm expansion. First, increased world demand for food, in their formulation, calls for converting more land into agriculture along with improving farm yields using "biotechnology, fertility, irrigation, and so forth." This first issue speaks to a Malthusian hunger crisis and a need for farmers in general to produce higher crop yields and expand cultivation. The second problem, of farm consolidation by "fewer entities," is a crisis for the farm itself. No longer able to "confine [their] thinking to tradition or locale," the Bender family had accumulated 13,259 acres of farmland near Luís Eduardo by 2006. They then sold the land to a private investment corporation. Adam Bender became the operations manager for the land, and the corporation later bought another 2,500 acres. Many farmers echoed the Bender family's juxtaposition of stiff barriers to farming in the United States with the seemingly boundless agronomic potential and limited government intervention in Brazil. The decision to purchase farmland at a commodity frontier is imbued with high expectations and deep uncertainty. When combined with the material attributes of land, being both finite and requiring some time to bring into production (Fairbairn 2020), the excitement around land sales as word of mouth spreads the gospel of high yields and cheap land pushes the limits of rational economic action. The boom-and-bust cycle of farmland can be partially attributed to the thrill of the land rush. As Madeleine Fairbairn notes in her study of land rushes and financialization, in land deals there is "a tendency to put too much weight on the experience of the recent past in establishing land-price expectations; after a few years of increasing land values, people begin to expect that prices will continue to increase indefinitely" (2020, 58). In the following sections I introduce a selection of US farmers in Western Bahia who will appear throughout the chapters of this book. Though the farmers have overlapping and competing interests, for clarity I group them here in terms of their motivations (profit, farming livelihoods, adventure, and religious mission) for migrating to Brazil.

Get Out and Get Big

In 2001 Paul Iowa was a commodities trading adviser in Northwest Iowa with an eye out for investment options. The first thing he told me during our first interview was that his family descended from a German farm family. They still own the century farm (a farm certified by the state to have been owned by a single family for 100 years). He operated the family farm from 1973 to 1990. Since 1990 the family has rented the land out to neighbors, and Paul has built his financial services and consulting business. Concerned about Brazilian competition for grain markets, Paul embarked on an agricultural tour of Brazil in 2001. Traveling with his son Jacob, his father-in-law, and prospective investors, he evaluated the agricultural potential of the Brazilian Cerrado and came back "really impressed with the size and scale that was potentially possible." He noted that Western Bahia has consistent rains, very flat land, and drainage from rivers—"Someday their agriculture is going to look like [what] we have [in Iowa]." They looked into a few other investment and production opportunities north of Luís Eduardo and in Mato Grosso, but farmland values were higher in Mato Grosso and logistics were worse north of Luís Eduardo. Western Bahia was situated close enough to

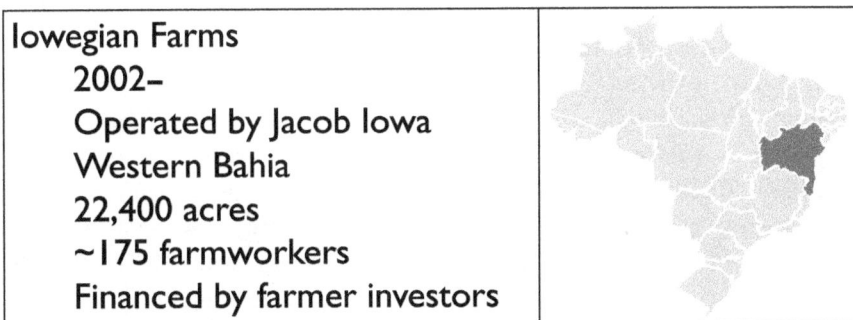

Iowegian Farms
  2002–
  Operated by Jacob Iowa
  Western Bahia
  22,400 acres
  ~175 farmworkers
  Financed by farmer investors

FIGURE 8.

the frontier to be inexpensive but far enough that it had well-developed infrastructure. The climate of Luís Eduardo made the production of high-quality cotton possible, but their first consideration was always the farmland itself, not crop production.

According to a PowerPoint investment pitch, what would later become Iowegian Farms was created "to provide U.S. agricultural producers a venue to participate in the growing agricultural climate that exists in the current economic model of Brazil." In 2001 the family pulled together "a few million [dollars]" through a private placement offering (a nonpublic funding stream that limits the investor pool to people with already existing business ties). They also sold a few hundred acres of Iowa land at $3,100/acre and then purchased Bahian land at $800/acre.

Paul's son, Jacob Iowa, a recent graduate of a large state university, packed his bags and, without speaking Portuguese or having much farming experience of his own, relocated to Brazil. Jacob felt adventurous in the beginning. "This place was way on the other side of the planet . . . someplace you're never going to go see, some place far off," but recently graduated and without a family of his own, he thought, "What the heck, let's try it." The Iowa family had purchased land from a fellow US farmer near Luís Eduardo Magalhães, Bahia, who then managed the farm under the employment of Iowegian Farms. Less than a year after becoming operational in 2004, management issues led them to turn management of the business over to Jacob. As of 2012, the farm employed ninety farmworkers, sixty workers for the cotton gin, ten office employees, an agronomist, and an operations manager. They cultivated 22,400 acres of farmland in cotton, corn, and soy, and owned 9,000 acres of Cerrado in Legal Reserve (land legally required to be set aside, to which we will return in chapter 2). Their farmland is divided between three farm sites (Iowa 1, Iowa 2, and Iowa 3) and several parcels (each named after Iowa counties).

The Iowa family had transitioned from production agriculture to commodity trading advising after the 1980s farm crisis; their purchase and operation of the Brazilian farm was their return to production agriculture. Soylandia for them was both a return to the family's farming past and a continuation of the family's farm consulting business. This intersection was especially useful in their endeavor to profitably manage production in the fields and investors in the boardrooms.

Dennis Tocantins, a fourth-generation farmer in Illinois, began farming on his own in 1979. He "worked [his] butt off to make fifty dollars an acre" on his 160-acre corn and soybean farm before quitting farming in 2000. In the 2000s he began a transition from farming to farm real estate. He visited Brazil on an Illinois farmer leadership program in 1998, then again in 2003. He noted that Brazil was expanding rapidly, and consultants were saying that in a year or two they

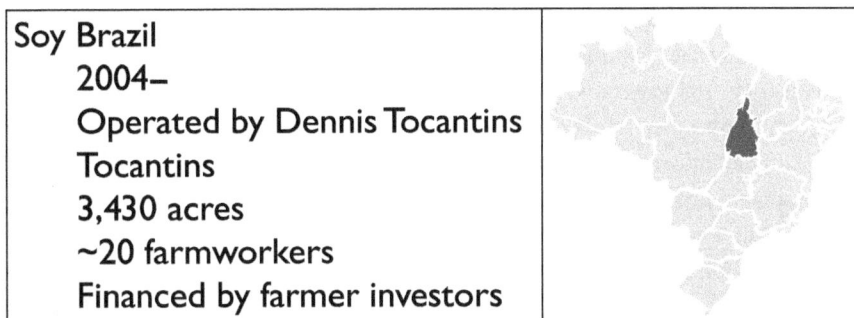

Soy Brazil 2004– Operated by Dennis Tocantins Tocantins 3,430 acres ~20 farmworkers Financed by farmer investors	

FIGURE 9.

would outproduce the United States (although he later complained that "they still say this"). While touring farms in Brazil he met a married couple in the state of Tocantins who was interested in selling land. He bought the land and opened up a test plot soon after, in 2004. Tocantins also drew his interest for its relative lack of US farmers compared to Bahia. He found the culture of the US farming community of Bahia unpleasant (as I will discuss in chapter 6).

In 2012 Dennis owned and operated 650 hectares, of which nearly 550 hectares were planted to soybeans, and rented 700 hectares, of which 660 hectares were planted to soybeans. Dennis and his agronomist also managed 280 hectares, and he and his investors had plans to add 1,800 hectares to their operation. In Brazil they have twenty workers, one agronomist, and a manager who handles the day-to-day operations. Dennis lives and works in Illinois and videoconferences weekly. People in his home community, according to him, like the idea of him going to Brazil and think it is adventurous, though a "really small percent of people have negative opinions, think you're helping the competitor, that kind of thing." Like the Iowa family, Dennis had left the farming livelihood in the United States because it no longer made financial sense and then entered a related occupation.

Though managed as a farm, Dennis's company, Soy Brazil, lists its mission explicitly as "buying, developing, and operating farms to capture appreciation." The company itself is a vehicle for real estate investment with nearly one hundred members and investors—most with connections to US agriculture and all with a long-term interest in real estate appreciation. As many US farmers felt squeezed off their land by rising farmland values, farm real estate kept him in the farm community and business but neutralized the disadvantage of high farmland values. In the United States, farmers were facing high farmland values, farm consolidations, and expensive startup costs. In 1982 the average US farm size was 589 acres, and in 2007 it was 1,105 acres. The consolidation of US farms can be credited to labor-saving technologies such as GMO seeds, reduced tillage, and larger equipment that allowed farmers to manage larger acreages. Farms there have also shifted toward specialization in which they focus on the production of fewer commodities. Together, US farmland value increased, and high rates of farm consolidation reduced land access. Farmers solved the problem of competing in a farm economy of shrinking profits and rising land prices by uprooting and starting anew. The Iowa family and Dennis Tocantins began their recollections of deciding to migrate to Brazil with their origins in agriculture and then told of their partial exit. For them, farming in Brazil is both a return to farming and a continued distancing from farming as they did it before. Both farmers highlighted competition and the potential for profit, yet both also made clear their desire to return to farming.

I Always Knew I Would Be a Farmer

Many US farmers' stories focused explicitly on their desires to farm and for their family farm to persist. Sitting in the shade on his Western Bahian soybean farm, John Illinois told me that his family "came from Ireland sometime in the 1800s and just always farmed." John owned and managed the farm with his son, Ian, who had farming experience and also had been through agricultural business training at a university. Ian grew up on a large family farm operated by his father, uncle, and grandfather and he "never had any doubt" that he was "going to farm."

Ian was studying business at a state university when, drawn by press coverage on the soy boom and by personal connections to tour operators, his father and uncle went on a short agricultural tour in Brazil's Cerrado. Months later they went on a second, longer tour. For Ian's father and uncle, Brazil was a means of acquiring more land to expand and maintain the family farm as well as to provide

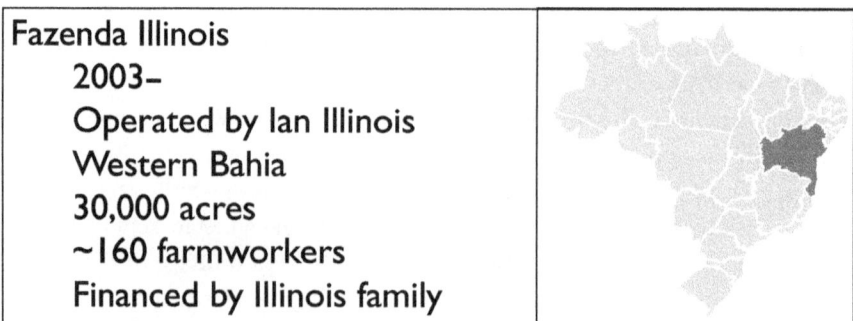

Fazenda Illinois
  2003–
  Operated by Ian Illinois
  Western Bahia
  30,000 acres
  ~160 farmworkers
  Financed by Illinois family

FIGURE 10.

more on-farm work opportunities to the wider family. John Illinois helped his father start the farm from scratch after the family had gone bankrupt and lost their land and farm during the Great Depression.

When I asked John when he had taken over management of the family farm he rejected the premise of the question, saying "I farm with my father and my brother, so I don't know if I ever really took it over. . . . I always just put my total commitment into it." The farm in Brazil was intended to supplement the family's farm income and allow them to expand in the United States. John explained that the farm in Brazil was "a way to make some really good profits, make some really good money and some of that will be used in time to further the US expansion."

For Ian, it was a means of starting to farm straight out of college, without heavy capital investment to buy land in the Midwest or waiting to take a more central role on the family farm. Land prices were high in Illinois at $3,000 per acre, and farming in Brazil seemed like it would be cheap and easy.[8] Ian's story is common in his difficulty of starting a farm as a beginner. Machinery costs, farmland values, and land availability impose restrictions on who can become a farmer and insurmountable debt on many who do. Before the completion of his MBA, he told his longtime girlfriend, Betty, "I'm going to propose. Say no if you don't want to go to Brazil." She said yes. Betty now does accounting for Fazenda Illinois.

The Illinois family purchased 4,400 acres in 2001 for a tenth of the price of Illinois farmland. Unlike most US farmers in Brazil, they self-funded their move to Brazil using capital from their farm in the Midwest. Their purchased land was cleared but not yet completely "developed," meaning they would have to use a crop rotation and heavy fertilization to make it ready for industrial farming. At the time Ian spoke no Portuguese and had relatively poor knowledge of the local agroecological conditions. Over the years he has learned conversational Portuguese and has developed a cropping rotation that is less focused on soy and more dedicated to cotton—a rotation that more closely resembles that of Brazilian producers in the region. At the time of my research in 2014, the farm had 30,000 acres of production land, 4,000 of which was cleared by the business, and the remainder cleared prior to being purchased. These 30,000 acres were in a rotation of corn, soy, and cotton, with the relative mix of the three crops changing year to year according to changes in commodity markets. In addition to their own land, they managed a sizable acreage for a midwestern farm investment firm.

Ian Illinois's story highlights issues with profitability and land access, but the main driver for him was to be a farmer—to maintain his family farming livelihood, inclusive of kinship, value, and community, by finding land abroad. This work maintained farming livelihoods, but it also deepened their relation with capital.

Brazilian Adventure

Eddie Upstate grew up on a Central New York family farm started by his grand-father where they grew sweet corn, field beans, soybeans, and field corn. He and his father found it was "gonna be hard to expand" there. The family saw potential in Brazil in terms of reduced land and labor costs and an increased potential for expansion. After touring rural Goiás, they settled on Western Bahia due to its proximity to Brasilia, reasonable access to ports, and its agronomic potential. They saw themselves as trailblazers and pioneers. When they came, Eddie told me, there was no infrastructure, it was very "primitive." "There was nothing in the area . . . a few gauchos, but not many. The land is on an escarpment and has regular and good rainfall." They purchased 1,600 hectares of land (half native Cerrado and half developed farmland) in 1999 that they quickly converted to all farmland; they bought another 800 hectares of Cerrado two years later to convert to farmland. Frontier Farm, as it was called, eventually grew to 18,000 acres.

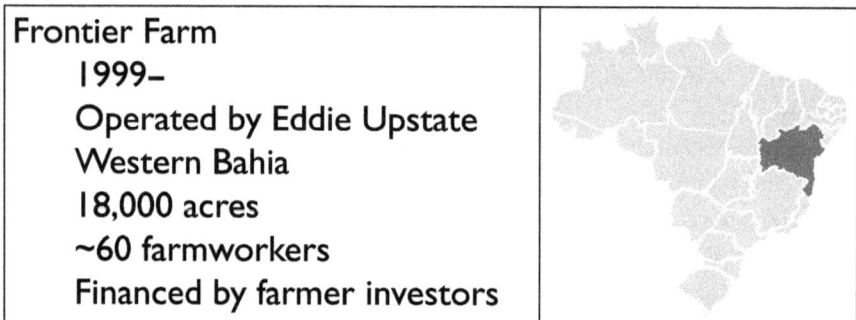

Frontier Farm
    1999–
    Operated by Eddie Upstate
    Western Bahia
    18,000 acres
    ~60 farmworkers
    Financed by farmer investors

FIGURE 11.

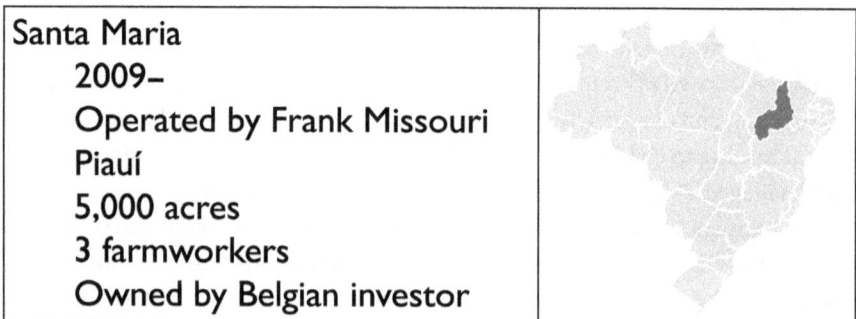

Santa Maria
    2009–
    Operated by Frank Missouri
    Piauí
    5,000 acres
    3 farmworkers
    Owned by Belgian investor

FIGURE 12.

The early days, Eddie stressed to me, were difficult. A worker they had brought with them from the United States only lasted five days before asking to go home because there was "no electricity on the farm, and it was a long way from home, and it was just scary." Eddie and his dad's plan was to "suffer in the first couple years, which is what we did, and then we'll have it pay off in the long run." At the time of the interview he told me it was just starting to get a little easier.

Frank Missouri told me he was from a long line of farmers. "As far back as we can trace, there's always been a farmer. My mom's from a farming family, my dad's from a farming family, both of my grandfathers were fairly well-known farmers in their county. My one grandfather was the first one to have a [hay] baler in our county."

The family farmed in Missouri near the confluence of the Missouri and Mississippi Rivers near St. Louis and in the flood plain. The area later became urbanized as a bedroom community of St. Louis. He studied, then taught and worked at a large public university in Missouri. He had decided to enroll in a master's program in agricultural economics and to work in policy analysis. This work and his friendship with a Brazilian in his old fraternity led him to Brazil, it was "the big answer to a lot of questions that were always being asked." They went on a tour, and he came back unimpressed. He went on another tour later and again was not impressed.

Later a group of Missouri hog farmers approached him to manage a farm for them in Brazil. The hog farmers feared growing regulation of livestock in the United States and expected that they would never be able to build another hog barn. Frank said no. As he remembers it, he told them "You're nuts. There's no way. You're crazy. You guys think it's so nice down there, it's not. . . . I think it's a bad idea." He crossed paths with them a few years later in Bahia and reconsidered. At the time (2003), Brazilian soy production had come to dominate farming conversations and press in Missouri. As he remembers it, an attitude of "we're never going to be able to compete with Brazil" encouraged Frank to think seriously about working in Brazil. The hog farmers weighed their options. They considered producing soybeans in Bolivia or Argentina where they expected the soil to be better but foreign control of land more difficult, or in the "black soils" of Ukraine or Africa, but they leaned toward coffee growing in Brazil early on because "some of those guys didn't want the political problems at home of farming soybeans in Brazil" (e.g., "neighbors calling you a traitor"), and because it seemed like coffee had a higher profit potential. He joined the endeavor because he saw potential in the venture but also out of a sense of "restlessness." He remembered thinking "Well, if I go to Brazil, and after five years the only thing I come back with is the shirt on my back, that's still a pretty good experience." Besides, even if the venture failed he would return with an improved resume, one with added proficiency in

Portuguese and Brazilian culture. In short, "there was this thing in Brazil that I knew would work, and actually my ideas did work. It was going to be tough . . . but it was also going to be an adventure. . . . So I saw a bigger risk in just staying [with] what I was doing."

The investment group faced challenges early on as the exchange rate shifted from 3:1 (reals per dollar) to 4:1 and the election of the leftist Luiz Inacio Lula da Silva worried them. The group quickly broke apart. One faction split off to buy land on their own, another (including Frank) decided to rent land and produce soybeans even though "the intention was to buy land, because that's what I had signed on to. I hadn't given up on what I had in America just to come be a renter down here—especially not to rent land for soybeans. I could have done that at home."

Frank's group rented land from another US farmer (the same farmer Jacob Iowa had hired and later replaced as farm manager) and their business relationship fell apart. Frank stayed in Brazil anyway. By that time more than six months had passed, and he was determined to make something out of his venture. He tried to explain the decision: "Tenacity. I don't know. . . . What's the difference between grit and being stubborn? You know? I would like to say I'm not a quitter, I stuck it out."

Today, Frank manages two small farms. The first, 5,000 acres in Piauí called Santa Maria, is owned by a Belgian investor. Settled near an old meteor crater, past long rows of sweet-smelling ten-year-old eucalyptus trees and a fence that was constructed to settle a debt, the farm has a small house, dozens of skinny pigs, a few dozen thin Brahmin cattle, and two workers who had not been paid in months. Without pay, transport to town, or food, the workers had made a deal with a grocer that he could keep his cattle on the farm in exchange for food. Frank also manages a banana farm a few minutes out of Barreiras, Bahia, with irrigated banana trees. The farm has a small house and garden, inhabited by a former MST (landless workers' movement) farmworker and his family. They take care of the farm, protect it, and earn a modest wage.

Eddie and Frank speak about farming and profit, but they also sought out adventure. Eddie found land where there was "nothing" and Frank found relief for his restlessness in Brazil. Neither one of them speaks of long-term plans in Brazil but rather focuses on stages of a plan—if it does not work out they can always return with the shirt on their back and a more interesting resume.

Soil and Souls

Not all farmers came for family, profit, or adventure. The Indiana family came to Brazil in 1972 after Kurt Indiana sold the Indiana farm to become a missionary

Oasis Farm 2004– Operated by Kurt Indiana Roraima 25,000+ acres ~50 farmworkers Financed by farmer investors	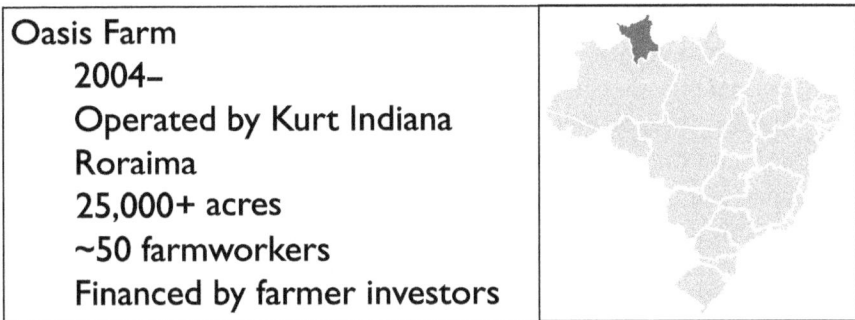

FIGURE 13.

in the southern states of São Paulo and Paraná. His son Brad stayed in Brazil until 1977 when, drawn by an interest in farming, he moved back to Indiana to work on his grandfather's farm and to attend university.

After ten years in Indiana, Kurt asked Brad to leave the Indiana farm for a few years to help out with the expanding missionary organization in Brazil. Brad left Indiana with his wife and ten-month-old son Caleb to work in the mission's accounting department. This work provided experience with Brazilian business practices and international money transfers that would later prove invaluable. After seven years of working for the mission, Brad's young family moved to the state of Mato Grosso to alleviate a perceived "spiritual burden for farmers in central Brazil, [where] there's no church, or Bible study or anything," and also as a means of reconnecting with agricultural production. Their early days in Mato Grosso were difficult. Procuring essential agricultural inputs like seed and herbicides was an uncertain and involved process:

> You had to stand in line and you made phone calls and you ordered it [inputs]. When it was time to pay for it, you would either write a check and someone would pick it up or you'd run to one of the towns south of us, four or five hours on a bus over a dirt road and go to the bank or however you thought to do it. A considerable amount of the effort was just in establishing the business relationships, getting suppliers and making payments and that kind of stuff. It's gotten a lot better, but it's still fifty percent of our time that goes to bureaucratic stuff. It's just a ton of paperwork in Brazil.

According to Brad's son Caleb Indiana, who now acts as manager on the family farm, "My parents made the decision from that standpoint to go to central Brazil, and agriculture was a little bit of a secondary question. They had to do something to be there in the community." As a way of financing this mission, and of reengaging with the agrarian life, Brad and Caleb courted like-minded investors, driven by missionary objectives as well as by financial profit, to start a soybean farm in Mato Grosso. Some investors were also missionaries and many were farmers. The farm grew slowly, and the family continued to do missionary work and grow the farm until 2001 when they perceived an economic and spiritual opportunity in the North of Brazil. Land prices were rising in Mato Grosso, but prices in the northern state of Roraima had remained low. Roraima also had extensive infrastructure and expected market opportunities with Venezuela. They sold the Mato Grosso farm for 40 percent over their expected market price and bought a midsize farm (more than 25,000 acres) in Roraima, christened Oasis Farm. However, the move came with difficulties. Land prices in Roraima at the time the family decided to move (2001) were forty reais but increased to 100 reais per hectare by 2003, then increased by another 800 reais per hectare in the next eighteen months. To make this turn of events worse, poor weather conditions in Roraima placed a stress on farming, as I will discuss in later chapters.

Leon Idaho tells a similar story. He and his wife owned a small farm in Idaho until he realized that he could not make a living from his 600-acre edible bean and sugar beet farm near Boise, and he wanted to build something for his children. Between 2000 and 2004, the family suffered four consecutive years of financial loss. While struggling with the farm, Leon received his calling as a member of the Church of Jesus Christ of Latter-Day Saints to serve the church and spread their teachings. Without "any kind of established location that the family's been for a hundred years," he "got on the internet and looked around" for a site to start a farm and spread the gospel. He considered farms in Mexico and Australia before stumbling on the FarmBahia (a company that specialized in consulting with farmers on agricultural investments in Western Bahia) website and signing on for an agricultural tour of Western Bahia. There he found the farming opportunities and the scale of agriculture impressive. More importantly, it seemed like

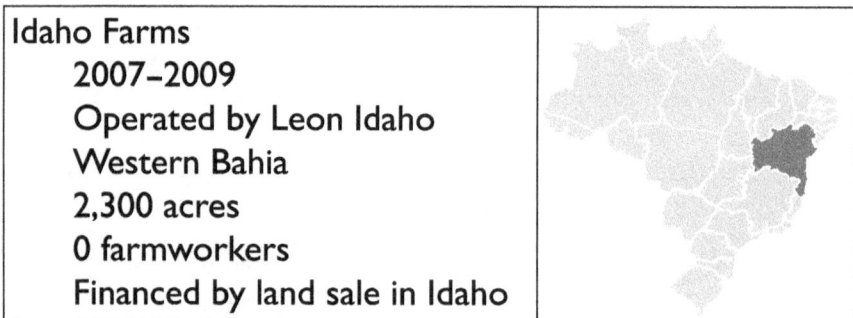

Idaho Farms
  2007–2009
  Operated by Leon Idaho
  Western Bahia
  2,300 acres
  0 farmworkers
  Financed by land sale in Idaho

FIGURE 14.

the kind of place where he could just farm, be part of a like-minded and friendly community, and raise his family. He sold his home acreage in Idaho and bought a piece of land in Bahia. He explained, "We had the choice between going broke in Idaho or going broke in Brazil."

Leon's dad was a farmer in western Idaho until he lost the farm in 1983. The family then went to California, where they worked on his uncle's farm. Leon left to study agriculture at an Idaho university while his dad, after working on his uncle's farm for eight years and saving money, had a chance to buy a farm to fix up and operate. They "grew sugar beets, and potatoes, and wheat, and corn, and hay, and beans—edible beans. Everything but soybeans . . . and cotton." At that time, the growth of Boise had led to increases in farmland values. Surrounded by big farmers, suburban development, and an inability to expand acreage or to make a profit with a small farm, Leon looked for alternatives. "Since we didn't have any farms, or any kind of established location that the family's been for a hundred years, I looked around. I looked at farms on the internet, in Mexico, and Australia—just wherever you could find them on the internet."

He found out about farming opportunities in Brazil through a popular information and tour website and was happily surprised to see the expansion of a frontier rather than the transformation of farmland into residential zones. "It showed that Brazil is making farm ground instead of building houses on it." He and his father took a tour, then sold their small Idaho farm. In 2004 Leon, along with his wife, Sarah, and their child, moved to Brazil.

First in Leon's mind was having a place to farm and to pass down to his children. He recognized and to some extent took pride in the differences between his farm and his neighbors'. It was a smaller farm, he was not supported by outside investors, and they did not have an "established, expensive farming operation like the other guys." Leon and Sarah's goal was to "grow a little bit . . . so my kids could farm if they wanted to." Luís Eduardo was attractive because it had cheap land but also because it had a farm community. "It was encouraging [that there] were other kids my age. . . . They were doing some fun things and trying to grow. And I didn't have that [in Idaho]." They purchased 2,300-acres near Luís Eduardo Magalhães in 2007 and named it Idaho Farms.

Making a Transnational Farm

"Get big or get out" rings true today. Wealthy farmers get big and continue to weather and profit from high farmland values and widespread farm consolidation. Many small farmers either adopt alternative farming strategies (e.g., community-supported agriculture and high-value produce production) or get out of farming. The farmers in this story, however, are neither small, nor elite. The incentives of lower labor and land costs in Brazil draw farmers to dusty Cerrado farmland, but farmers' access to capital makes the migration possible. These farmers financed their migration through private placement (piecing together investors from neighboring farmers, business associates, and family), open calls for investors and for those who had farmland, through the sale of US farmland at high prices to be used as capital to invest in Brazilian land purchases. The assembly of a transnational farm can require a "shepherding" (Fairbairn 2020, 95) of small plots into the formal market, adding value to the land along the way by formalizing the land title and consolidating smaller properties into larger holdings (Fairbairn 2020).[9]

Typically, investment capital is used to purchase land, machinery, and inputs and to pay farmworkers, managers, lawyers, and accountants. These farmers used investment capital in place of government or bank loans for operating costs. The exception to this arrangement was Dennis Tocantins's farm in which investments were structured as loans to either the US-based corporation or the Brazilian corporation. Like most US-based farmers, Dennis used loans to rent land and purchase inputs at the beginning of the growing season and paid out profits from crop sales at the end of a project term. Project terms lasted between one and ten years, after which capital was repatriated and distributed to investors. Most farms requested investment up front and distributed profits annually.

A pitch for a $10 million investment in what I will call Global Farmland Investments (GFI) illustrates the narrative and financial elements of a Brazilian farmland investment pitch.[10] The cover page of the document shows an image of dozens of combines marching through a soybean field. A slide from their investment pitch presentation asks, "Why Brazil?" and lists the reasons:

- Land in Brazil is 80 percent cheaper
- Production inputs are 10 percent cheaper
- Production returns are 25 to 50 percent greater
- Asset appreciation is double the US rate
- Highest quality cotton and grain products in the world
- Strong market for Brazilian agricultural products
- Government is pro-agriculture and foreign investment
- Agriculture is the backbone of an already strong economy, the strongest in South America
- Climate is similar to California, where climate and seasons are highly predictable
- There are a growing number of foreign agricultural investors, generating interest and value in land and production in Brazil.

The investment opportunity was framed thus:

> The GFI Fund I, LP (Limited Partnership) provides investors with a vehicle to invest in U.S.-managed agriculture in Brazil. The Fund will utilize Brazil's attributes of affordable land and ideal agriculture conditions and the expertise and experience of a U.S. large farm operator and manager. Fund resources will be applied to land, management, operation, and the renting of machinery. The properties will be located in Western Bahia, Brazil ("investment territory") and will be managed and run on site.

The "investment strategy" was to rent 3,000–8,000 hectares of already established farmland on 7–10 year contracts. Most US farmers in Brazil had a mixed financial interest in crop production and land speculation; renting land placed GFI squarely in the field of crop production without the potential to develop and sell farmland. This strategy is common in farmland investment strategies as managers focus on "cash returns" (income from yields and rent after subtracting operating expenses) and "capital gains" (returns from the sale of land) (Fairbairn 2020). The GFI Fund strikes a balance between cash returns and capital gains in its investment pitch.

The GFI Fund projected extremely optimistic goals—namely, an average annual return to investors of 25–40 percent. Further, they anticipated that investors would be paid back in full within 2.5 years of production. According to their investment pitch, this incredible rate of return would be possible insofar as investment would capitalize on "cheap land" in Brazil and the introduction of "farming innovations" from the United States. Investment would pay for renting farmland at $25–40 per hectare, machinery costs of $950,000, management and labor costs of $230,000 per year, and input cost of $2.5 million per 2,500 hectares per year for cotton and $575,000 per 2,500 hectares per year for soybeans.[11]

GFI was created by an Iowan farmer, Ted Burdside, in partnership with an investment banker from Texas. Ted "manage(d) all investments and runs all operations in Brazil, including budgeting, marketing, risk management, crop produciton, and labor management." His pitch highlighted his own farming experience and knowledge alongside market opportunities in Brazil. This included growing up on a family farm, comanaging crop production and labor on his Iowa farm, earning a degree in agriculture (though no degree by that name actually exists at the university named in the pitch), and frequent public presentations.

In face-to-face investment pitches, GFI made investment in Brazilian agriculture an easy choice. According to a PowerPoint presentation, in Brazil farmland is cheaper, inputs are cheaper, and returns on production are higher. A pro-agriculture government, strong economy, and predictible climate in Brazil made the investment not just profitable but safe. The only associated investment risks were the political risk of foreign investment, currency fluctuation, and weather— "a risk in any agriculture investment." These risks were mitigated by, respectively, the Brazilian government's "pro-agriculture" and "pro-foreign investment" stance, the Brazilian government's "active . . . effort to control the fluctuation levels of the Real," and the fact that the farm is twelve degrees south of the equator and therefore "temperature is never a factor."

Investors were attracted to the confident and optimistic outlooks for their farm investment. They were also drawn in by personal relationships. One document, made available due to an ongoing lawsuit between investors and GFI (which will be explored in greater depth in chapter 6), details the importance of word-of-mouth in attracting investors.[12] According to the account, two entities were responsible for bringing in a large proportion of the capital investment: Donna and Craig King and Brad Hill. Donna and Craig King introduced the fund to their longtime neighbors who in turn invited their father to invest $300,000 in the fund. They also recruited Brian Theisen who would become the aforementioned US agronomist on the Brazilian farm. Via Brian, the Theisen family collectively invested over $1.4 million in the farm. Brad Hill, on the other hand, owned an investment firm in Minnesota. Besides investing $870,000 of his own capital in the fund, he encouraged his clients to invest. They collectively invested $1.3 million, for a total of over $2.1 million between Mr. Hill and his clients.

For investors, it was an opportunity to invest for retirement in a productive asset that made sense to them. It also offered a chance to gain firsthand knowledge of markets and production in Brazil that could be used to guide their farming decisions on midwestern farms. For farmers, private investors provided quick capital for farm purchases and development. However, in their shift from bank loans to fund production in the United States, to private investments to fund production in Brazil, farmers also relinquished a measure of control as they now had to answer not only to family members but also to stockholders (Ofstehage 2018b).

Financing for US farms in Brazil often comes through personal contacts, much in the way that investors for ethanol plants in the Midwest are often local farmers. For farmers who distrust the stock market or other investment funds, ethanol plants and international production groups organized into limited liability companies offer an expected return on investment; they also offer a measure of legibility as less-abstract, more personal and material investments. Nearly all US soy producers in Brazil have formed corporate bodies such as LLCs or corporations or are moving toward that model. This reflects the nature of large-scale production in Brazil as much as the changing landscape of family farm corporatization in the United States. Farm investments also mirror global trends of farm financialization (Fairbairn 2020). Thus, financial motives, markets, actors, and institutions take on a larger role in farm production and capitalization. Financialized land is both a productive asset and a speculative one. While farmers do intend to profit annually from sales of their harvest, they also expect to sell their developed land at a profit.

Farmer-investors get involved for a variety of reasons. They see production agriculture as both a safe investment and one that makes sense to them. Investing in Brazilian soy farms can provide them with insider information on the climate and market in Brazil and—at least as seen in producer magazines—Brazilian soy can appear to be an inevitable out-competitor of US soy. They see investing in it as a way to ameliorate this loss. In a Skype interview, one such farmer-investor reported hearing and enjoying a farmer's investment presentation in Chicago. He was attracted to the presenter's honest and forthright communication style. He invested a small amount for multiple reasons: to stay informed about production costs and the production environment, gain contacts with US and Brazilian farmers in Brazil, and gain profit.

Another farmer-investor I happened to meet on a rural bus on his way back from an American's Mato Grosso farm (where he works a couple of times per year) also suggested that farmers' investment presentations informed investment decisions. Speaking of one infamous farmer, he mocked, "He's a smooth, sharp talker, [who] says you'd have to be stupid not to invest, with how good ag[riculture] is in Brazil, how cheap land and labor are, there's no downside." A small-town newspaper (Zippay 2003) reported the reasoning and process of another farmer-investor's decision to become a "pioneer" in international farming. While doing missionary work in Brazil, the family had met Brad and Caleb Indiana. Encouraged by the Indiana family's qualifications and Christian work ethic, and assured they would not "take down the rain forest for farms," the family visited and then invested. One of Eddie Upstate's farmer-investors saw the Brazil farm as a way of diversifying and minimizing risk. The investor still owned and operated an Iowa farm but was "always looking for other opportunities, and we're doing research around the world where there can be interesting opportunities." They settled on Brazil as an investment. Eddie described his investors' interests as varied and complementary: "I think any time you're investing, you put this large amount of money into something; you have to have more than just dollars and cents in your mind if you're an educated investor. I think, generally, there has to be a second reason and possible third and fourth yet—I would say." According to him, some business partners report investing in order to have something to pass down to their kids and grandkids and "actually defer to their kids on some decisions." Their investment group was made up of retirement-age investors "thinking about their legacy."

Investors also find an opportunity to learn about the Brazilian way of farming. One of Dennis Tocantins's primary business partners told me that he had not learned very much from the agronomic practices of Western Bahia because "the areas are too different" and "we no-till anyway," but that they had learned new business practices. Farmers in Brazil, he told me, determine crop rotations based on expected profitability, "whereas in the US we try to grow [corn and soybeans] and then try to sell it." This array of shifting priorities and opportunities the US farmers in Brazil came to use exemplifies flexible farming.

Besides the financial and productive potential of investing in US-owned farms in Brazil, investing without actually farming in Brazil offers a level of plausible deniability for investors. A report by the Brazilian nongovernmental organization Rede Social de Justiça e Direitos Humanos finds that cases of land-grabbing are not only profit-seeking but also a means of distancing investors from the effects of agricultural investments. Relating the process to *terceirização*, roughly defined as outsourcing, but better understood as a process of detaching capital and capitalists from work and workers, the report finds that investors and investment funds exempt themselves from responsibility for community land dispossession, poor working conditions, or the environmental consequences of industrial agriculture (Rede Social de Justiça e Direitos Humanos 2018).

Leon Oster described the process of setting up a Brazilian farm as a two-headed problem: first, the issue of titles, corporate bodies, and certifications; and second, elements of trust that fit hand-in-hand with the process of attaining these documents. The first step is to start a Brazilian corporation and get a permanent visa. The process requires partnership with a Brazilian citizen and often costs tens of thousands of dollars in legal and administrative fees. A partnership with a Brazilian citizen is required due to the enforcement of a foreign land law, which is easily bypassed using a "shell" or *laranja* or joint partnership with a citizen who acts as a figurehead but holds little real power over the farm (Castro, Hershaw, and Sauer 2018; Fairbairn 2020).

Forming a Brazilian corporation as a noncitizen requires that a farmer give power of attorney to a Brazilian citizen to file for a corporate title. As a migrant in a foreign country, Leon found it "hard to trust people down there," but he asked Frank Missouri and Ian Illinois for recommendations and partnered with an associate of Ian's. Unfortunately for Leon, his partner soon after began working full-time with Paul and Jacob Iowa, which meant "there was really no time for him to do my stuff." His partner had told him that Leon "was just a very small fish in the pond." Leon's challenges did not end with difficult-to-trust partners. In later chapters, I describe Leon's eventual farm loss in Brazil due to a variety of issues including difficulty with attaining machinery and titles as well as agronomic issues, but he identified untrusted business partners as his main regret. The "real part that hurt me was my partner . . . my partner killed me. If I would have had a different one . . ."

New farmers often turned to more experienced US farmers in the area (and rarely to Brazilian farmers) for advice, and almost all of them turned to US consultants for advice. One such adviser advertised his services to those with a "critical mass" of investment who were prepared for the "isolation, language and cultural barriers, and lack of first world comforts." Another consultant limited his work to clients with at least $2.5 million of investment capital. He provided tours; helped identify investment opportunities; identified "virgin" and "developed" tracts of land for sale; and guided farmers through the legal process of starting a Brazilian corporation, becoming a Brazilian resident, and buying land.

With few exceptions, US farmers own the land outright under a registered Brazilian corporation. In fact, many of them pitched Brazilian farms to investors primarily in terms of land speculation, not crop production. They do not expect to stay in Brazil for the long term. Instead, their plan is to clear and develop the land, make a profit from production for a few years, then sell the farm, farmland, and farm corporation and repatriate any profits to shareholders. Registered capital can be repatriated without authorization, though funds in excess of registered capital are subject to capital gains tax in Brazil.

Brazil was an attractive site for land speculation because of its openness to foreign investment. The Federal Constitution of 1988 gave the government the power to regulate the sale and leasing of rural land to foreign entities. Before that, Lei No. 5.709 of 1971 had limited the size of foreign-owned landholdings and the proportion of land held by foreigners per municipality. An attorney general's decision in 1994 significantly weakened these regulations by interpreting corporations with majority foreign capital as Brazilian corporations and thus unrestricted from land control. This decision opened Brazilian farmland up to the US farmers who trickled in during the early 2000s. When they toured and purchased land between 2000 and 2005, a Brazilian corporation, even if majority foreign owned, had no restriction on landholding. Then, in the midst of the 2007–2008 food crisis, there was an increased concern over land-grabbing, which placed national security and sovereignty at risk (other concerns included rising land prices, food prices, frontier expansion, and land appreciation and speculation). The Lula government criticized the earlier deregulation of foreign landownership and in 2010 the attorney general issued opinion LA-01, which re-established limits on landownership by foreigners—reverting the definition of foreign landowners to include corporations with majority foreign capital, restricting land purchases by foreigners to 5,000 hectares, and instituting a 25 percent cap on lands owned by foreigners per municipality. While certainly there are legal loopholes (Fairbairn 2015), foreign landownership regulations would severely impede the production-speculation model favored by US farmers in Brazil until the Bolsonaro administration began to dismantle them again (Sauer, Leite, and Tubino 2020).

Crisis–Migration–Crisis

US family farmers migrated in response to different perceived sociocultural and socioecological crises. They experienced a sense of hope in the Brazilian Cerrado but then their plans unfolded messily into improvisation. Their migrations demonstrate power and powerlessness, capital and culture, and crisis and hope. Much like their Brazilian counterparts who left southern Brazil for Western Bahia, US farmers' migration is not so much a case of US farming elites wantonly grabbing land as mid-level farmers becoming elites via migration to Brazil and the courting of investor funds. In contrast to the farmland investors that Madeleine Fairbairn describes as "becoming farmers overnight" (2020, 74), this is more akin to farmers becoming investment managers overnight. To understand this movement as well as its later fall-out, we need to consider care and maintenance along with land and commodity markets. This land grab is not an outcome only of state incentives, deregulation, or profit expectations. Farmers are also supporting personal and family ideas of progress, future, preservation, and heritage. Yet this work, as the following chapters demonstrate, is made possible only by the dispossession of people and degradation of the land. It is also a displacement of the farm family moving to Brazil. Even so, their giddiness about the scale of land, the growth of Luís Eduardo, and the adventure of farming in far-away Brazil make clear that their work in Brazil is not just about capital but also about belonging, progress, and joy.

The migration of family farmers from the US Midwest to Brazilian Cerrado reveals a pathway for surviving on a damaged planet (Tsing et al. 2017), though not a sustainable one. The farmers respond to challenges to their livelihood and dreams by engaging with capital. They depend on hypermobility and finance to maintain farming livelihoods. The fallout from crisis is not capitalist ruin but frontier expansion and the generation of new capitalist relationships—between farmers and investors, farmers and the Cerrado, farmers and farmworkers, and farmers and their neighbors and families. There is a decoupling, a disaggregation, and a distancing at play, but there is also the beginning of a new process of coupling, aggregation, and generation. The farmers adapt their plans, practices, and even values in response to Brazilian regulations, Bahian farmworkers, and the Brazilian Cerrado itself while also keeping a close watch on changes back home in the United States and opportunities to either increase investments or return to the family farm. We will explore this generativity and encounter in the coming chapters.

WASTELANDSCAPES AND SACRIFICE ZONES

US farmers converged on Luís Eduardo Magalhães and its surroundings in search of profit, cheap land, cheaply paid labor, farming livelihoods, and a bit of adventure, however they could have found cheap, fertile farmland in the Ukraine or Australia. They could have found similar farmland in Argentina or Bolivia. What made the Brazilian Cerrado and Luís Eduardo in particular a destination for transnational farmers? The incorporation of the Cerrado into greater Soylandia; the arrival of US farmers in the Cerrado; and subsequent encounters between Soylandia, Cerrado, and transnational farmers depended on the making of farmland. The making of farmland in turn depended on waves of dispossession and enclosure of common land and traditional territories. The Brazilian government was an active agent in expanding the soybean production frontier. In the 1970s the state subsidized rural credit and technical assistance for soy producers through the Sistema Nacional de Credito Rural and created Embrapa to develop new seeds, germplasms, pest control methods, and soil fertility management practices. Further, in 1996, Lei Kandir (the Kandir Law) incentivized raw grain exports through the provision of tax breaks. Together, these policies not only supported the expansion of soy production but also "negate[d] the possibility of other uses of the land" (M. Santos and Silveira 2001, 119). The state made the hinterlands, and the Cerrado in particular, into an object of development through material incentivization (rural credit, agricultural research, and tax breaks) and discursive framing of the Cerrado as wasteland, or *vazio agricola* (an agricultural abyss). In this chapter, I ask how the Cerrado was made into investable farmland and how US farmers take part in this framing to give meaning, authority, and authorization to their work.

The development of what US farmers call "degraded pastures" into "productive farmland" constitutes, for them, both an underexploited investment opportunity and merited behavior. Land is not just an asset or commodity—it is a site of imagination, dreaming, and memory. It is a site of negotiation in which the owners do not just possess the land, they work to control the narrative around it and define it. The Brazilian government invested heavily to fill the so-called Cerrado wasteland with cities, roads, and commodities. Not fitting the aesthetic or visibility of landscapes that merit conservation, there were few inducements to conserve the land and plenty of technologies, infrastructures, and practices to transform it. Farmers reproduced the wasteland discourse to dismiss allegations of deforestation, celebrate their contributions to development, and connect to family histories of settler colonialism (Ofstehage 2024). I use the frame of wasteland and wasted land to explore how transnational farmers engage with the Cerrado landscape and how farmland is physically and discursively cultivated.

Labels of waste and value lend authenticity to development and conservation projects and delegitimize resistance. For example, agricultural development and a land rush in the Nacala Corridor of Mozambique is predicated partially on imagined wasteful land use by peasants and the potential of turning wasteland into productive territory despite counternarratives by Mozambican farmer organizations that industrial agriculture of the Brazilian Cerrado was the real wasteland (Wolford and Nehring 2015). In fact, a member of the Mozambican Rural Association of Mutual Aid commented about a tour of the Brazilian Cerrado: "All we saw, for hundreds of kilometers, was huge soya fields. No farmers, no villages. There are no trees, and there is no animal life, because heavy use of pesticides and fertilizers has turned the area into a desert. We were horrified to think that our home could become an empty wasteland like that" (Liberti and Parenti 2018).

Landscapes of waste are defined by what they lack. Things as well as people are alienated, becoming standalone objects to be used or exchanged; that alienation is never complete, as connections endure and new relationships are generated. The processes of alienation and dispossession on the land generate social and material arrangements between humans and nonhumans as well as generating ruin, rubble, and residues of success and failure (Gordillo 2014). This is the case with flexible land. It is made to be alienated and commodified, and part of this process is ascribing meaning to it as wasteland, investment property, or productive farmland. Capital operates alongside social and ecological processes, sometimes in opposition, other times in conjunction, and often in ambivalent relationships.

To make landscape into land, it must first be made tradeable, investable, private property; second, it must be made free from protected, sacred, or taboo status; and third, it must be made to be productive for cash crops. Government encouragement of development and neglect of local people creates wastelands and paves the way for frontier development (Bastos Lima and Kmoch 2021).[1] Wasteland discourse supports this process by defining land as unworthy of protection and in need of redemption. Land is redefined in relation to new property regimes, erosion, financial investments, crop rotation, and labor regimes. Marginal, waste, or idle lands are made out to be "empty of people, histories and claims, but full of potential for new and improved use. To classify land as underutilized requires discounting current uses" (Li 2014b, 592). These frames overlook decades of labor and life in the region and build on myths of frontier capitalism, Malthusian futures of famine, high farmland values, high food prices, and yield gaps. The naming of waste—whether applied to forest, mountain, or swamp—is a call to action: to "improve." Improvement begins with enclosure, including draining the swamp, clearing the forest, mining the forest, and plowing the prairie. I follow Tania Li (2014b) in exploring how land is made investable and, further, in tracing how it becomes enrolled in a development project, not just an object to be destroyed. Land is rendered investable with surveys, maps, and titles but also by framing the land as wasteland, creating spectacles of hidden treasures in wild frontiers, and highlighting crises and scarcities. The drama of potential yield gaps on idle lands awaiting technology and capital is enticing to landowners, investors, and governments. "A striking feature of the global land rush" Li writes, "is the prominence of moral arguments and references to the social value of investment" (2014b, 597).

Whether cynical or not, landowners' narrative work and references to feeding the world, creating jobs, building infrastructure, and improving the land serve to further consolidate landownership in the service of the development project and offer protection from accusations of land theft, deforestation, and dispossession. This book tells the story of how US farmers encounter Soylandia and this chapter tells an important part of that story—how the Cerrado itself became a target for transnational land investment and how farmers turned it into a productive and speculative asset.

From Acid Land to Global Breadbasket

"In the beginning, there was a great deal of unproductive land . . . areas that were previously unoccupied or under subsistence or low-input production systems" (Chaddad 2016, 22). In this somewhat biblical opening to an overview of natural resources in the Cerrado, the land is unpopulated and unproductive and its development was made possible by agricultural technology and farm policy.[2]

This framing of the transformation of the Cerrado features man as creator and redeemer and is echoed in transnational farmers' claims that before "we came there was nothing." Further, this legitimization of land dispossession and conversion with reference to improvement speaks to elements of Brazil's land reform legislation that gives protection to landholders who have made "improvements" to their land by bringing it into production (Alencar et al. 2016; Pereira et al. 2022; Lopes and Lima 2022; Wright and Wolford 2003).

Awareness of the Cerrado pales next to the international concern and imagination around the neighboring Amazon, but the narrative power of the Cerrado is evident in the rich stories people tell about it. These stories tell not of different experiences but of a different world entirely. Norman Borlaug, father of the Green Revolution, described it as a nearly uninhabited wasteland, an "acid land":

> Until 30 years ago, the Cerrado was sparsely inhabited and generally considered to have little value for agriculture. Some agriculture was practiced on strips of alluvial soils along the margins of streams, which were less acidic and where there had been an accumulation of nutrients. In addition, there was some cattle production although the natural savanna/brush flora characterized by poor digestibility and nutritive quality resulted in low carrying-capacity production. Today, a great agricultural revolution is under way in the Cerrado, the result of a long process of research and development that began more than 50 years ago. (Borlaug and Dowswell 2003, 10)

This view is common in agronomy and rural development circles. The Cerrado is a dark space on the national map in need of filling in. Agronomists and farmers define the Cerrado by what it lacks. Its soils are less fertile for industrial crops than soils of southern Brazil or the US Midwest. Its trees do not tower above like those of the Amazon. Sometimes they are not even recognized as trees but rather as overgrown shrubs. Its people are in need of modernization, development, and civilization. Accordingly, the flora and fauna are insignificant, the people backward, and the soil toxic. The hope in these circles is that this wasteland can be turned into something valuable and soy offers that transformative potential. The emergence of Soylandia, according to this perspective on land, is not degradation or dispossession but development and creation.

For many inhabitants of the Cerrado, the transformation of the Cerrado into farmland is not development but dispossession and despoilment—a loss of livelihood, home, and community. Traditional, Indigenous, *quilombola* (Afro-Brazilian), and peasant communities were thriving in Western Bahia long before the introduction of Green Revolution technologies. The Cerrado biome itself is a biodiversity hotspot and a critical landscape for water recharge (Durigan et al.

2022) and water use (Barbosa de Jesus and Geralda de Almeida 2022).[3] Though threatened by land grabs, loss of water access, agrochemical pollution, and outright violence, many of these communities persist today. The portrayal of the wasteland ignores and delegitimizes alternatives to Soylandia and at the same time opens up the land to investment and development.

Narratives of wasteland, salvation, improvement, and creation do important work for both the state and for farmers in the Cerrado. The discourse and framing of land as just another frontier to be made productive and the Cerrado as undeserving of protection do important work for the farmers. It celebrates the spirit of frontier farming, dismisses concerns of deforestation and dispossession, and naturalizes the transformation of Cerrado to farmland as inevitable and as progress. Evidence of this is visited and revisited throughout this book in the words of the farmers. This narrative work, while ethnographically interesting in itself, calls for narrative counterwork to denaturalize the process of making soil and landscape into land.

Construction and Destruction of the Brazilian Cerrado

The wide-open fields that farmers find on tours and purchase for farming are products of a decades-long political-economic strategy. Brazil's "March to the West" in the 1930s and 1940s created soy fields in the Cerrado, a tropical wooded savanna in central Brazil. Public policies incentivize soy production in order to populate and make productive territory where previously there was "nothing," according to many US and Brazilian farmers in the region. From the air, this transformation is stark; the curves, colors, and topography of the Cerrado contrast with the monochrome, flat, geometrical appearance of soy fields. A ruthless geometry is superimposed over a gnarly landscape.

"The Cerrado Is Where We Hunt, Where We Harvest Our Foods; It Is Where the Spirits Reside"

The encroachment of Brazilian and foreign farmers, dispossession of Indigenous people, and conversion of the Cerrado made this geometrification of a wild landscape possible, and those processes in turn were made possible by state developmental interests, entrepreneurialism, and violence. Unsurprisingly, Cerrado dwellers' perceptions of the land are starkly different from that of industrial farmers. Indigenous children perceive the Cerrado with affection and deep knowledge (Bizerril 2004), and local populations depend on the Cerrado for

FIGURE 15. The escarpment at the western edge of Bahia draws a sharp line between farmland and Cerrado.

both their livelihoods and cultural reproduction (Graham 2009). Nevertheless, the despoiling of the Cerrado is already transforming how local people perceive it. Schoolchildren in Brasilia espoused low identification with the region and little appreciation for the region's natural landscape. Though children with greater exposure to the Cerrado showed greater affinity, many echoed farmers and soil scientists in calling it ugly and empty (Bizerril 2004). Students in Barreiras, Bahia, represented the Cerrado in drawings as nonhuman spaces (with some exceptions with reference to the past), stereotyped occupation (conflict, confrontation, degradation, people versus land), and futures of urbanization and desertification (Rigonato 2013).

The Xavante activist Top'Tiro marks the destruction of the Cerrado not just as a loss of diversity but also a loss of a set of knowledges and practices essential for life:

> The Cerrado is where we hunt, where we harvest our foods; it is where the spirits reside and where we make our rituals. It is also the location of the Village of the Dead. The Xavante world is the 'Ró, the Cerrado. The Cerrado is made up of many parts, which we call mará, itehudo, ambu, apê, and so on. It is all part of a single complex whole. As we

go through certain rituals, we acquire greater knowledge of the Cerrado, and when we get older we have even more knowledge. But for our knowledge to continue, the Cerrado cannot disappear. How can we be good hunters if we don't have Cerrado animals to hunt? How can we be good healers if we don't have Cerrado herbs with which to cure? How can we be good warriors if the spirits of the Cerrado don't have a place to stay? Our marriage ceremonies and ear-piercing rituals that transform boys into adults, all of this—everything—comes from 'Ró, the Cerrado. (Top'Tiro 2009)

Engineers, agronomists, and explorers have defined the Cerrado as a wasteland in spite of examples of abundance and thriving populations. An engineer on the Roncador-Zingu expedition in the 1940s, Manuel Rodrigues Ferreira, wrote that "these Indians live in a region which is hostile to animal life, since the soil is not fertile, watercourses are few, and the vegetation consists predominantly of wizened scrub. . . . To survive the Xavante struggle against the hostile nature that surrounds them" (Ferreira 1946 as cited in Coimbra Jr. et al. 2004, 151). Julian Steward and Louis Faron defined it as "relatively arid and unproductive uplands" and an "infertile plateau of sandy soil covered by scrubby xerophytic growth" while also observing that the Indigenous people subsisted well (Coimbra Jr. et al. 2004, 151). Some indeed recognized that humans could thrive in the Cerrado. The ethnologist and founder of Survival International, David Maybury-Lewis, noted Indigenous Cerrado dwellers' ability to "make use" of an "uncompromising environment" (Maybury-Lewis 1967, 61). This emphasis on scarcity allows landscapes as well as people to be defined as wasted and discarded (see Millar 2018).

The term *Cerrado* comes from Spanish references to *mato Cerrado* (closed forest) and identifies the area as wild, difficult to cross, and inhospitable (C. M. da Silva 2019). Previous agricultural development and industrialization production systems included extensive pastoralism on common land (100–150 cattle per 500–700 hectares); small agricultural areas (three to four hectares cultivated per fifty hectares of land); traditional farming systems in wetlands that mixed crop production (potato, maize, and beans) with fishing; and traditional farming systems in valleys—similar to that of wetlands but with higher productivity (Diniz 1984). In the local vernacular, the flat, dry region of Western Bahia that is now mostly soy fields is called the *gerais* or *fechos de gerais* (commons), reflecting a collective, hospitable, and noncapitalist relationship to the land. Few communities made their homes in the gerais, but it was a collective site for collecting firewood, hunting, gathering wild fruits like pequi (*Caryocar brasiliense*), holding livestock, holding festivals, and performing religious ceremonies. While agriculture in the valleys (*fecho de pasto*) exploited *terra vermelha* (red soil), *terra preta* (black soil), and *terra de cultura* (extremely fertile loamy soil) work in the *fechos de gerais* was adapted to the low water availability and low soil fertility of the uplands by using extremely low-intensity land-use practices (Barreto, Barreto, and Figueiredo 2017; Alcântara and Germani 2010). This low-intensity adaptation to the gerais was common throughout much of the Cerrado (Nogueira 2009), including the São Francisco River Valley communities of Formoso do Rio Preto and Correntina in Western Bahia (Sobrinho and De 2012; Krone 2023). When outsiders call this region unpopulated, they are disregarding land-use practices outside of intensive agriculture and urban living. Indigenous communities utilized valleys with plentiful water for agriculture and settlement and used the gerais for wood collection and hunting. So even if the soils of the gerais were not useful for farming prior to the use of heavy fertilization to modify the soil, they were of vital importance as a "land of no one, and therefore the land of everyone" (Moraes 2000, 267).

The maligned Cerrado has some of the oldest soils on Earth, which soil scientists describe in oddly anthropomorphic terms. They write that due to nonextreme soil and climate factors, "once established, the Cerrado [vegetation] tends to maintain itself with more tenacity than other vegetation formations" (Motta, Curi, and Franzmeier 2002, 13). Ecologists understand that plant life in the Cerrado biome itself evolved in the Pliocene and Pleistocene in response to an arid climate, the presence of fire, and acidic soils (Pinheiro and Monteiro 2010). The earliest record of "Cerrado-type vegetation," by analysis of plant pollen, dates to 32,000 YBP, while vegetation that closely resembles present-day Cerrado occurred in 7,000 YBP in central Brazil and 10,000 YBP in northern Brazil (Ledru 2002, 47). Indigenous and *quilombolo* (Afro-Brazilian) communities in the Cerrado continue to use controlled burning to promote native plant growth and manage wildfire fuel (Eloy et al. 2018). Fire-management of the Cerrado has been shown to revitalize the landscape under certain conditions (Welch et al. 2013).

The Cerrado, to use a Brazilian phrase, is *uma floresta de cabeça para baixo*, or an upside-down forest, with a high belowground root mass of living and dead roots and a relatively low aboveground biomass of leaves, stems, twigs, and trunks (Abdala et al. 1998). This contributes to the perception that little vegetation grows since much of it is out of sight. Deep-rooted plants contribute significantly to water availability in Cerrado ecosystems, and the replacement of deep-rooted woody plants by exotic grasses and agricultural crops may change the biome's hydrological cycle (R. S. Oliveira et al. 2005). Land-use intensification threatens the Cerrado's future in terms of both agricultural productivity and ecosystem stability, due to agrochemical overuse, mineral leaching, and groundwater contamination (Hunke et al. 2015). Furthermore, soil erosion and degradation increase in step with the expansion of "modern" agriculture in the

FIGURE 16.   The Cerrado as seen in passing from a bus window.

Cerrado (Batistella and Valladares 2009). Thousands of years of weathering, along with careful indigenous land management, have produced soils that make the Cerrado resilient to change. Cerrado communities such as the Canela people to the northeast of Luís Eduardo value, use, and recognize this land by living with it, not trying to control it (T. Miller 2019). Its transformation into a global breadbasket depended on both a radical agricultural intervention and the violent intervention of settlers and capital.

Filling the Abyss

The Cerrado is a site of ever-moving encroachment of farming into *quilombola*, Indigenous, and other local smallholder communities; this encroachment is a violent process of land-grabbing and dispossession. Distant from the Bahian capital of Salvador, and occupied by three *sesmeiros* (Portuguese land colonizers) with land claims dating back to the Portuguese colonial administration, Western Bahia was seen as a reserve and used primarily for extensive pasture by distant landowners. It was ignored by the state until industrial agriculture innovations promised both increased agricultural production and a more significant role in the national economy (Barreto, Barreto, and Figueiredo 2017). Since the early years of Portuguese colonialism, bandeirantes from São Paolo invaded indigenous territories in the Cerrado in search of gold and slaves. Bandeirantes occupied an important role in a strategy to expand the Portuguese Crown's territorial borders and are still celebrated for expanding Brazil's national frontiers (Garfield 2001). The feting of the occupation of Brazil's interior frontiers is based on myths of heroic, brave bandeirantes pitted against a hostile nature and hostile inhabitants. This myth places progress and development of natural resources against barbarity and backwardness. The political consciousness of Brazil remembers that "todo brasileiro que abre caminhos novos é um bandeirante" (every Brazilian who opens roads is a bandeirante) (Ricardo 1956, 391), allowing for a heroicization of progress and a vilification of environmentalism (Duarte e Silva 2010).[4] This system continued more or less from the nineteenth century up until the 1970s when *grilagem* (land-grabbing) displaced *fechos de pasto* (mixed farming and animal farms), and mechanized agriculture began to dominate the landscape (Imbirussu, de Oliveria, and Germani 2017). *Grileiros* (land-grabbers) took possession of vast swaths of land in the region through missions such as "operação limpeza da area" (Asselin 1982). In one move they dispossessed local people and introduced a more capital-centered and power-dependent model of property. "The moving frontier" was made possible by the "availability" of land (made available through state and parastate power) and enabled a rapid response to commodity booms—a rubber boom in Amazonia, mining in Minas Gerais, ranching in Goiás and Acre, and soy in Goiás and Mato Grosso (Foweraker 1981). This long process of enclosure of the gerais and dispossession of land has had the continued support of the Brazilian state, and Western Bahia is still a hotspot of land conflicts (B. de C. D. Moura and Lavoratti 2012).

The history of agricultural development in the Cerrado is not a story of farmers exploiting fertile soils and ideal growing conditions but one of intentional, state-led, and capital-dependent development. Embrapa developed fertility practices to "correct" acidic, low-fertility soils; tillage practices to "build" fragile soils; and integrated pest management to reduce pest and disease pressure, where no winter frost or high biodiversity created ideal conditions for pests and diseases. Rural credit and price supports in the 1970s and 1980s, economic liberalization in the 1990s, and a commodity boom in the 2000s supported the economics of soy production.

The Cerrado is the subject of a rich narrative and a leading narrative comes from the ruralistas. Proponents of the land use change in the Cerrado argue that agricultural research, rural credit, and the pioneer spirit transformed the Cerrado from a green desert, barren land, or acid land into a global breadbasket, a driver of national development, and a model for agricultural development. Intensive fertilization, hybrid seed varieties specifically bred for production in the Cerrado, and a set of farming practices I call the "Brazil Model" (Ofstehage 2019) made industrial agriculture possible, but narrative work made it heroic.[5] Supporters tell a clear-cut story of transformation from a wasteland to a breadbasket: "The agricultural sector incorporated a large area of degraded land from the Cerrado into national production, and today this previously abandoned zone accounts for almost 50% of national grain production" (Klein and Luna 2018, 163). Herbert Klein and Francisco Luna continue to describe the Cerrado as "the part of the rural world that would become modern," with "parts which were left behind and still practice subsistence agriculture" (Klein and Luna 2018, 3). In an edited volume on the Cerrado and sustainable agriculture, the president of the Japan International Cooperation Agency (JICA) writes that "Brazil achieved an epoch-making breakthrough to become a net exporter of grain by converting barren land into one of the most productive agricultural areas in the world" (Tanaka 2016, x). In the introduction to the same volume, the editors argue that this "epoch-making breakthrough" converted the "barren land" (Hosono, da Rocha, and Hongo 2016, 6) of the Cerrado into not only a source of local employment and an impetus to regional development but also into a major factor in national poverty reduction and the reduction of global hunger.

The creation of the Matopiba development project in 2015—as discussed in the introduction—occurred after the arrival of many US farmers to the region, but its emergence and political framing speak to the interests of the ruralistas and their perspectives on the region. Along with earlier development programs for the region—including POLOCENTRO, PRODECER, and PROTERRA—the Plano e Agência de Desenvolvimento da Região do Matopiba was created to funnel private and public investment into the region. According to *deputado* (member of the Brazilian Chamber of Deputies) and ruralista Carlos Henrique Gaguim (Tocantins), this investment was expected to contribute to "the generation of employment and of production, which is of fundamental importance for Brazil, especially for the people of the States of Tocantins, Bahia, Maranhão, and Piauí" (Bezerra and Gonzaga 2019, 56).[6] In a Chamber of Deputies session he argued that "there are thousands upon thousands of hectares in need of industrialization. And what is the mechanism of that industrialization? It's money" (56).[7] In another session the deputy argued for this development to be open to both Brazilian and foreign farmers, saying, "It is necessary that the Government allows anyone, foreigner or not, that wants to buy land here, has the right to buy it and produce on it" (58).[8] A deputy and ruralista representing Bahia, João Carlos Bacelar, supported this call to amend the foreign land law, saying, "It is agribusiness that is employing [workers], it is agribusiness that is generating manual labor, it is agribusiness that is paying dividends for these states [of Mapitoba] and for all of Brazil" (58).[9]

Producer organizations defend their own role by arguing that they are the real protectors of the Cerrado. The two major trade federations of large-scale farmers in Bahia, the Associação de Agricultures e Irrigantes da Bahia (AIBA) and the Associação Baiana dos Produtores de Alagadão (ABAPA), contend that they are saving the rivers and improving the infrastructure of the region. The AIBA's annual report for the 2015–2016 crop season announces soy farmers' contributions to employment opportunities, to an increase in the Human Development Index of Brazil, and to environmental sustainability.

Yet there is nothing wrong with subsistence agriculture (Ofstehage 2020), and so-called underdeveloped spaces are not empty (Ofstehage 2021a). Local populations did use and occupy the land but in ways that have either been rendered invisible or ignored by proponents of industrial soy farming. Before land appropriation, Indigenous, *quilombolo*, *ribeirinho*, *geraizeiro*, and local smallholder communities thrived in river valleys where water was plentiful and the soil was favorable. Their use of the gerais for livelihood and ceremonial purposes was less visible to outsiders but of great importance to them. Defenders of the Cerrado describe the inseparability of the landscape from daily life, its biological endemicity, and even the ability of the Cerrado to fight back.

Ecologists and agroecologists have critiqued the Brazil Model as environmentally destructive of a fragile and highly endemic ecology. Activists and researchers have critiqued the model for providing little local economic benefit at best and for endangering the health and livelihoods of local communities at worst.

Consequences of the "Miracle of the Cerrado"

Besides producing uneven development with relatively few low-paid positions, soy production inhibits local agriculture by capturing massive amounts of water, creating pest outbreaks, and applying illegal agrochemicals (R. F. M. Moura 2017). *Comunidades geraizeiras* (people living in the gerais) and *ribeirinhos* (people living near the rivers in the valleys) frequently have conflicts with farmers over land but also over water access (B. S. dos R. dos Santos 2020). Geraizeiras communities warn that the overuse of limestone and gypsum for industrial agriculture have made the soil impenetrable, causing both decreased water infiltration in the upland soils and increased nutrient discharge on lowland springs, waterholes, and marshes (B. S. dos R. dos Santos 2020). Soy production disrupts carbon flows in the Cerrado (Sawyer 2009) and represents a great threat to tropical ecosystems in Brazil (Fearnside 2001). With only 2.2 percent of its land legally protected, between 1970 and 2005 nearly half of the Cerrado was converted to agricultural use (Klink and Machado 2005). Negative environmental effects are concentrated in hotspots of agricultural development and contribute to the rapid decline of

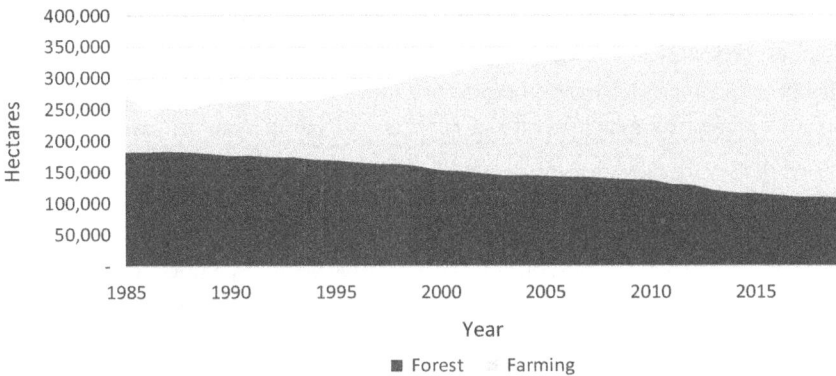

FIGURE 17. Conversion of Cerrado to farmland, 1985–2019, created by the author based on data provided by MapBiomas.

the Cerrado biome (Brannstrom et al. 2008; R. S. Santos et al. 2021). Land use changes in the Cerrado, even early in the historical process, provoked the influx of "agents of modernization" (capitalized farmers, economic groups, and the state) and fomented social unrest and violent conflicts between local communities and newcomers (Diniz 1984). These conflicts—including those over poor working conditions for farmworkers (Silva Coutinho, Germani, and de Oliveira 2013) and the dispossession of land from Indigenous and peasant groups (Alves 2009)—continue apace.

The Brazil Model emerged out of engagements between scientists, farmers, and the Cerrado. The "miracle of the Cerrado" is often attributed to two major breakthroughs: deriving soil management practices to coax production out of the "barren" land, then developing hybrid soybean seeds to adapt to the climate of the Cerrado (Nehring 2016).[10] Brazilian government research into suitable seed varieties and soil management processes made soy production in the Cerrado possible and profitable, while government support programs induced farmers, primarily from southern Brazil, to migrate to northeastern Brazil.

In the 1970s and 1980s, a rapid influx of capital and "agents of modernization" transformed the region from one that was isolated and based on low-density cattle ranching and shifting cultivation to one based on capitalist agriculture. This provoked conflicts between capitalist farmers and peasant families (Diniz 1984). In the 1970s the region was settled by people from northeastern Brazil as well as by gauchos from the far South; both imposed capitalist ways of exploiting land and opened the Cerrado to industrial agriculture (Diniz 1984).

Oral histories of early southern Brazilian settlers tell a story of hope and challenges. In the 1980s they came for flatlands and the opportunity to farm and had to contend with soil that "wasn't corrected yet" and a lack of "practically everything," including yeast and flour for bread, drinking water, and fuel (Schlosser 2014, 17). Many brought their families and reproduced aspects of the South by creating gaucho cultural centers and competing in community soccer games (Schlosser 2014).[11] These early migrants to the region often presented themselves as entrepreneurs and adventurers in the mold of bandeirante heroes of old. However, they brought with them the same patrimonialism, violence, and land theft that the bandeirantes have always been known for and their presence has brought economic growth along with growth in inequality and poverty (Favareto et al. 2019).

White southern Brazilians battled what they saw as poor soils and government neglect. Meanwhile, displaced communities of Western Bahia faced and continue to face the loss of gerais land, reduced water availability, exclusion from hunting and foraging territory, agrichemicals contamination, and more intense pest infestations in the valleys (Calmon 2022). In an online profile of Lusineide dos Santos, a Cacimbinha community member in Western Bahia, she laments that "[the Cacimbinha community] (is) down here and [soy farmers] are up there, dumping all that poison into our springs" (L. dos Santos 2021). Further, the arrival of agribusiness brought few jobs and little infrastructural development besides that which supports the importation of farming amendments and exportation of farm products. Many with access to land have sold it and moved on; others pursue work on soy plantations themselves (Lima 2019). In nearby Piauí, peasants fear retaliation if they speak out against farmers and companies. Resistance is impeded by geographical isolation and invisibility along with a weaker presence of the MST compared to the South (Calmon 2022). Where the MST does operate in the region, it has found space to create viable agrarian communities that place great significance on community and the Cerrado, though not without challenges from the state and local agribusiness powers (Q. L. da Silva 2018).

A study by Gabriela Russo Lopes, Mairon G. Bastos Lima, and Tiago N. P. dos Reis explores the memories of land use change in Mapitoba from the perspective of pioneers, local community members, and workers. The results reveal a complicated reality. Smallholders recall early land deals with regret, relief, and resentment.[12] For many, these early land deals were sometimes voluntary and sometimes involuntary but always coercive. Those who refuse to sell are subject to violence in the worst cases but also the closing of schools, hospitals, and roads, making life unlivable for them. Even those who resisted selling land suffered for that choice. In the case of one smallholder farmer, "they came here in the small hours and poisoned all our hens. The other day they shot our goats. Then they came again and offered us money to leave, but we didn't take it because we have nowhere to go, and we don't want to leave" (Russo Lopes, Bastos Lima, and Reis 2021, 9).

Those who did continue farming were excluded from former common use land and the degradation of valley land and water.[13] Access to water is severely restricted by large landowner exclusion, government conservation restrictions, and poisoned water supplies (Russo Lopes, Bastos Lima, and Reis 2021). While soy farmers take pride in feeding the world, their work threatens local food production by destroying native fruit trees, reducing the water supply, often killing wild and domesticated food plants through glyphosate drift, and intentional destruction of farming livelihoods.[14] One smallholder farmer remembered, "Three times they burnt out our cassava mills. Other times, when it was the season to harvest our vegetable gardens, they would come and smash it all with tractors" (17). A rural workers' union member summarized: "Soy employs too little, pays too little, and large landowners profit a lot. . . . In our region, they leave only holes, diseases and dust—and a meager salary" (19). A smallholder farmer added that "soy for them is important. They deal in dollars, but they do not put anything on Brazilians' tables. Milk, [cassava] flour . . . it all comes from smallholders. Their thing is earning dollars and pushing people to the streets. If they

FIGURE 18.   Photography of change I.

FIGURE 19. Photography of change II.

FIGURE 20. Photography of change III.

are God's children, so are we. Deforestation, water problems . . . their children will also suffer from this, it won't be only ours" (19).

Just as epic narratives are espoused by the Brazilian government and promoted by agribusiness-friendly media to valorize agricultural development in the Cerrado (Cabral, Pandey, and Xu 2022; Boaventura, da Silva, and Dutra e Silva 2023), politicians tie their fortunes to visible and spectacular growth and improvement. Changes in Luís Eduardo itself were stark even in the relatively short duration (spanning eighteen months) of my fieldwork there. Hoping to record this change, I placed myself in designated sites across the capital of agribusiness to take pictures of each site over time and write fieldnotes on what transpired during my time there.[15] Much of this exercise documented ongoing business and residential construction, but in the case of the central highway, BR-242, I documented a kind of permanent construction frozen in time with little change occurring. In the month leading up to the 2012 Brazilian presidential election, construction crews came to life and construction proceeded rapidly. This election season–driven construction frenzy demonstrated yet again that development is perceived as a winning electoral strategy.

Getting to Know the Cerrado: The Arrival of US Farmers in Brazil

US farmers knew of these conflicts on the Cerrado and a few took part in them, but most of these farmers understood the region as an investment and farming opportunity. The Cerrado—supported by government programs to incentivize deforestation and development there—offered cheap land, cheaply paid workers, and boundless opportunity. It was a wide-open space, not unlike what their predecessors are said to have witnessed in the Great Plains of the nineteenth century. Several interviews with farmers began with a retelling of where the farmers' ancestors came from and where they settled, connecting their own migration and settlement of a distant grassland to that of their forefathers.

Farm Tours

For many of the US farmers, their first encounter with the Brazilian Cerrado was on farm tours—some led by private consultants and tour operators and others operated by farmer leadership councils—where they could witness the endless fields of soybeans, the clearing of Cerrado land for frontier expansion, and the growing city of Luís Eduardo Magalhães. According to a tour operator based in South Dakota, many farmers take agricultural tours in Brazil out of curiosity and a desire to learn about their competitors. Farmers are interested in seeing how Brazilian farmers manage their workers and fields, how they use technology, and how they incorporate practices such as no-till, *safrinha* (second crops), and cover crops. The highlight for many farm tourists, however, is witnessing the clearing of Cerrado, though this can be difficult to arrange. The guide himself expressed awe in the clearing itself and the "frontier spirit" of Brazilian farmers in the region.

Jacob Iowa, who manages his family's 20,000+ acre farm in Western Bahia, remembers the wide-open possibilities of open and cleared land as the most exciting part of visiting Brazil on his first trip:

> You could see that this town, Luís Eduardo, had sprung from nothing; and there's incredible people coming from every corner of Brazil, and in some cases the planet, just to get a part of it; and it was just a boom-town and we were really excited about it. . . . I remember I couldn't sleep the first three nights 'cause I was so excited about it. You come from Iowa and . . . [there are] these 80-acre fields; and you come down here and you see everyone has these 1,000-acre fields, and you didn't even know stuff like that existed; and you'd go home and explain it to people, and they'd either think you're exaggerating, or they don't believe you.

On the same tour, Jacob's father Paul saw the Cerrado as a blank slate without vegetation, fertility, or people "[Brazilian farmers] were clearing trees and brush. It was Cerrado, pasture and shrubs. Not much besides ten-foot trees, grassland." Paul noted that there was a nearby limestone quarry for pH amendments and that without amendments, the "corn would grow a foot tall and die" because "there was no fertility" and the "soil profile goes down 100 feet deep." To change the pH they would need to "correct" the soil with a four-ton lime application. Jacob's Iowegian Farms is not a dead place as some would say of plantations and monocrop farms. Visiting the farm I heard sertenejo music coming from the married and single farmworkers' housing buildings, the clanging of machinery from the machine shed, and native birds singing. As the red dust that covered the concrete buildings of Luís Eduardo made land degradation in Western Bahia easy to see in the City of Agribusiness, songbirds on soy farms reminded me that the rhetoric of "nothing besides ten-foot trees" ignored the persistent and vibrant life of the Cerrado.

Jacob shifted our conversation from the infertility of the soil to his impressions of the scope, which he called "impressive." You could "see the horizon in all four directions" and see "guys (farms) as far as you can see." Based on these impressions, he predicted that someday Brazilian agriculture would "look like what we have [in Iowa]" once they have proper infrastructure, but "with the technology that we have [in Brazil], it is going to happen a lot quicker [than it happened in the United States]." This juxtaposition of the infertility of the Cerrado soils with their boundless scale and opportunity is odd, but it is supported by both the potential for farmers to "correct" the soil (as we will explore in chapter 4) and the optimism of agricultural consultants in Brazil.

After confirming their interest in investing (sometimes following agricultural tours, other times not), many prospective farmers hired US agricultural consultants based in Western Bahia to identify pieces of land for sale. Consultants supported the farmers' dreams of boundless and easy opportunity by emphasizing opportunity and minimizing climatic risks, environmental destruction, and the difficulty of starting a new farm. One consultant's website framed the potential as endless, stating that "Brazil's frontier region is booming, and the boom is destined to continue long into the future. The potential of this vast and largely untapped area—the largest virgin land mass on earth—is beyond rational speculation." At the same time, the consultant—who wished to remain anonymous—translated *Cerrado* into English as a "closed, inaccessible wasteland" and pronounced this a "good description" of the region prior to settlement by farmers. The Cerrado, the website states, "was literally an inaccessible, useless wasteland [that] produced little of value." The consultant provided guided investment tours, identification of profitable investment and agribusiness opportunities, research services for land investments, identification of "virgin and developed" tracts of land for sale (between 1,000 hectares and 50,000+ hectares), guidance in establishing Brazilian corporations, capital registration and repatriation, identification of business services, credit negotiation, and assistance in obtaining local forms of identification. They only worked with prospective investors with access to liquidity of no less than $2.5 million. The US-owned consulting agency warns of the risks of buying land in Brazil in general terms and specifically from those who speak English, "including North Americans and Europeans," who are "looking for another sucker."

The Cerrado presented by farm tours was a *terra nullius* ripe for implementing soy production while leaving local communities and ecologies either invisible or portrayed as wastelands awaiting redemption. According to the farm consultant, that redemption was made possible by science, farmers, and men: "Cerrado land produces nothing of value without fertility improvement." The fertility of Cerrado soils is "man-made" in the sense that "extremely low fertility," "deficient" soils were made productive through intensive fertilization ("correction" in farmers' vocabulary) and soil management.

Prairie and Cerrado as Spaces for Conquest

The Brazilian Cerrado and the American Prairie share some basic characteristics as grasslands and upside-down forests; more importantly for many US farmers and investors is the fact that they share a history of settlement, enclosure, and agricultural development. Jacob and Paul's Iowegian Farms promotes this connection on their website, reminding the public that Iowa is known for its contributions to agriculture as much as the "hard working spirit (of) the farming community." Iowegian Farms "share[s] that same vision" in Brazil. "The Brazilian Cerrado" their website states, "is undeveloped and sparsely populated and good conditions for workers are required to attract appropriate talent." The reader is left to complete the thought, *just like the Prairie was before settlers arrived.*

The American Prairie—where many US farmers in Brazil come from—and Brazilian Cerrado share a narrative of conquest, development, and progress. Colonists in each place identified the respective frontier regions with "wilderness, emptiness, the savage, the Indian, the slave, the colonized, the atheist, the heretic, the weak, the backward" while "settled places" were identified as spaces of "civilization, the civilized, the crowded, the urban, the white man, the colonizer, the Christian, the strong, the advanced" (Amado 1990, 53). What survives of the Prairie and Cerrado is their potential to transform ordinary people into champions of enlightenment, democracy, the nation, and progress (Cronon 1992). This transposition of geography and temporality, connecting the nineteenth-century American Prairie to the twenty-first-century Brazilian Cerrado, allows farmers to embody practices and ideas of development and progress—neither place nor time is essentialized but rather generalized as a process of becoming. The rhetoric of "backward" land use is a common settler trope.[16] Whiteness, manhood, and patriarchal authority gave meaning and authority to settling the US frontier (Sachs 2015). F. J. Turner famously idealized the American frontier as a meeting point of "savagery and civilization." "That coarseness and strength combined with acuteness and inquisitiveness; that practical, inventive turn of mind, quick to find expedients; that masterful grasp of material things, lacking in the artistic but powerful to effect great ends; that restless, nervous energy; that dominant individualism, working for good and for evil, and withal that buoyancy and exuberance which comes with freedom—these are traits of the frontier" (F. J. Turner 1893, 9).

Transnational farmers in the Cerrado echo the claim that "nothing was here before." Caleb Indiana arrived in the Cerrado (Mato Grosso) in 1994 as a prospective farmer and missionary. He remembered that "there was *nothing* [his emphasis], there was nothing," but "now [2012] I'm guessing there are about 1,000,000 metric tons annually of soybeans. . . . There wasn't a bank in town, there weren't phone lines, it was just a little place dug out of the woods." Caleb celebrates the transformation of the Cerrado as an untouched, forgotten place becoming productive. This framing erases not just the value but the very existence of Indigenous and quilombolo communities (the Gamela in Piauí, the Akroá in Maranhão, Tupinambá de Olivença in Bahia) and the biodiversity of the Cerrado itself just as discourses on the conquest of the American Prairie depend on tropes of wastelands, lazy natives, and backward landscapes. The trope "This isn't the Amazon, this is the Cerrado" reflects the farmers' disregard for wildlife on the Cerrado and serves to disarm critiques of dispossession and deforestation. It offers acceptance that the people, plants, and animals of the Amazon are deserving of protection while, at the same time, naturalizing and valorizing industrial agriculture in the Cerrado as victimless modernizing development.[17]

This Isn't the Amazon: Wasteland Aesthetics

Land is a financial and legal claim of possession that is defended in fields and courts, sometimes with pistols drawn and other times with handfuls of tattered documents. It is also a material and social landscape made up of plants, soils, animals, and humans as well as boulders, toxic residues, and the remnants and memories of past occupation. Wasteland connects definitions of land as property, land as landscape, and land as soil in that a normative definition of waste supersedes protection and opens land up for development. Physical landscapes such as swamps, grasslands, and jungles are marked as ugly, wild, unruly, and in need of taming and soils that are not fertile enough for intensive agriculture are read by farmers and agronomists as in need of "correction" and "improvement."[18]

US farmers described the Cerrado in a manner similar to that of Brazilian farmers and agronomists. A website operated by an agricultural economist, who worked as a consultant and tour guide for US farmers and investors interested in opportunities in Brazil, described the Cerrado as a "worthless space" where the vegetation is a sparse combination of shrubs and grass and "trees seldom exceed 10 meters in height or 250 mm in diameter" (Ag Brazil 2012). An online report by Iowa State University agronomists listed the limitations of the Cerrado before concluding that it held yield potential:

> The Cerrado area has been defined as a wasteland with stunted twisted trees. The cerrados are not rainforests. The soils of the Cerrado are highly acidic, saturated with aluminum, deficient in phosphorous, and have low water-holding capacity. Early on many felt that the land could not be cultivated. Contrary to popular belief, the soils in the cerrados proved to be deep and well drained with excellent physical

characteristics suitable for mechanized crop production. . . . It is clear that there is potential for large increases in crop production in the cerrados. (McVey, Baumel, and Wisner 2000)

A call for investment for one US-owned farm tells potential investors that "Western Bahia is not a rainforest. In its natural state, the Cerrado in Western Bahia is generally characterized by thinly populated small trees." Alone, this statement plainly states a fact, but it also tells investors that this investment is safe from both government intervention and public outcry.

The Cerrado is not the Amazon; Bahia is not a rainforest. These truisms, often repeated by US farmers, first struck me as inane but later as a meaningful statement on why the Cerrado is open for business. The statement does several things. First, in the face of environmental and human rights activism, it points out the relative ignorance of many who assume soy production in Brazil means soy production in the Amazon. Second, it is an implied concession that Amazonia indeed deserves some protection. Third, it implies that the Cerrado does not deserve the same.[19] The aesthetics of wasteland identifies beauty and ugliness, especially by contrasting stunted, twisted, ugly trees of the Cerrado with the towering trees of the Amazon rainforest. The statements of farmers and other actors involved in its transformation into farmland all imply that the Cerrado is ugly and infertile, but that with proper management it can become productive. This narrative—built on the material landscape of the Cerrado, ingrained landscape aesthetics, and visions of modernity—effectively disarms concerns over degradation, dispossession, and deforestation while also celebrating the transformation from waste to value. In essence, intensive agriculture in the Cerrado allows the Amazon to be spared and the Cerrado to become a sacrifice zone.

Farmers use the differences in material appearances and public interest in the Amazon compared to the Cerrado to assuage investor concerns; they also use these differences to argue forcefully against conservation measures in the Cerrado and protection of indigenous land. Legal land reserves in Brazil, legislated by the federal Forest Law, require landowners to set aside protected land. In Cerrado states, farmers are required to set aside 20–35 percent of their land, while those within the Amazonian ecosystem are required to set aside 80 percent—further evidence that Amazonian landscapes are valued more highly than Cerrado landscapes despite the fact that the Cerrado is a highly endemic tropical savanna with a diverse population of plants, birds, fish, reptiles, insects, and amphibians. Infrastructural improvements and government-funded agricultural research further induce farmers to make the Cerrado "productive." The incentivization of the Cerrado-to-soy farmland transformation—via legal land reserves and government incentives for Cerrado soy production—has also displaced rural

Bahian communities off of the commons on which they depend for subsistence agriculture and ranching (Diniz 1984). The Forest Law is critiqued by farmers and ruralistas as impeding development and increasing costs, and by environmentalists as not enough and too easily evaded (Azevedo et al. 2017; Soares-Filho et al. 2014).

Farmers framed the land itself as inherently worthless without agriculture because, as they saw it, the stunted trees were of little aesthetic, economic, or natural value. They also painted the region as a whole as in need of development because of its poor infrastructure and the lack of built cities. Farmers often described the region as being "nothing" before they arrived; one went so far as to say it was like a picture in *National Geographic*. "I certainly felt like it was adventurous at the beginning. . . . I thought this place was way on the other side of the planet like . . . crazy pictures you see on *National Geographic*, someplace you're never going to go see; some place far off, that's how this place was when I first got here." Today, in the view of many, the area's improvements—like roads, electricity, and buildings—should be mostly credited to the farmers. Said Eddie Upstate of his predecessors, "When they arrived here, there were very few poor roads, no electricity, a lot more forest. Now, roadwork has been done twice, both at expense to landowners; and electricity goes out frequently when it rains; but it's much better, less primitive." This narrative work by farmers again defines the land as neither beautiful nor useful, with agricultural development as the only rational pathway.

This devaluation of the Cerrado landscape and concomitant valuation of its improvement reflects the farmers' sentiments about land, progress, and development. However, the similarity between farmers' interview responses and their public comments in newspaper and farming magazine articles suggested that this framing was more than just a reflection of ideas of progress and land. In interviews, farmers used this discourse to speak directly to US investors, potential investors, and the US public to defend their work in Brazil as *not* deforestation ("this is not the Amazon"), *not* degradation (you have to spoon-feed the soil), *not* dispossession ("there was nothing here") but only improvement (job creation, road building, connecting electricity). This discourse is built from an ideology of settler colonialism, individualism, and productivism, and also out of self-interest in shirking blame.

Considering this valuation of the Cerrado in contradistinction to the value of farmland, farmers label any environmental protection efforts there as backward. After I asked him about the challenges of farming in Brazil, Dennis Tocantins quickly listed regulations as the most difficult aspect of farming in Tocantins, particularly the environmental protections inscribed in the Forest Law. He explained that the law "was widely ignored until around 2000." Until then, rural parts of

Tocantins had no reserve, no trees, "no nothing," but in more recent years surveillance, enforcement, and sanctions had lessened. He then proceeded to describe in detail his view of what was justified deforestation and what was not:

> I've been to the Amazon before on vacation and you see guys on the river who are doing real slash-and-burn agriculture; that's how the process starts with guys like that. Not always; sometimes it's the bigger ones. Then, next, somebody will come in and buy it up; the first guy sells his plot to someone else who has a cattle farm. They'll sow grass and then raise cattle out there. Then ten, fifteen, twenty years later a soybean farmer will come in and say "I can farm here," and he'll start a soybean farm. . . . I don't believe in deforestation, but I also don't believe that the WWF [World Wildlife Fund] and Greenpeace have the best interests of the people at heart. This was prairie here, we converted it.

Dennis highlighted the issue of what counts as valuable natural space. He states that slash-and-burn agriculture in the Amazon should be stopped because the Amazon should be protected, implying that slash-and-burn is an illegitimate land use strategy. He then justifies land use in the Cerrado because "this was prairie here" and "we converted it." At the same time, he speaks to a different measure of environmental care. Large-scale farmers use environmental regulations to argue that they are doing no harm because the law says they are allowed to deforest a given amount of land, and they generally stay within those boundaries. This allows large-scale farmers to place more blame on a colonist who illegally clears a 10-hectare piece of land for slash-and-burn agriculture than on a landowner who legally clears 800 hectares and reserves 200 hectares.

The Forest Law—originally passed in 1965 and relaxed substantially during the adminstrations of Michel Temer (2016–2019) and Jair Bosonaro (2019–2023) with strong support from the *bancada ruralista* (a powerful faction within the National Congress allied with the interests of commercial agribusiness)—places protections over forest cover along waterways and steep hillsides and requires a "legal reserve" of undeveloped land left in natural vegetation. Yet the Forest Law is violated by 51 percent of soy farms in the Cerrado biome (Rausch et al. 2019). The law has not only been limited in terms of conserving land; it has also been a further force of enclosure of the gerais as land placed under legal reserve is protected from both industrial soy agriculture and traditional common-use access by Indigenous communities. This has affected hunting, fishing, slash-and-burn practices, removal of timber and fiber, extraction of wild honey, picking of flowers, collection of medicinal plants, production of coal, and gold mining (Ribeiro 2008) and given political cover for the expansion of both soy farms and eucalyptus plantations.[20]

Ian Illinois, always proud to show me his farm and extensive fields on the very western edge of Western Bahia, often described his reserve Cerrado land, legally required to be set aside by the Forest Law, as something just to make bureaucrats happy. This was partially because he'd never seen it and could not provide any detailed description of what it really looked like. "I don't really pay that much attention to the reserve, I just have to have it, own it; you never do anything with it. I've never even seen it; you just buy it and there it is, just to make the environmental departments happy. You can't do anything with it." When asked how much land he owned, he often did not include the reserve land. It was owned, but not available to be farmed, so for Ian it existed only on paper. Similarly, another farmer described the Forest Law as superfluous in an online post. He stated that their farm was over a thousand miles away from the Amazon but that they fulfilled their legal environmental responsibilities.

In contrast to the tepid support from Brazil agribusiness and in conjunction with many Brazilian soy farmers, US farmers find the Forest Law to be unnecessarily supporting a worthless landscape and overly interventionist. Ian explained that the "environmental laws" (the Forest Law) were easier to comply with than labor laws (see chapter 3) but had heavier fines. He described environmental governance in Brazil as opaque and slow, giving the example of an environmental license (to cultivate a piece of ground) that had been held up for years after they had purchased the reserve land, applied for a license, and had the deed confirmed. The license, according to Ian was held up in Salvador where paperwork is piled in endless stacks. "It's this building and you go in and there's this lady sitting at the window. You take in your paperwork and she takes your stack of paperwork. She puts a stamp on top of it and gives you a slip of paper with the number that was on that stamp, so that's your proof you delivered it, and then she sets it on these stacks of paperwork that are just stacked to the ceiling all over the building." At the time we spoke, he said "[We can't] get the environmental license until we get the reserve approved, and they're both in the hands of the same governmental organization, but the environmental license side wants to fine us for not having the license, but we can't get the license because they haven't looked at our reserve! It's not like that in the US." Ian's frustration with Brazilian bureaucracy is hardly surprising, but this specific frustration speaks to more than the red tape involved in getting environmental licenses. It stems from both a general distaste for government regulation (despite their enjoyment of Brazilian government protection of their land and investments) and specific opposition to the regulation of what US and many Brazilian farmers consider a wasteland.

Jeremy Campbell writes that "colonists [of the Amazon] build alienation into property, settler consciousness in which wilderness inevitably yields to the progress of the plow and the paper deed" (2015, 31), and that they use discourses of development and progress and specific policy evidence to authorize and celebrate their work. The true destroyers of the forest, according to Amazonian colonists, were "the sem-terra (MST) who use fire to clear their fields, a primitive farming method that leads to uncontrolled wildfires" (140). The settlers interpret the development desires of the state and flexibly claim to be working toward those goals. In the case of US farmers in the Cerrado, I contend that they do the same. Not only do they argue that they are developing the region; they say they do it better than the Brazilians and that the government is just getting in their way. This framing is necessary to make the Cerrado fit for agriculture and to make it investable.

The farmers' narratives of the Cerrado resemble the phenomenon of wastelanding (Voyles 2015), in which landscapes are defined to advance political arguments about land use and control as well as to define a politics of waste vs. development. In orienting the land as a landscape of development, it becomes territorialized by capital; by describing native Cerrado as wasteland or as "nothing," farmers confuse difference for deficit.[21] It allows them to claim not only legal authorization to clear land but also a moral authority over it as job creators, developers, and farmers. The long process of commodification, simplification, and colonization of prairie historically in the United States has obvious current-day parallels in the Brazilian Cerrado.

Back to the Future: The Dominance of Farming Narratives

The transformation of the Cerrado and the Prairie—in terms of conquest, colonization, and modernization—have been similar. And both have experienced possibilities other than extractivist productivism. Their histories also exhibit the limitations of the extent to which visions of landscapes can be enacted in isolation.

Wasteland is a normative classification given to a defined area that identifies it as neither productive nor valuable nor worthy of conservation. It is defined by landscape appearance, current land use, alleged infertility of soils, or in some cases arbitrarily (often as a colonial claim on land). Narratives of waste and value can be connected to landscape, land use, and soils, but such narratives can also be materially arbitrary and racially constructed.[22] Environmental changes compound over time to impose settler land use; to subject Indigenous populations to environmental degradation and risk; and to erase, delegitimize, and ignore alternative relationships with and uses of the land.[23] The classification of wasteland is thus meant to discredit current occupants' claims to the land; to authorize land use change (regardless of whether this results in degradation, deforestation, and so on); and to disregard conservation.

Statements by farmers, agronomists, and government officials are based on heterogeneous but identifiable factors including landscape, work, built environments, and production practices. What they allow is more homogeneous—they allow settlement, authorize land use change and occupation, and authorize a treatment of and opinion on both land and people. Wasteland can be deforested, denuded, and plowed with minimal complaint because, as farmers often reminded me, "it's not the Amazon." It is not the kind of natural landscape that merits protection and not the kind of productive landscape that merits congratulations; therefore, it is a landscape that is best off torn asunder. Likewise, the people of the land do not merit protection because their culture, work, and economy have not fostered the kind of economic and agronomic production that is valued and respected by the dominant culture. The local people are either paternalistically taught the agricultural ways of the settlers; removed from the land (forcibly or not); or otherwise marginalized on the landscape. The narrative work described above opens up the Cerrado for investment and the creation of flexible land.

WORKING SOYLANDIA

We boarded Ian Illinois's fixed-wing airplane at the single-runway airport outside of Luís Eduardo Magalhães. After reviewing two preflight checklists, he piloted us down the runway and we lightly lifted off. Ian had invited me to accompany him to his soybean and cotton farm while he was in town for a few weeks. I had been to the farm several times, usually taking a few hours' drive by pickup on BR-242, a busy highway used by speeding trucks hauling cotton bales, cotton seeds, soybeans, and agricultural inputs. By plane our commute was thirty minutes to his soy farm at the edge of Western Bahia. The plane was expensive, Ian told me, but the mileage is about the same as his pickup; mostly it saves him commuting time.

As we moved across the landscape, the geometry transformed below. Circles of dark-green, irrigated produce fields near to town became square blocks of bright-green grass seed fields; then massive rectangles of soybean, cotton, and corn fields became visible near the escarpment that divided the states of Bahia and Tocantins. These shapes of crops stretched to the horizon, only divided by the jagged outlines of the Cerrado where rivers cut through fields and by stark, straight lines of Cerrado where farmers had left legally mandated forest reserves. At the end of our flight, we passed over Ian's farm, Fazenda Illinois. As we neared the farm, he identified fields and farms. He pointed out a tractor planting soy and indicated that it was a Texan worker, Eric, driving a John Deere tractor with John Deere implements, on land owned by an Illinois farmer in the middle of Brazil.

We landed at an old farm that, since my previous visit, had been sold back to the Brazilian farmer from whom Ian had originally purchased the land. The Brazilian farmer had offered a good price and was "someone [Ian] could trust." It

FIGURE 21. Ian's airplane.

FIGURE 22. A Texan worker, operating an Illinois-made tractor, on a field owned by an Illinois family, in the center of the Brazilian Cerrado.

was a safe deal because the farmer had money coming in from the sale of his other pieces of land and could pay Ian as the money came in. The new owner allowed Ian to use the runway where we landed. Ian had a red pickup there and we took it out to check in on the farmworkers planting corn. The first thing we did upon our arrival at Ian's main farm property was to wash the pickup. I helped, brushing off some dirt with a soapy brush, and he sprayed it down. I told him about how Frank Missouri had explained that in the United States you want to have a dirty pickup to show how hard you have been working, but in Brazil you want a clean pickup to show that you have laborers to do the dirty work. He laughed, "I guess I'd never thought of it that way."

Ian's office was small, perhaps 100 square feet, and has four desks and a bathroom. The walls were adorned with a poster about identifying soybean rust, a map of Brazil, and a whiteboard listing seed varieties applied to different fields. As I looked around, Ian told me that Iowegian Farms had much nicer, cleaner offices, despite having a smaller farm. Ian's desk was indistinguishable from the three other desks in the office except, perhaps, for the larger stacks of papers and the presence of a few English books. He sat at his desk for the first hour or so that we were there and spoke with managers who came into the office—a very casual, easy atmosphere.

As soon as we landed, Ian was talking with his farmworkers via CB radio to ask about planting progress in the field. He talked about which fields to plant first; chitchatted mostly with Eric, the Texan farmer in the John Deere tractor; and asked about the impact of potential rain on planting. We spent the morning stopping each tractor driver to ask about their planting progress. At almost every stop he found a planter checking on smoke coming from an engine, taking a break, checking on seed depth, or consulting a manager about something. At each stop Ian helped determine what the problem was and often helped solve it. When we loaded Eric's planter, Ian operated the small tractor to lift the large seed containers over the planter. Later we drove by a tractor emitting an excessive amount of black smoke. Ian hailed the planter by radio and explained that the worker needed to replace a filter. He also checked seed depth in every field and advised planters to plant either deeper or shallower. While checking seed depth he looked at the spacing, making sure it was not too dense or too sparse. Throughout the morning and afternoon, he demonstrated his farming know-how—checking seed depth by hand, kicking the dirt to check compaction—and his farming "know-what," including chemical application, planting rates, and mechanical issues.

For lunch we went back to the farm. The workers had their lunches brought to them, and we ate what was left of the *feijoada* (a standard Brazilian bean dish) and spaghetti. We ate quickly, then Ian headed to his office in the main building

FIGURE 23. Unclogging the bean planter.

to check emails and Skype messages for about an hour. Later, Ian held a meeting with all the farm managers, seven in total. Each took a turn giving a statement on the progress in their area and answering questions. Afterward, we went back out to the fields and continued to check on progress until 4:30, when Ian flew us back. Betty, his wife, picked us up at the airport with the kids in the backseat, and they dropped me off at my place.

This division of labor, the contrast between farmwork and office work, and the division of city and farm life are common themes on transnational and Brazilian farms in Soylandia. Typically, farmers visit the farm a few times per week to meet with managers, to check on progress in the fields, to make sure things are in working order on the farms, and to make an appearance. Otherwise, they can be found in their offices completing paperwork, communicating with investors in the United States or with workers on their farm, and managing their office staff. Farmers operate farms from nearby urban centers or from as far away as the United States. Work is alienated from the farmer by outsourcing the labor and by the bureaucratization of worker relations. Care for, or more aptly maintenance of, farmworkers is governed more by minimal work requirements determined by Brazilian law than by reciprocal worker-capitalist relations common to plantation economies. Altogether, it was more reminiscent of a man camp or oil rig than a family farm. Groups of single men working on oil rigs—far from land, home, and kin—and their bosses model the modularity of capitalism in which they appear to be estranged from local entanglements (Appel 2012). Flush with cash and far from the watchful eye of elders, family, and non-business authorities, the workers live in a kind of disconnected world. Vignettes of oil rig workers point to disconnection and a world with different rhythms, social relationships, and work than in their homelands. One Texan explained that he felt he had two parallel lives—one in Houston and one wherever he happened to be posted—each of which stopped when he left that place and started again when he came back, "like pressing stop and start on a DVD," as he put it. While on the rig, the workers' three- to six-week hitches were characterized by grueling 24-hour workdays in which shifts lasted 12 hours. Given that the rig ran constantly, however, everyone was on call at all times (Appel 2012). Yet, as Hannah Appel reminds us, these seemingly detached workers and modules are enmeshed and entangled in the infrastructures, economies, and ecologies of the places they occupy (Appel 2019). Life on a flexible farm is modular. Work is divided by specialized teams, each with their manager, and life for the flexible farmer is divided between home and office. Workers, members of these teams, are disposable and replaceable.

Working on a Transnational Farm: Hoes, Gins, and Newsletters

As my interlocutors often told me, sometimes impatiently, a typical US soybean farm in Western Bahia looks like a typical Brazilian soybean farm in Western Bahia. Large farms have a machinery/mechanic shed, barracks for workers, a mess hall, an office for the farmer, and often a soccer field. Most have barbed-wire fences surrounding the farm and a small garden to provide otherwise hard-to-get greens. The farms are designed as a worksite, a housing site for workers, and a well-defended base of operations. Farmers' impatience with my queries about the differences between their farms and farm practices and those of their Brazilian neighbors stemmed, in part, from their inability to bring something different to Brazil. Instead of introducing an "American model" of farming as many expected to do, they largely adopted the "Brazil Model" of industrial farming. Their boredom with the question also stemmed in part from the general lack of importance they placed on the aesthetics and livability of the farm itself. The farm, after all, was where laborers worked, lived, and relaxed while farm-owners' lives were in the city. This disconnection between farm and farm-owner is a characteristic of what I call flexible work, an important part of flexible farming.

Although virtually invisible in investment pitches, the narratives of migration, stories of success and failure, and career histories are evidence that farmworkers are ever-present on transnational soy farms, even on relatively small ones. Workers only enter the conversation when they are asked a direct question or when farmers are asked about their challenges—as if the workers are an external issue like weeds, investor demands, or environmental protection, not an integral aspect of the farm. There is a dissonance when a farmer describes their farm as a family farm yet, on the ground and on paper, it is managed more like a plantation. This disconnection speaks to what I call flexible labor. Flexible labor is a worker-farmer relationship with little reciprocity, no kinship, and no long-term commitment, in which workers are marked as unskilled and easily replaceable. This flexible labor arrangement allows farmers to hire and fire workers with little concern for the welfare of the business or the workers. The flexible farm resembles a plantation or even a slaughterhouse when a "worker in the boar stud experiences only boars, a person in finishing barns works only with grown meat hogs, and a given employee on the cut floor might interact with thousands of left hams every day" (Blanchette 2015, 648).

US farmers in Brazil embrace this flexible labor arrangement. When Frank had first arrived from Missouri, there was no auto-steer, no lightbars, no GPS (global positioning system, for self-driving machinery). He once told me a joke passed on to him by a Brazilian farmer. The farmer had the first GPS ever. It was used for spraying chemicals from an airplane. A worker, Geraldo Pahera Silva (GPS), would stand with a flag to mark where the plane needed to spray. Once it passed over, he would move eighteen meters down the field and mark the spot for the next pass. The fictional Geraldo Pahera Silva directs our attention to slow progress in working conditions, the replacement of labor by machines, and the continued disregard for workers, real or imagined. Frank uses this joke to distance himself from the very worst accusations against soy farmers in Brazil.

Expendable labor is not new to the industrial economy, nor to family farms that depend on farmworkers. The soy farm first removes people from the land; then it brings in workers from outside to cultivate but not to connect with the land. This disconnection is always incomplete as workers do create durable relationships with the land. Flexible farmworkers are housed at farms, but it is not their home; eat at farms, but do not grow food; cultivate the land, but are separated from it by chain-link fencing. While monocultural soybean fields are not strictly plantations, they do resemble them in terms of the racialized use of labor, use of crop monocultures, and ideals of control over plants and people. The next section explores how flexible labor is made possible, what is generated from it, and how one manages the work on a transnational farm.

While Jacob Iowa managed the family's soybean farm in Western Bahia, he (and his father Paul) also helped manage the family's investor relations, most of whom were back in Iowa. Part of this management was a defense of the farm's environmental, economic, and social impact in Brazil. In one LinkedIn post he defends his family farm's impact on human rights in Brazil. He recalls purchasing the farm and finding employees living under black plastic tarps and sleeping on sacks of fertilizer; the previous owner stated that they did not have the capital to invest in housing. Jacob's family built "one of the nicest employee housing units in the region, complete with a lighted soccer field." At the same farm, he found workers bathing under a shower that was designed for chemical applications; asking the farm manager about this, he learned they were employees from a neighboring farm and quickly put a stop to it. These experiences speak to the farmers' newfound need to manage labor; to their newfound value in being a good boss; and to their courting of investors by demonstrating their ability to manage investment in labor while avoiding the ire of government bureaucrats. All of this was new for farmers raised on farms where the majority of the labor was provided by the household. In this new world of farming they struggle to manage workers, investors, worker regulations, and paperwork.

Care for farmworkers often resembles an insidious gift in which acceptance of care by the worker comes with obligation. New York Dairy farmers sometimes welcome dairy workers into their families with expectations of working according to family dynamics, not work contracts, as well as an expectation for workers to contribute social labor to the family by attending get-togethers (Sexsmith 2019). Iowan organic farmers work alongside their employees to provide a good example and to show that they are "not just off eating donuts somewhere . . . not just being lazy or whatever . . . come in to work early and . . . always stay later than the employees do" (Janssen 2017, 125). The existence of these relations between farmers and workers in the United States shows that farmers cultivate a social relationship with their workers that blurs the worker-farmer distinction—one that reveals a certain discomfort with capitalist relationships. This mixed feeling toward workers exists among US farmers in Brazil too. Frank once told me that MST activists were thieves who try to get something for nothing, but in the next moment he admitted that were he in their situation, he would participate in land occupations. On another occasion he remembered that when he first arrived in Brazil he thought "learning plant names, insect names, learning to farm here" would be hard, but "that's easy. Crop scouts, farmworkers know everything here. They tell you all you need to know; [and they] know how to operate machinery."

Managing Workers

Workers move quickly between farms and between different tasks on farms. At Iowegian Farms, according to Jacob Iowa, workers change jobs throughout the year. They may be assigned a piece of equipment for a season—for example, operating a sprayer for four to five month, then, come harvest time, switch to operating a cotton harvester. With three farms—Iowa 1, Iowa 2, and Iowa 3—Iowegian Farms divides up workers into mini-units on each farm while managers move between farms. The division of workers according to farm sites is primarily to save transportation time. It takes time and labor to transfer farm machinery between farms—disassembling them, and loading them each time. Jacob also recognized moving workers between farms would be a hassle for the workers, explaining that "all the workers have to . . . every few weeks, every few months, pick up all their belongings, not that they have a whole lot with them at the time, but they pick it up and go to the dormitory on the other farm. . . . Maybe it's a little uncomfortable for them, but you're always moving people around constantly. It's a hassle."

Profit-making on transnational soy farms is divided between on-farm crop cultivation and off-farm cultivation of financial processes (e.g., land speculation, attracting and retaining investors) as well as defending against liabilities (e.g., lawsuits and governmental fines). On transnational soy farms, work is divided between farmwork and office work, and farmers struggle to manage both. Eddie—who grew up around dairy farms in Central New York and was perhaps more familiar with farmworkers than some other US farmers in Brazil—retains a lawyer, an agronomist, six farm scouts, and a team of twenty to sixty farmworkers. In his office in Luís Eduardo, he told me that to farm in Brazil you have to become a manager, and that transition can be difficult. "Usually in the States you might have five employees; often [they] are family members; here you're not an independent farmer but a manager of people, land. That's a different job entirely." He lamented that education and training are low among workers but that his formerly "primitive, illiterate" team is now "trained, educated, and many can read." Though he and his father saw themselves earlier as trailblazers and pioneers, he now took pride in what he perceived as a "massive change" they had brought to the training and employment of workers.

On US- and Brazilian-operated farms in Brazil, the farmworkers are divided into two racialized groups of laborers. Generally, white sulistas operate heavy machinery and work in managerial positions, while local Baianos (primarily Afro-Brazilians) from the surrounding area and from south of Luís Eduardo Magalhães work as manual laborers. Of these two groups, the second is far more likely to be seasonally hired or released, replaced by machinery, and treated as unskilled workers. I had heard of Brazilian (but not US) farmers saying they would "never trust a Baiano with a tractor," and Ane Gracia, in her ethnography of farmworkers in Western Bahia, cites Brazilian farmers calling local farmworkers "rascals" and "lazy." Bahian workers are excluded from spaces of power occupied by gauchos from the South because, according to the farm owners, they lack leadership qualities "intrinsic of gauchos" (Gracia 2017, 36). Farmworkers come primarily from Western Bahia and maintain homes in their original communities. According to Ian Illinois, "most [farmworkers] are from around here, so they live on the farm. . . . We're required to give them a day and a half a week off, so every other week they get three days."

According to Gracia (2017), farm owners consider a good farmworker to be one who is not temporary, who stays loyal to the farm, and continually improves the quality of their work at the farm. In other words, a good worker is not necessarily the most skilled laborer, but one who is willing to stick around. Workers on a Bahian soy farm are essential but, with the exception of tractor drivers, replaceable. Farmworkers in Gracia's research did see some of the progress alluded to in Frank's story of Geraldo Pahera Silva. One native of West Bahia remembered driving open tractors through dusty fields, but now, "with the air conditioning, the music, and everything closed off? Oh child, you don't know how much it's improved" (Gracia 2017, 77).

Though US farmers rarely mentioned race, their farms were delineated along the same division of trained workers who manage, consult, and communicate, and untrained workers who perform manual labor. On Jacob's Iowegian Farms, the cotton hoeing crew, about forty-five workers, work temporarily for four months removing weeds from cotton fields. He characterized them as generally unskilled: "Those people came from south central Bahia and those are probably the very bottom rung that make the very least amount and have no education and no skills or training." But he added that there is a path out of the hoeing crew: "Every year we pick off a few from that group and slowly over time they get trained and start to work as small machinery operators and kinda work from there." The relatively high turnover of workers, especially manual laborers, became a concern not in terms of retaining specific skills or people but in maintaining the workforce as a collective. When I asked Jacob if turnover was low, his eyes opened wide. "Turnover!?—I wish it was!"

Fazenda Illinois employs 11 managers and 165 workers, including 50 workers at the cotton gin (the cotton crew is cut to fourteen workers in the off-season). The workers labor in teams such as soil fertility, harvesting, and public relations; they live in on-farm housing, typically leaving the farm once every two weeks for three days. The workers represent one of Ian's greatest frustrations. Ian explains that Bahia is not a traditional agricultural region, so workers are not used to the odd hours and the realities of agrarian production. "Agriculture's also new to this area so, really, even when we came ten years ago there was only half as much ground as what's being farmed now, so it's really fast. That's kinda a struggle because they haven't worked on a farm, and just beyond the technical side of it, the culture of it is different too. You know, not having [to just work] nine to five and [get] two hours off for lunch-time."

In his eyes they are uneducated, untrained, and often lazy. Fazenda Illinois offers some training on the farm, providing a six-month internship for crop scouts pursuing a two-year degree at the local university. Of the fifteen to twenty interns they host each year, they try to keep six to eight.

Ian makes farm decisions based on market trends and climatic trends but also based on minimizing his use of farm labor to reduce hassle and risk with regard to worker protections. He told me about how they had cut back cotton production for a period because "the market is not calling for cotton" and were able to shut down the cotton gin. This allowed him to reduce the labor force from 140 to 40 workers. Besides the cost savings, and implied less hassle in dealing with workers, he could "cut the fat"—to keep on the workers he trusted and get rid of those he did not. He paid unemployment for those who were laid off, but "you

FIGURE 24.   Farm machinery and farmworker transportation.

have to do that with anyone eventually," he said. Instead of "turnover," Ian talked about "weeding out" bad workers.

Even worker injuries were described as a hassle. Ian spoke of a worker who lost "a finger and a half" in a gin accident. The worker went on disability paid by the government; then he came back and lost another finger in a similar accident. The worker sued Ian, but as of 2014, Ian would not settle. He explained that he trusted the law to make a fair judgment and did not want to incentivize future lawsuits. This legal accountability to workers became a point of contention for Ian, especially as he considered how much the region had "improved" since he had arrived. Increased enforcement of already existing worker protections led him to pursue technological fixes, even at a financial cost to the farm. When they arrived, he remembered, "it was commonplace for employees like these seasonal employees that come through to live in plastic tents out in the Cerrado, out in the trees; and now you can get a fine for not having the right brand of fire retardant paint on the door of the worker house; it's just really crazy." The problem, he found, was that the labor laws did not differentiate between city workers and rural workers, so "workers have to have a restroom within so many meters all the time, and if you're in a tractor in the middle of the field that's kinda tough. So we've had to buy mobile cafeterias and restrooms we have to park out by the tractors that are working; we used to just take a little toilet paper with us in the tractor and we were ready to go!"

Ian actively pursued technical and agrochemical strategies to replace labor— not necessarily to reduce costs, improve productivity, or improve yields but to reduce liability and hassle. He had stopped hiring cotton hoers so they would not have to "deal with them" anymore and had switched to a heavier dependence on herbicides, saying, "We . . . sort of eliminated all those jobs and we will make a significant capital investment if it reduces the number of employees because of the liability issues." He continued on this point: "Yeah, it's about reducing liability. The other thing is if somebody gets hurt down here, on the job, the employer is 100 percent liable. The employee has no responsibility to use their safety equipment that you've given to them. Or if they just do something stupid, it's always the employer's responsibility, you know, to get them fixed up plus pain and suffering and paying damages."

Workers' jobs are regarded as low-skilled positions and they can easily be replaced by other workers or machinery. The cotton gin continued to depend on workers to function and, unfortunately, that was the site of the majority of their injuries.

On Oasis Farm the Indiana family pursued a different tactic with their workers. They chose to invest in long-term employee relationships, paying over market price for labor in hopes of retaining workers for long-term employment.

They employed a foreman who manages the farm, one or two operators, and seasonal help. The Indiana family employs what Caleb calls objective-driven management—meaning that they intend and are required by investors to produce an economic profit—but that their management decisions are driven by an interest in treating workers well and in being stewards of the land. Leon Idaho did not hire farmworkers at all. "I wanted the traditional, you know, American farm. You live out on the farm, and you go into town when you need to, and your kids work with you and all that kind of stuff. . . . I wanted that traditional experience. But I ended up spending more time dealing with problems in town." The Indiana family and the Idaho family are exceptions.

Beyond high turnover and high liability to worker protections, farmers complained about a lack of work ethic and know-how among farmworkers, especially field-workers (everyone but agronomists, tractor drivers, etc.). John, Ian's dad, told me their family's contribution to Brazil was limited in that "we just really try to have a culture of . . . telling the truth, doing it like it's supposed to be done, save money, you know, when you do it. You know, put some numbers behind the decisions, good numbers. You can find any numbers you want, but find accurate numbers to base decisions off of, to really try to get down to what's really true, what's right." Farmers reported needing to check up on work to make sure jobs got done. Ian's father, John, reported one of the biggest challenges of managing workers on Fazenda Illinois was getting them to complete a project, "not just the easy 80 percent." For this, they had created layers of accountability—having multiple people watching the workers, documenting the work, and accounting for the work—because, he explained, "it's a different culture here about getting some money for free, you know, [people are] more deceptive [in Brazil]." For him, it was "about making sure everything's done right, having control over everything, and doing double-entry accounting on everything."

This framing of the worker as hopeless and lazy not only recalls descriptions of the Cerrado itself as a barren wasteland but it also identifies the workers as replaceable cogs in the farm operations.[1] Flexible labor is outsourced, easily replaced, and detached from place. It enables a flexible farmer to manage a farm without being physically present, reduces commitments to whatever is minimally required by contract, and distances the farm owner and farm family from in-field labor. Hiring on-farm managers, writing mission-vision statements, the standardization of work, and modern lines of communication (i.e., email, Skype, and the like) allow the farm owner to "farm by email" (Lapegna 2016). But becoming a manager of workers is not an easy transition.

Jacob Iowa defined successful farming in Brazil as a matter of finding and holding on to the right people. It is the same in Iowa as in Brazil, but "here it's just that the sample pool that you have to pull from are uneducated and illiterate and unskilled and so it creates more of a management problem." One of the most important teams on his farm was the Human Resources Department, responsible for maintaining both the workforce and keeping the farm in compliance with worker protections. Despite his complaints about Brazilian workers, Jacob avoided bringing down Iowa workers:

> You really need to have the local manager from that country managing a lot of that day-to-day stuff. I could try and find some Americans to come down and help run things on the farm more but . . . I would have a hard time . . . finding people that can really adapt to the culture, be among the workers and learn the language and stay around here for a long period of time, so I strongly prefer having a local manager and . . . training those types of guys.

Eddie from New York explained the differences between US and Brazilian farming in terms of transitioning to a managerial role and learning to work within Brazilian cultural norms:

> The biggest challenges are culture, regulations, agronomics. Culturally, one has to learn Portuguese, and learn to be flexible, patient, be *tranquilo* [easygoing]. Many who failed here got burned out, frustrated, and left. You need a longer term, more patient mindset—[to] change your mindset. . . . You can't come down and just farm. You can't just farm. The business side here takes a lot of time and a lot of patience and a lot of know-how.

But not everything can be solved by an easygoing mindset. The labor ministry and IBAMA (Instituto Brasileiro do Meio Ambiente e dos Recursos Naturais Renováveis, the federal environmental agency), Eddie said, "are difficult and expensive to deal with—that is a challenge." Ian too complained of labor protections as both unnecessary and inefficient: "Labor laws are unbelievable, they're so invasive. . . . It's a way to regulate, to increase income to the government without raising taxes." He gave an example of cotton hoers, who are required by labor laws to be wearing protective shoes and clothing. Labor costs were so low that it was cheaper to hire workers to remove weeds than to use herbicides. They hired 100–150 temporary workers for a few months a year until one day a ministry of labor inspector showed up. They were fined 5,000 reais for two infractions of improper clothing. The labor department, according to Ian, can either multiply the fine by the number of infractions or the number of workers, and the auditor chose to multiply it by the number of workers (Ian employed 102 workers at the time). They settled out of court.

Section 31.23.5.1 of Brazil's regulatory laws for agricultural work is the target of many North American farmers' contempt: "Worker housing must: have beds with mattresses, be separated by at least one meter, be limited to two beds in height, and have at least 110 centimeters in height between bunk beds." For North Americans like Ian and Jacob, rules like these are both overly constrictive and illogical—an opinion repeated by Brazilian farmers in the region. Labor laws restrict more than bunk bed arrangements. Worker protections limit daily hours in the field, provide days off for workers, and protect them against unwarranted termination. For his part, Jacob recognized the need for worker protections but believed they went too far: "It's not fair for the employers, it's not practical, but I can understand it to a certain extent 'cause I think, there is a huge index, a difference between rich and poor and the rich do, or have a history of exploiting the poor in Brazil. . . . But it's unfair to those that are trying to do what they can."

Labor laws that govern rural farmworkers in Brazil emerged from post-military-coup Brazil of the 1960s in which reforms such as the *estatuto do trabalhador* (rural worker statute) instituted simple protections over working hours, wages, and conditions (da Silva Coutinho, Germani, and de Oliveira 2013). The reform also brought rural workers in line with an "industrial model of regularity and organization." Reforms created better working conditions and disrupted workers' dependence on *senhores* (bosses) but created new forms of dependence on workers' unions and state courts. Workers in sugarcane fields of the Northeast came to "[see] themselves, their hopes and their aims, differently. Land was no longer the sine qua non of freedom. Mobility was now important, along with reliably paid wages, and the terms of captivity now were understood in the dichotomy between the *engenho* [sugarcane mill] and the street" (Rogers 2010, 178). Despite the unrealized judicial potential of the labor laws for workers (French 2004), the protections nonetheless are perceived as a great burden by soy farmers.

Labor laws, Ian complained, "are so detailed that [the labor ministry] can literally come in and measure your living space and be really anal about that." From Ian's' perspective, they provide housing, transportation, and three meals a day; "all of that is required" and still they have to hire a São Paulo accountant to keep them in line with labor regulations. He took umbrage that any workers' rights violations had become framed as slavery in Brazil:

> If the government decides that your farm, that you're involved with slavery, the government can take your farm and give it away to poor people; and at that same time, when they approved this law they set up a committee to define what slavery is. So we don't know, if someone works 15 extra minutes, is that slavery? . . . The bunk beds have to be 100 centimeters apart; if they're 95, is that slavery? . . . If you're in a dirty or unsafe environment, that's considered slavery [in Brazil]. For me, it's like, if you can't leave [the farm], then that's a slave.

Eddie recounted his own struggles with the Department of Labor:

> I'll tell you a quick story. This is how the ministry of labor works now. I had a guy who worked for me for five years. He was in a pretty good-paying job for me, pretty high up there in the company. We decided to let him go. So I sat down with him, went through all this stuff, his severance, you know, and got the number—like 8 percent—I said, "I'll give this, and a little bit more." He said, "Oh great. Thanks so much. You're a great boss!" We had a great talk. Shook my hand right at the table here. Walked out the door. I thought, "OK. Good. Paid him. Great. Done." Well, about three weeks later, I get a notice in the mail. "You've been summoned to a worker hearing by such and such guy because he says you didn't pay him"—what was it?—"back bonus for 2009, 2013, that you had agreed to." I said, "This guy never had a bonus. I don't understand. . . . He was in accounting. Accountants don't get bonuses for Christ's sake." So anyway, I said, "It looks like an open and shut case. He has no proof. They're just going to throw the allegations away." I go to my lawyer, and I say, "Hey. Here's the case." And the guy says, "Oh God. This is really bad." I said, "What do you mean?" "Well, he doesn't have proof, it doesn't really matter. It's his word against yours, and you don't have any proof that says he didn't have a bonus." I said, "Well, how else would you—he didn't have a bonus! I mean, there's no paperwork, that's as good as it gets."

Labor protections restrict hours worked, ensure safe housing conditions, and require protective clothing. To transnational farmers they pose a threat to the business and are cast as unnecessary, unreasonable, and inefficient; indeed, Brazilian bureaucracy is infamous. Jacob called the labor laws unfair and impractical. "I can understand it to a certain extent 'cause there is a huge index, a difference between rich and poor. The rich do or have a history of exploiting the poor in Brazil, but it's unfair to those that are trying to do what they can." Partially for the reason of this pushback from workers and labor laws, Jacob has dismissed his own early concern for providing work and training for Brazilians. Several farmers claimed an intent to bring jobs and opportunities to Brazilian workers before finding out that workers in Brazil had the backing of relatively strong labor laws and the farmworker federation.[2] I understand this as a kind of bureaucratization of worker relations. Farmers expected reciprocation for their jobs and wages in the form of appreciation and loyalty but, instead, received demands for better living quarters, more pay, and days off. In turn, most farmers care for workers just to the extent that contracts and workers' laws are enforced. Care on these farms becomes maintenance of the workforce as a collective thing and is focused on retaining enough workers rather than on caring for people in a more holistic sense. This fits with their relationship with workers, which for the most part is antagonistic, and their flexible labor strategy, which minimizes long-term commitments to people. Thus, farmers often expressed worker relations through iterations with government auditors and paperwork, not through face-to-face interactions with workers. Ian once described a government building where the paperwork died:

> It is unbelievable, this place. . . . It's this building and you go in and there's this lady sitting at the window. You take in your paperwork and she takes your stack of paperwork; she puts a stamp on top of it and gives you a slip of paper with the number that was on that stamp. So that's your proof you delivered it, and then she sets it on these stacks of paperwork that are just stacked to the ceiling all over the building; so there's a lot. So this new guy is guessing that they'll just start over and do it electronically and just forget about everything . . . 'cause they don't know that they'll ever be able to find it and figure it out.

This specter of mountains of paperwork constitutes a second branch of transnational farmers' work in Brazil.

Managing Paperwork

On a Monday morning I took the hour-long bus ride from Luís Eduardo Magalhães to Barreiras. As we watched sertanejo music videos on the bus, the landscape transformed from the dusty urban streets and buildings of Luís Eduardo to flat fields of soy, then to patches of Cerrado brush. This eventually ceded to large tracts of nonagricultural land, broken up only by the large Chinese-owned tree plantation with its square blocks of tall, straight eucalyptus. I was meeting Frank Missouri in Barreiras to accompany him on a quick trip to Bom Jesus, Piauí. Frank began his career as an agricultural economist at a large public university in Missouri and came to Brazil to manage a farm with a group of investors. Since arriving he had worked with several failed US-owned farms and then stuck around to salvage his move. At the time of our interview, he owned and operated an English-language school in Barreiras, owned a small banana farm outside of town that was managed by an ex-MST worker, and managed a mixed-use farm in Piauí for a Belgian retiree. He once remarked, "I'm like the A-team."[3]

Frank drove three and a half hours to the town of Bom Jesus to check on the farm, where two trusted workers kept it in operation. More immediately, he went to handle bureaucratic and legal business related to the farm. For years, Frank and the Belgian landowner had been working to wrest control of their farm from another North American who had first gained the trust of the Belgian owner; and who then allegedly misused farm finances and assets for his own profit. On the side, this man had allegedly also purchased a plateau of native Cerrado land to convert to charcoal production without an environmental license.

The business of the day in Bom Jesus was to fire a lawyer who had been working for the Belgian landowner. Frank suspected the lawyer was working solely in the interest of the other North American and needed to be removed. In order to fire the lawyer, Frank had to file papers in person, have them signed by a judge, and receive a copy of the signed document. Bom Jesus hosted a special agrarian court that had been set up specifically to handle agrarian court cases, primarily land disputes. Coming from Espirito Santo, the judge had bodyguards and wore a bulletproof vest out of fear of violence—a common precaution in the land frontiers of Brazil where the state has a reduced presence and where landowners have competing and overlapping claims on the land.

Having filed the papers with the young judge, we drove next to the land title office to ask about removing the other farmer's name from the company's documents—an issue that had so far prevented Frank and the landowner from effectively taking control of farm assets and finances. The government worker explained that Frank needed to go to the capital, Brasilia, to arrange the paperwork. Frank replied that he had already been there and they told him to come to Bom Jesus. She offered the name of a specific official in Brasilia, and Frank was satisfied with that progress. On the return trip I brought up another farmer's comment that farmwork in Brazil is 50 percent office work. Frank countered that it is more than that, often significantly more.

Paperwork comes to dominate the transnational farm. Most US farmers believed they would come to Brazil and do some amount of farmwork at least, but as Eddie says, "You're really more of a business manager first and foremost here, than you are a farmer. . . . The farming comes afterward. . . . I was ready to get on a tractor and drive. But we realized pretty quick—in about ten days—we can't do that."

Managing Investors

Paperwork keeps farmers in their offices; so does another kind of labor, rarely complained about, but ever present. That is the work they do to update, appease, and satisfy investors. You can see this in vision statements, remarkable not only in their content but even in their existence. Ian's statement gives few clues that it is even about a farm—with references to professionalism, agility, and rationality:

> We want to be known and recognized for our operational excellence, for our rational use of assets, for our competency in agribusiness, for our

professionalism in our commercial relationships, and for punctuality in meeting our obligations. We want to be a business that is agile, lean, and competitive that utilizes the latest in proven technologies. We want to be a business that values and betters the lives of our employees on their merit, always producing in an economical, rational, and self-sustaining manner when compared with other local and international agricultural producers.

The Indiana family farm in Roraima claims to be "the best Brazilian agricultural investment opportunity for US investors in terms of long-term profitability and net worth accumulation" and "to improve the position of the US farmer in global agriculture through sound and profitable investments in Brazilian agricultural operations." In their "Commitment to Workers' Rights and Sustainability," Oasis Farms pledges "Honesty at All Times"; maintenance of environmental licenses; responsibility to investors, employees, and the land; full compliance with all labor and wage laws; continual training for workers; a commitment to sustainable agronomic practices; and the use of GPS-applied inputs. They offer "agriculturally-oriented investors" participation in farmland appreciation, and production in regions with "globally comparative economic advantages relative to U.S. agriculture": "[Our farm] has been committed to good working conditions for its staff and their families and will insist on the same with the new acquisitions. The Brazilian Cerrado is undeveloped and sparsely populated and good conditions for workers are required to attract appropriate talent. This is all geared toward workers AND investors—to say you don't need to worry about slavery allegations or anything like that."

Transnational farm mission statements allow a farm owner to impose a philosophy of work on their workers but also to speak directly to potential investors. They institutionalize a set of ideal practices, to be enforced by managers; and they let farmers focus on finance work—filing updates, communicating with investors, and managing investment funds. Farmers regularly send investors agronomic updates on field conditions, rotation decisions, planting or harvesting progress, and pest pressure; economic updates that cover markets, politics, and infrastructure; and general farm updates on decisions about land sales or purchases. A 2010 update for Fazenda Illinois lists new machinery purchases with a justification for their purchase, introduces a new hire for the operational management team, and announces changes in their gin management structure. The update then covers field conditions for soybeans and cotton, detailing pest pressure, crop stands (the population of germinated plants per hectare), required replanting, and general conditions. It is illustrated with photos and a chart of recorded rainfall. The update ends with charts on market prices in Brazil compared to the United States; estimated yields compared to past years; and an update on upcoming travel plans for Ian, Betsy, and their daughter. Other farmers manage blogs to keep their investors up to date, which also may raise their public profile and aid in courting investors.

Managing investors require careful management of expectations. Many farmers have monthly or biweekly virtual board meetings; some have regular newsletters or email updates; others have regular guest columns for newspapers or farm magazines; and still others have blogs. Most have farm websites. Farms in the United States and Brazil are increasingly visible virtually as farmers shape public opinion, market their produce, and connect with other farmers (Riley and Robertson 2022).[4] Eddie held weekly FTA (Findings, Tax, and Audit Committee) meetings with his investors. It was a chance for them to ask any pressing questions about farm production, the farm business, or other agronomic, political, or economic issues in Brazil. They also held quarterly investor meetings, to be "painstakingly transparent." There, he would give estimates on inflation and its impact on labor and fuel costs, expectations for shifts in the exchange rate and other general business climate updates, updates on weather and pests, and an overview of the financial health of the farm. I asked if this was primarily for legal liability purposes and he pushed back, "Yeah, there's always the legal side to it and all that, but I generally just try to be as transparent as possible. It's good business. It's good practice. If people want to get upset over what I'm telling them—hey, it is what it is. I can't change it." The meetings can get contentious. "There's real bullets flying, and it's real big, so if anything goes wrong, it's a big problem. You're talking about 20,000 plus acres. If you mess up 10 percent of your farm, that's a heck of a big loss. So . . . you're always thinking about, 'Well, can I explain what I'm doing?' [laughs]." Going through the questions weekly is stressful, he told me, but it is a good barometer of how things are going:

> You've got to answer [the investors]. It makes you think about things and analyze them. And there are times when we've had investors come down here with great ideas. And there are times I've had investors come up with terrible ideas. . . . Some are too nosy, some don't care. They get frustrated because, they say, "Why is this all happening to us? This would never happen in the US." . . . It's hard to explain some days, to be honest. And it gets tiresome.

Investors—who are mostly retired or current farmers in the United States—often share their own agronomic, mechanical, or financial ideas, and sometimes these ideas are incorporated.[5] One of Eddie's strengths as a farmer, he told me, was transparency: "We're very good at being transparent." I believe he was comparing himself with other US farms in Western Bahia when he continued, "There are a lot of farms [where] generally it's going to be a shred of the truth."

While tasked with ensuring timely planting and harvest, managing pests, and keeping in line with government regulations, farmers must also satisfy investors—lest they lose their investment, or worse, have their investment moved to a competing farm. Eddie explained his good treatment of workers as something demanded by investors. Many investors would be upset or angry if you mistreated workers. They preferred better people and better pay in order to maintain workers and reduce turnover. "[You] can't afford to have too much mobility, turnover. Investors aren't necessarily interested in the workers' improvement, but in the negative—do no harm. You also have to maintain a good reputation to reduce turnover, attract better workers." While workers may be replaceable, investors are not.

"Investors," Chad Davis (investor in Dennis's Tocantins farm) told me, "need to see return on investment, but they are also interested in yield as a benchmark; cost structure; critical success factors. . . . They want to do things the right way." The farm is not just run as a business, but as a financial asset to satisfy investors. Farmers are in direct competition with each other not only for land but also for capital; and they compete by demonstrating their ability as managers of capital. This is the work involved in managing a transnational industrial soy farm. To make work flexible, skilled and unskilled workers do the farmwork; the farmer is responsible for managing the workers, the paperwork, and the investors and investments.

Becoming Flexible Farmers

In becoming a manager of labor rather than a farmer, most North Americans are taking steps toward the Brazilian model of industrial soy farm management. This role allows many North Americans to claim that farming is easy in Brazil; it is getting used to Brazilian culture and regulations that are difficult. Flexible farming entails a distancing of farm owners from fieldwork and fieldworkers, and a concomitant engagement with the work of farm management, farm finance, and investor relations. US farmers adopted commodified and corporatized managerial practices similar to the Brazil Model and large-scale farms in the United States, but they also devoted time to tending to investors and capital. It is a mix of both productive work (checking seed depth and choosing seeds) and financial work (talking with investors and writing farm updates), just as farmland is at once a productive asset and a speculative one. Financialized work practices now more directly reflect the pursuit of capital accumulation. Farmers abandon the tractor seat in favor of a pickup cab or a swiveling desk chair as they manage workers and handle bureaucratic and logistical matters to keep the farm in operation.

While traditional notions of family farming can be framed as self-exploitation as farmers tighten their belts, reduce profit margins, and endure hard times, this work is more clearly characterized as the exploitation of farmworker labor. These farmers also become capitalists in the political and economic sense, as they come to see their role of providing work as a rejected gift and take on an opposition role toward workers while depending on workers for producing capital. They have participated in a further hierarchical, structural shift which places financiers in a position of authority over decision-making processes; now, farmers must court them, compete for them, and report to them.

FLEXIBLE FARMING AND THE WEEDINESS OF SOYLANDIA

The paradox of the Cerrado landscape is that, to supporters of agribusiness, it is both wasteland and breadbasket. The paradox of industrial farming in the Cerrado is that, according to US farmers in Western Bahia, it is both so easy that it is boring and also requires "spoon-feeding the soil" with intensive soil amendments and near-constant applications of herbicides, insecticides, and fungicides. Early in my research a US agricultural consultant in Brazil discouraged me from studying the farming practices there at all, saying that US farmers simply adopted the practices that "the market called for" and that they placed little aesthetic, cultural, or ecological value on farming practices. For the most part, farmers agreed with the consultant.

"You can't get farmworkers to do it the American way," Frank Missouri told me. According to him, many farmers told their investors that they would "show people how to farm, but they ended up learning from Brazilians." In order to succeed as a farmer in Brazil, "you need to understand, learn. . . . Americans have no real impact on Brazilian farming techniques, and Brazilians refuse to plant like Americans. [Brazilian farmers] go all the way up each row, stop, turn around in the road, and come all the way back down. Then plant around everything. . . . No American has taught a Brazilian anything."

"Planting like Americans," to Frank, means planting end-rows at each end of the field in which tractors have space to turn around, just like farmers do back in Missouri. These end-rows are planted perpendicular to the rest of the field, as practiced by many midwestern row-crop farmers. It also means planting an entirely cleared field without trees, shrubs, or sheds.

Dennis Tocantins spoke with frustration of trying to manage his Brazilian farm from his Illinois office and facing pushback from his Brazilian agronomists: "What I bring to the company is more of the management. . . . In terms of agronomics, honestly I don't really think that I bring much to the table there. I rely on our agronomist to tell me what he thinks we should do." These were striking statements to me, especially after seeing farmers' investment pitches that highlighted their farming skills and ability to bring "American farming" to the Cerrado.

Farming is easy for transnational farmers in Brazil (Ofstehage 2016). Frank recounted thinking the biggest challenge of farming would be learning plant names, insect names, and best practices, "but that's easy. You have crop scouts, agronomists, managers, and farmworkers that know everything here and tell you all you need to know; [they] know how to operate machinery. The most important thing is city work—paperwork, legalese, culture. You need a good scout, a couple tractors, a couple good tractor drivers, and everything else is easy." They hire agronomists and managers to advise and direct the work, and farmworkers to do the work, but they recognize that developing the land is hard work. As Jacob Iowa explained, "We didn't realize at the time how much it took to really develop the properties. It's not even a matter of just adding fertilizer. It takes years to build up the fertility and soils and build them up to the point where you produce optimal yields. . . . We kinda learned about that the hard way." But, as Jacob went on to argue, the benefit is that "newer ground or raw land" is cheap.

This struggle over good farming practices was an unexpected turn for me. I had come to Brazil expecting US farmers to have implemented their own expertise, know-how, and practices. From interviews with them and documents, they had expected the same, to implement something called "American farming." Instead, they deferred to agronomists and farmworkers on many agronomic decisions. In this chapter I address that very issue: How do transnational farmers farm? I propose that they pursue flexible farming by disentangling and alienating work, plants, and land, but that they also engage with material realities of farming through two processes. First, they engage with the social and physical life of soil; and second, they engage with the life of plants, pests, and other life through what others call the weediness of soy monocultures. Finally, I propose that these encounters, despite farmers' attempts to separate, disassemble, and alienate agricultural life, produce emergent ecologies and new farmers. In a world of spreadsheets and paperwork, the Cerrado's soils and pests became a matter of concern for farmers, despite being framed in investment pitches as easy farming.

Soylandian Soils

The Cerrado's relatively sparse aboveground vegetation is unimpressive to many outside observers—a grassland dotted with short, gnarly trees and prickly shrubs; yet underground there is a rich ecosystem of deep plant roots, soil bacteria, mycorrhizae, worms, ants, and termites. Industrial landscapes and ecologies are emergent and so are industrial soils. The soils are the material remnants of geological weathering, biological life, and human use. The processes of desertification, soil genesis, aggregation, and degradation imply a past state of the soil, an active and dynamic present, and a future trajectory. Soils are also enrolled in very human processes as they are named, remembered, cared for, and valued—not to mention their significance in territorial and nationalistic discourses of homelands, national soils, and belonging. Even outside of the soil science frames of soil quality and soil health, soils are named as good or bad, ours or theirs, and meaningful or commodified. I define these complex engagements between farmers and soil as anthropedological encounters—or the mutual becoming of humans and soil in which soil is biophysically transformed: farmers adopt tillage, cropping, and fertilization practices; farmers and farmworkers construct memories, values, and names for the soil; and alternative (human or nonhuman) relations are severed, disrupted, and forgotten.

Scientific studies of the Cerrado have generally focused on its limitations and strategies for making it productive. Early scientific assumptions and findings were that the Cerrado lacked adequate rainfall, but in the early twentieth century, the Brazilian geologist Miguel Arrojado Lisboa proposed that it was the soils of the Cerrado that limited its agricultural potential, something the locals already knew. They told him that "the soil is bad" (C. M. da Silva 2019, 6). Agronomists turned to the Cerrado as a site for experimentation and improvement. Later, increasing farmland prices and worsening soils in the South of Brazil (caused by poor land use, according to the São Paolo agronomist Rafael Vasconcelos) led farmers to seek cheaper and less-degraded land elsewhere (C. M. da Silva 2019). In the 1950s, Rockefeller Foundation agronomists found similarities in Brazilian and US experiences of a Dust Bowl and saw the potential to fulfill the American dream (or myth) of converting desert to garden in the Cerrado (C. M. da Silva 2012). Researchers determined that agronomy and plant science would be the best tools for converting "desert" into "garden," declaring that "these areas are capable of supporting a much more intensive agriculture than they do at present, and there is an indication that economic returns may be obtained through improved fertility practices. Systematic examination of the soils of the 'campos cerrados' are needed" (C. M. da Silva 2012, 151). Together Brazilian and North American agronomists identified soil acidity, toxic levels of aluminum, and limited availability of soil micronutrients as the primary limitations of plant growth. They resolved to eliminate aluminum toxicity by adding dolomitic calcium, fertilizing with calcium and magnesium, and modifying the availability of other nutrients.

Industrial soy farmers clear the Cerrado and denude the soil, but their relationship with Cerrado soils is more complicated than degradation. As we saw in chapter 2, most Brazilian and US farmers consider the Cerrado a wasteland and soy fields as progress. Within that narrow frame of value, they consider themselves to be improving and caring for the land. Through that productivist lens of soil fertility, it is hard to argue that the soils are degraded—they have a pH that is more appropriate for crop production, more nutrients that help crops grow, fewer nutrients that are present at toxic levels, and so on. As I argue here and elsewhere (Ofstehage 2023), farmers frame their work, and especially their soil work, as care for barren soils in which they are making, building, and improving soil—and in the process becoming better farmers. Maria Puig de la Bellacasa writes that "not all relations are caring, but very few could subsist without some care" (2017, 70), and I agree. So, what kind of work is necessary to maintain a transnational flexible farm? My work as an anthropologist is to unpack these signifiers to understand what farmers need to do to maintain their soil, how they create meaning from this, and what this means for the future of farming. I explore transnational farmers' relationship with the soil through material and social encounters of clearing, fertilizing, and tilling the soil. Thus, soils are emergent in two senses. First, they change in relation to both human and nonhuman processes and become new assemblages of inert and live matter. Second, they are emergent in the sense of being catalytic of change. The material properties of soil make certain farming futures possible or impossible. They also change the ways farmers see themselves and their relation to the land. Thus, people change the soils, but soils also change people.

Opening New Ground

Off the dusty streets of Luís Eduardo and inside an innocuous business building, we sat in a nondescript meeting room. I sat across from Eddie, farm owner and manager of Frontier Farms with a taste for adventure, and next to Jonathon Smith and his son Jeffrey, investors in the farm. It was an opportunity to have investors and farmers in the same room. We spoke mostly about their different reasons for coming to Brazil and their relative involvement in farm decisions, but the conversation took a turn when I asked Eddie about clearing the land. He sat up a little, his eyes brightened, and he excitedly explained,

> I don't know, where do I start! When you're opening Cerrado, anytime you're opening new ground, it's like a hundred years ago in the Midwest

or several hundreds of years ago in Europe or now in Brazil. You're gonna find different things. Number one, when you're opening land on a 10,000-hectare farm and it's full of trees . . . sometimes there's pieces of ground you don't expect. Root structures are something that you come across, that was a big problem for us.

It is of little surprise that farmers here refer to land conversion as "cleaning" the land.[1] Farmers, investors, and farm tourists alike describe clearing these ten-foot trees in romantic terms. When I spoke with farmers about the various topics of interest to my research, they would dully list yields, weather patterns, markets, and infrastructure; but, like Eddie, their eyes lit up when they talked about clearing land.

Eddie's casual, humble tone belied his pride in transforming the land. He reminded me more of a Dakotan than a New Yorker:

> The county, Formosa, was pretty primitive; [Jeffrey, Jonathon, and I] were talking the other day, we were kinda trailblazing a little bit. . . . The landscape was pretty rough, you had to be patient, tough, adventuresome; we'd go up there weekly. So we started from scratch there, . . . and we had a lot of difficulties. Opening Cerrado is like—how should I say—it's a bag of surprises. . . . We went through a lot of [surprises] and now our ground is developed. We've invested a lot in it, and now it's producing ground.

Eddie's framing of his difficult work in "opening Cerrado" and "producing ground" speaks to the taming of the wild, surprising, impenetrable Cerrado and the consequent creation of knowable, productive land. The chain, not the chainsaw, features in many accounts of clearing the Cerrado. Farmers typically would drag a heavy chain with a heavy tractor through the shrubs, bushes, and trees to knock everything down. Some would then make charcoal from the wood, but many would simply burn the rubble in the field. This was a process of taming the wild, uncovering the unknown, and making the illegible legible. This is only the first step of making the Cerrado produce soy.

A consultant's website portrays the clearing of Cerrado forest as a straightforward process. Initial clearing is done by dragging a 100-meter long, one-inch-thick steel cable between two large tractors. A heavier, shorter 75-meter chain can be used where vegetation is thicker. This is best done during the rainy season when roots are more easily pulled out of wet soil. After uprooting trees, larger trees are harvested for firewood, brush is burned in the field, and a chisel cultivator can pull remaining roots from the ground. A disc cultivator breaks down large soil aggregates, two to three tons of limestone are added, and the disc cultivator passes through the field again to work in the lime. The first crop planted is upland rice, after which soy, cotton, or corn can be incorporated. Upland rice tolerates "poor soil fertility" and although yields and profits from its cultivation are low, it acts as a cheap, intermediate crop while the soil undergoes biochemical reactions to the clearing and soil amendments.

The clearing of native Cerrado vegetation was also a favorite story of farmers; for many, it signified the beginning of a battle between the wild and unruly Cerrado and the controlled progress of soybean fields. Clearing the Cerrado holds special value for transnational farmers as a singularly tangible achievement. It is the transformation from a wild, messy, uncontrollable wasteland into a tamed, clean, and manageable cropland. The bravado with which Eddie told me of his clearing, and the deep interest of farm tourists in seeing trees fall, remind farmers of family stories of settlement and conquest. Perhaps more than any other work in Brazil it expresses their masculinity—not a New Age farming masculinity of caring for the land, nor that of being a businessman farmer. It is the masculinity of their grandfathers, which was built not just on production and profit but on conquest, settlement, and transformation of the land itself.

"Putting on Fertility"

George Lake settled in Western Bahia with his family in the 1970s; the family accumulated 250,000 acres of land before being forcibly evicted. He remembers the soil being "aluminum toxic" and Brazilians wanting nothing to do with the "desert." A local agronomist recommended he add magnesium to neutralize the aluminum; they bought a sprayer to apply it and planted a successful crop of rice. "[Brazilians] thought we were crazy—until we showed them how to make the land produce. One could say we started the hell that followed (his family's later eviction) by being successful." Few of the later US farmers made claims of showing Brazilians how to farm or of innovating soil management strategies, though US Mennonites certainly do so (Ofstehage 2018c). However, many described their engagement with the soil as a generation of fertility rather than as degradation. Soil erosion is a serious issue in converted Cerrado farmland. Soil erosion is a foundational concept in political ecology (Blaikie and Brookfield 1987), and the concept of fertility is problematic, but here I adopt a frame of soil building and soil genesis over one of soil degradation.[2] This allows me to address the matters of concern to my study population since soil building was both their main concern in farming and their main social connection to the land. This framing also contributes to a critical understanding of soil fertility.

Fertility for soil scientists is a scale of how apt a soil is to produce a high yield of a given cash crop. For permaculturalists, agrologists, and agroecologists it is akin to soil health or vitality; for socialists, it may be a measure of how well the

FIGURE 25.   Heaps of lime keep a field fertile.

soil supports both community and ecology. For industrial midwestern farmers in Brazil and in the United States, fertility aligns somewhat with the definition used by scientists; but rather than a measure of a soil it is a thing to apply to soil. For them, whether using manure, or more commonly synthetic fertilizer, fertility is defined as the NPK (nitrogen, phosphorous, potassium) content and is something that can be "put on." "Putting on fertility" contrasts with permaculturalists' concepts of "building" or "growing" the soil.[3] Like the clearing of the Cerrado, putting on fertility expresses a masculine ideal of farming—fertilizing an otherwise barren landscape (Ofstehage 2022). Fertility here is not a property of the soil, a value given to represent health, or an indicator of the human-soil relationship but something that farmers apply. Jacob Iowa illustrated this point in his explanation of how he planned his crop rotation: "The soybeans are following the cotton . . . because usually you put heavy fertility on the cotton, so there's a lot of residual fertility . . . so you don't need to invest in the soybeans, which is a cheaper crop, and the soybeans don't need as much fertility."

Once we understand that fertility is something to be applied, we can better comprehend transnational farmers' engagement with the soil and their understanding of their relationship with it. According to Jacob, "the clearing is really the easy part; it's the development that's the hard part. It takes a lot of time, it's

[an] expensive process; once you get your clearing license you can just put a big chain together and knock it down. It's pretty shallow and it comes undone pretty easily." Soil fertility itself is not that important to flexible farmers; but a soil's potential to be developed into fertile ground is more important. They add phosphate, potash, gypsum, magnesium, nitrogen, and lime every year.

Jacob's thoughts here speak to an important characteristic of flexible land—that it can be made productive. The potential to put on fertility advances two goals of flexible farmers. First, it means the farmer can buy marginal land cheaply, fertilize it, and produce well enough to make a profit from crop production. Second, it means that the farmer can sell that developed land at a speculative profit once the land has been "developed."

After clearing the land, farmers add large amounts of lime and gypsum the first year and then supplement with phosphate, potash, gypsum, magnesium, nitrogen, and lime thereafter. They also integrate no-tillage cultivation, which minimizes or eliminates tillage in fields to conserve soil moisture and increase organic matter in Cerrado soils. By comparison, midwestern row-crop farms often only fertilize with NPK and are just recently transitioning to minimal tillage.[4] US farmers in Brazil learned these practices from Brazilian agronomists, soil scientists, and farmers.

FIGURE 26. Straight rows in the field are no longer indicators of "good farming" for US farmers in Brazil.

Brazilian soil experts describe Cerrado soils as infertile, ancient, and acidic, and also perfect for agribusiness. The dominant soils of the Cerrado are latosols, defined as soils in an advanced stage of weathering and "virtualmente destituidos" (nearly stripped bare) of primary and secondary minerals (Embrapa 2013, 93). Latosols, with little nutrient reserve for plants, are therefore "são solos com grandes problemas de fertilidade" (they are soils with big fertility problems) (J. R. Correia, Reatto, and Spera 2004, 43). According to soil scientists, latosols are suited for mechanization due to their high water permeability and poor chemical makeup; they are "apt for agribusiness" (Sano et al. 2007, 96). Latosols are generally well-drained soils and extremely deep; the topsoil rarely measures less than a meter, and there is little distinction between soil layers. The limiting factors of latosols are low fertility, susceptibility to erosion, and low soil organic matter. Embrapa soil scientists recommend that Cerrado farmers use the soil according to its agricultural potential; correct the soil in terms of acidity, aluminum saturation, and low fertility; take care with soils with high clay content; maintain soil cover for the longest period possible, especially during the rainy season; and adopt, whenever possible, agricultural conservation like minimum tillage and no-tillage (J. R. Correia, Reatto, and Spera 2004).

Soil infertility in the Cerrado is not what it seems to outsider investors, agronomists, and farmers. The Cerrado is home to many plant species that thrive in its low phosphorous, low pH, low water, and high aluminum soils. Hans Lambers and his colleagues argue that transforming the Cerrado into farmland can lead to the extinction of the plants that are suited to that ecology (Lambers et al. 2020). Many Cerrado plants survive and thrive in low phosphorous soils by creating symbiotic relationships with mycorrhiza (J. B. Moura and Cabral 2019). In his 1956 dissertation, Reeshon Feuer identified 40 percent of soil in the federal district of Brasilia (in the center of the Cerrado) as latosols of "excellent physical properties for agricultural crops, but reaction and nutrient status is often unfavorable." Cropping, he argued, was "not possible on the scrub-savanna uplands under a continuous cropping type of soil management, involving existing technique and management." Moderate yields would be possible with "use of rotations, mulches, cover crops, animal manures, and small amounts of industrial materials," while excellent yields would be possible on all latosols with "full use of scientific soil and crop management principles, machinery and industrial materials" (Feuer 1956, 349). While outlining the same issues with Cerrado soils as other soil scientists, Feuer is unique in outlining them in relation to various types of land use. This distinction is important; fertility is relational and dependent on land use, farming practices, and plants. The distinction of fertile/infertile is based on the production of certain cash crops, not a reference to the overall health or quality of the soil.

Caring for the Soil?

Because of the differences between Cerrado soils and soils in US farmers' home states, farmers often spoke of the neediness of Cerrado soils and the need for intensive soil maintenance. Dennis Tocantins once described to me the extra care needed to fertilize "weak" Cerrado soils. They begin with a heavy application of gypsum (two tons for 1,500 acres) and continue applications of lime for two years to "bring it up." They reapply lime every third or fifth year, depending on the soil sampling. In the United States they sample every two to five years, but they test in Brazil each year because the soil "needs to be taken care of." Further, in Brazil they take a more targeted approach of applying fertilizer in bands where seeds are planted rather than broadly in order to save money:

> [In Illinois] you can almost skip applying fertilizer for a year, whereas down there [in Tocantins] you literally can't. There are severe limitations, the areas with new soil; there's an area where we took out a new pasture and the fertilizer bander got clogged up and so fertilizer wasn't applied in spots. Where the fertilizer skipped, the plants were 1–2 feet off the ground and the other plants were 4–5 feet tall. The newer the soil, the more you have to add fertilizer. You're talking about 440 kilos per hectare, moving a lot of product and tendering a lot of product.

A major challenge to farmers' conceptualization of fertility as something to be added is the need to address pH in the highly acidic soils of the Cerrado. I asked Jacob, "What do you have to do to bring it up to production level?"

> The first thing you do is you add a lot of lime. Lime is kinda the key ingredient to neutralize the acid in the soils here, probably about 6 tons of lime per hectare in the first year alone and probably a ton of gypsum per hectare; and then you put on phosphorous as well, so you're basically correcting the soil because the natural pH of the soil's real low. About four and a half. [Lime] reduces the acidity so it increases the pH. The lime is basic. The gypsum is for the sulfur; it has a high content of sulfur, and the potassium is one of the main macronutrients.

Farmers often compared the fertile soils of the Midwest and the infertile soils of the Cerrado in terms of soil testing, micronutrients, soil pH amendments, and banding of fertilizer. These comparisons demonstrated differences in soil management practices. They also demonstrated farmers' perceptions of Cerrado soils. Using words like "weak" and phrases like "bring it up," "correcting the soil," and "taken care of" allows farmers to claim that the soil is in need of care and that they are caring for it. This distinction likewise allows farmers to claim that their practices are improving the land and gives them firmer ground to stand on from which they can make this claim.

Human relationships with the soil can be classified under the dominant technoscientific interventionist extractive mining of soil or as antiproductivist, affective, care for the soil (de la Bellacasa 2017). In what Maria Puig de la Bellacasa calls the "utilitarian-care vision," worn-out soils are "put back to work" using technoscientific practices at "the expense of all other relations" (186). This industrialist approach to soil contrasts with the anthropological approach to indigenous soil classification, care, and relations. The US farmers of Western Bahia do not pretend to love Cerrado soils, but for them Cerrado soils do become a "matter of care" insofar as the soils need to be corrected, built, and generally maintained (177). The relatively infertile Cerrado soils—compared to the black soils of the Midwest (which have been similarly eroded, made toxic with fertilizer, and are now extremely low in organic matter)—require increased maintenance because they are already fully degraded. Therefore, they can only be improved.

The ability of the concepts of soil fertility and soil quality to represent holistic soil health is questionable (Engel-Di Mauro 2014), but these concepts are very real in their potential to motivate farmers' practices and narratives. US farmers create discourses and values around adding fertility and improving land; they claim they are not degrading the soil but building it. Both the discourse of soil as barren and worthless and the agronomic reality that the soil requires extra care to make it productive for industrial agriculture support the mistaken belief that without soy farmers the landscape is barren. Further, this framing supports their politicization of soil with claims that this is not soil degradation but rather soil building and correcting the soil.

Of course, this notion of soil building is easily dismissed from either a perspective of the farmers' own disinterest in improving Brazil in other ways and in terms of the farmers' overall impact on the habitat and ecology of the Cerrado. But this is also an argument made by other "conservation farmers" who reduce tillage with one hand and increase herbicide use with the other. Beyond the *need* for soil maintenance in any kind of farming situation, these farmers are also using this discourse to defend against investor and public concerns about deforestation and degradation.

Building the Soil

No-tillage soy production became widely adopted by Brazilian farmers in the Cerrado to maintain soil moisture, reduce soil erosion, and also to reduce production costs (Kiihl and Calvo 2008). It is also closely tied with the expansion

FIGURE 27. Many US farmers adopted no-till in Brazil to suit the soils and climate.

of soy production, increased use of agrochemicals to control weeds, and land dispossession (Ofstehage and Nehring 2021). Soil conservation itself is rarely on the minds of transnational farmers, though most of them practice no-till farming. Rather, no-till is seen as a means of reducing the number of workers, preserving soil moisture, and increasing organic matter content. In their words, it is a necessary practice, not a choice driven by stewardship. Further, it is made possible by the availability of Roundup Ready soy varieties that are not susceptible to glyphosate—an herbicide widely used in the United States and Brazil—to control weeds in the absence of tillage.

On his decision to adopt no-tillage, Jacob Iowa said it was not really a matter of reducing erosion but "a matter of trying to improve the organic matter and reduce field costs, wear and tear on equipment." Their rotation of corn, soy, and cotton required some kind of removal of cotton (a perennial crop) in order to plant another crop the next year. Without tillage, they would use a stalk chopper to mow the plants after harvest, then "burn [the cotton] down with chemicals; that's all you really do."

A high-level worker for the USDA-FAS in Brasilia explained the rapid adoption of no-tillage in the Cerrado: "They don't want to mess with the land; it's tropical so you don't have the requirement to open up the soil to warm it up for germination. The soil is so depleted here and so poor that in their mind you always want to have some kind of cover on it."

Likewise, Dennis reported that in Western Bahia no-till was necessary because of the high temperatures that quickly dry out Cerrado soils: "You have to leave organic matter on soil to protect it." But no-tillage comes with its own limits. While walking through a harvested cotton field, Ian from Illinois pulled a cotton plant from his field to demonstrate how the taproot went straight down for a few inches, then spread sideways, unable to penetrate the compacted soil. He said this was a problem in dry years when it needs to reach deeper for moisture.

Farmers are unconcerned about conserving the soil itself and find little reason to. As quoted earlier, a common sentiment was that "there was no fertility. . . . [The] soil profile goes down 100 feet deep." No-till is agronomically necessary to preserve organic matter and to conserve soil moisture, but it is also mobilized by farmers to argue that farming in the Cerrado requires extra care and skill. In their view, the soil is more vulnerable and less robust than the soils of Illinois, Indiana, or Iowa.

While at each step there is a set of material requirements that farmers meet, there is also a social meaning and value given to that work. Clearing the land is necessary to plant row crops, and it is also deeply valued and confers masculinity to farmers. Soil fertility needs to be increased to produce soy and cotton; it also gives authorization, value, and meaning to farming in the Cerrado. Tillage is necessary to maintain soil moisture, but it also becomes about building the soil. This intersection of the materiality of soil, care work, and value demands a reassessment of industrial soils and care. If soil care is the material maintenance of soil, farmers' adoption of new fertilization and tillage practices qualifies. Despite the destruction, degradation, and dispossession wrought by soy cultivation in the Brazilian Cerrado, it is clear that care, value, and work are integral in industrial soils. Yet this care work that is necessary to maintain agricultural production on flexible farms also sustains violent ecologies. But the discourse of soil care helps farmers assuage investor concerns about the environmental impacts of soy farming. It also creates emergent ecologies that, despite farmers' best efforts, run wild.

Weediness and the Smell of 2,4-D: Soy and the Making of Capitalist Nomads

On a farm visit with Ian, I watched and listened as he checked in on planting progress in the fields from his pickup. As we drove through a rain shower I mentioned offhandedly that I like the smell of rain and he replied, "I love the smell of

2,4-D; it means the weeds are dead."[5] Americans in Bahia needed to clear trees, shrubs, and grass; to "make" soil; and then to "build" it. Once they supplanted Cerrado for soy, they needed to engage with soil, plants, fungi, bugs, and weeds to defend Soylandia from the weediness of the Cerrado. This engagement meant changing the practices, values, and know-hows of the farmers themselves. As they changed the soil fertility and pH as well as the plant population, they battled the Cerrado; they also became different farmers.

Soy dominates landscapes in Soylandia where farmers have "turned huge areas of the mixed landscape . . . into something alien—a blanket monocrop crawling with giant machines and soaked in pesticides (Hetherington 2020, 5). As Kregg Hetherington and others recognize, this taming of the land is an ongoing process of combating weeds, fungi, and insects. Crop monocultures are ideal conditions for fast-growing annual plants, plant diseases, and herbivorous insects that take advantage of the ample sun and sustenance and lack of competition—they are weedy landscapes. Industrial agriculture depends on controlling the diseases, pests, and weeds that thrive in such conditions (Guthman 2019).[6] The plantation—of which monocultural soy farms share many characteristics—is home to two landscape disturbances: simplification of plant, animal, and soil life in vast fields of monocultures; and weedy proliferations of disease, noncrop plants, and insect pests (Tsing, Mathews, and Bubandt 2019). Care for the plantation entails the eradication of all species except one within a boundary. While the framework of care provides a way to understand the maintenance work on the plantation, the field of emergent ecologies provides a framework to understand this process as a generative one that creates life out of the rubble.

Capitalism is always generating new nomads, or "agents capable of adapting to varied political, cultural, or ecological contexts" (Stengers 2010, 390). Flexible farmers, in their mobile, financialized livelihoods certainly qualify as capitalist nomads. Soy too has shown that it adapts well to habitats, economies, and social spheres. Flexible farmers' capitalistic nomadism requires adaptation to biodiverse life that threatens agriculture; some adaptations prove remarkably effective while others threaten the existence of the plantation itself. The soils, insects, weeds, and fungi of the Cerrado make farming difficult and expensive and create friction—in some cases impeding development and in others fine-tuning it.

"Soy can be produced by a boy, but cotton is man's work." Or so I was told by a foreign agricultural service agent in Brasilia. Farmers frequently complained about the difficulty and expense of growing cotton, especially when compared to soy. Cotton requires much more labor, extra attention, and even a totally different managing style. Ian likened it to raising livestock. A common saying, he told me, "is that if you ask someone if there is anything wrong with your cotton and they say no, they're lying." Cotton requires more fertilizer because it does not fix nitrogen like soy does, and it grows best with micronutrient fertilization. For Jacob, cotton was a headache. "Fertilizer is our single greatest expense; [cotton] just requires more nutrients to grow." Cotton also calls for more pest management and, produced in industrial monoculture, that means more pesticides. According to Jacob, "You have to spray more fungicides, more insecticides. . . . We'll do seventeen applications [of pesticides] for the cotton in a year and we'll do five for the soybeans. Seventeen applications of actually running the sprayer through the field; now within that sprayer there may be two or three different chemicals; last year we bought something like forty-one different insecticides— it's something you have to monitor daily and you're spraying weekly."

Farmers apply additional applications of pesticide because cotton is more susceptible to pests and producing high-quality cotton requires minimizing aesthetic damage to the cotton fiber. Most pesticide applications for cotton are preventative, not prescriptive because, as Jacob told me, "the insects can really go through the boll pretty quickly if they get away from you." To add another element of complication and expense, since cotton is a perennial it has to be killed in the field in order to plant it or another crop the next year. Further, the state requires the farmers to kill cotton plants in between seasons in order to reduce insects and disease on host plants. This requires either using tillage to pull up the cotton roots or spraying a maturing agent on the plants two weeks prior to harvest in order to kill the plants—sometimes both.

In addition to the finicky growing conditions of the plant in monoculture, cotton production requires a large capital investment for machinery and a cotton gin; or if the farm does not own a cotton gin, payment for harvested cotton to be ginned. Owning and operating your own gin can provide control over the process and cotton storage, but it entails more laborers, requires financing to build, and is expensive to operate.

Still, cotton offers access to a lucrative market and for most US farmers it is worth the effort. Eddie, speaking of the possibility that agricultural development in the region had plateaued, looked to cotton as the future:

> I think for Bahia, I think for us here, the one thing we can do here that nobody else in Brazil—or probably the world—can do [is] produce world-class cotton on dry land farms at a very high yield. And we have to continue to hang on to that. As long as we can continue to do that, we're going to have a value here. Now, it'd be a lot better if it weren't $0.65 cotton out there, right now. With $1.00 cotton, I think our region would be a lot more excited. But prices are low. And I think that's something we have here—that's our competitive advantage. And that won't change.

But cotton—with one primary use in textiles, intense pest pressure, heavy fertilizer requirements, the necessity of either operating a gin or paying for cotton to be ginned, and the need to kill the plant after harvest—is a difficult crop to produce, especially when compared to soy.

Meanwhile, Roundup Ready soy is the ideal industrial monocultural crop. The soy plant provides its own nitrogen, and it requires little postharvest processing. But although soy is the ideal flexible crop, it is not as easy to grow as it sounds. Soy farmers, after having built and corrected the Cerrado soils, need to reckon with the weediness of the Cerrado and monocrop agriculture. Weeds themselves are easily managed using glyphosate, more commonly known by its tradename as Roundup.[7] Roundup Ready soybeans are engineered to be resistant to glyphosate which would otherwise kill the plant. This broad-based herbicide, along with 2,4-D, effectively kills all other plants in the field, with the exception of some glyphosate-resistant plants, leaving a "clean" field (Ofstehage 2022). Weed control thus requires only frequent applications of glyphosate.

The flexible farmers' fiercest opponents are the tiny whitefly and microscopic soybean rust. Asian soybean rust is caused by the fungus *Phakopsora pachyrhizi*. Regarded as the most severe plant disease to affect soy, it can cause yield losses of up to 90 percent. It was first identified and reported in Brazil in 2001. Due to the year-round survivability of both soy plants and the fungus, it has been aggressively controlled using regulatory measures and fungicide application, but compliance with the regulatory measures is inconsistent and the fungus is growing resistant to fungicides. Plant scientists advise integrated pest management and biotechnological strategies to replace increasingly ineffective fungicides (Godoy et al. 2016).

Soybean rust looms over the soybean farmers of Western Bahia. The specter of rust hangs in Ian's office next to a map of Brazil; it shows the stages of soy rust with a sequence of ever-deteriorating soybean leaves, reminding managers and agronomists who pass through the office to beware. In 2003 Western Bahia lost 30 percent of its soybean crop to soybean rust. As of 2012, when I began my research, the fungus was under control but only with heavy applications of fungicide. One investor reported touring Brazil not for adventure or profit but for answers to how Brazilians controlled rust since it had recently entered the southern United States and begun to spread northward. The social connections he made on that tour led to his later investment in a large US farm. Others, like Frank, identify fungicide applications as a practice they would introduce on farms in the Midwest. "We've never talked about putting fungicide on soybeans. Soybean rust hit so hard here, everyone had to think about it. And suddenly we figured out we probably should be using these fungicides even if you don't have rust." At the time, in 2012, midwestern farmers were applying insecticides and herbicides liberally, but they rarely used fungicides. Frank remembers conversations with farmers in Missouri who said "Hey, you might think fungicide is something just for European wheat farmers, or something. But you need to start trying it."

Farmers generally saw soybean rust as an expensive nuisance to keep an eye on but one that could be managed well with heavy applications of fungicide. When his family arrived in 1999, farming had been simple, Frank explained: "You'd plant a crop, you got to treat the seed and all that, but all you did was [apply an] herbicide, maybe you [applied] an insecticide, went to the beach, slept a little bit . . . and you did pretty well." And then pest management grew more complicated. When rust arrived in 2003, they started applying fungicide and they have been able to manage that, but "in the last five years what's happened is the insect pressure. . . . The cost to control the insects today outweighs the cost of fertilizer. . . . It used to be you'd talk about 'I'm going to spend ten sacks [of soy] on fertilizer and five on chemicals.' Today, you're saying 'OK, I'm going spend ten sacks on fertilizer, I'm going to spend about fifteen, twenty on chemicals.'"

Insects continue to be out of control. Worms are a particular issue for farmers in Western Bahia, but none more so than the whitefly. Eddie pointed to the pesky whitefly as the villain responsible for his family considering an end to their thirty-year Brazilian experiment. Along with flexible farmers and soy plants, it too is a nomad. Whitefly is one of the most important pests of tropical and subtropical agriculture; it adapts easily to new host plants and geographical regions, has been reported on all continents except Antarctica, and feeds and reproduces on six hundred different annual and perennial plant species. Biological control by predators, parasitoids, and pathogens, not insecticides, are the most effective control (Togni et al. 2019). The absence of a "nice freeze," as Eddie told me, means insect pests live undisturbed throughout the year. "The best we can do," he said, is to "kill everything you got living in the ground. Anything green, you kill it, and don't give any habitat for worms, or whatever it might be. But still, they find ways to live through it."

Whiteflies are extremely resistant to insecticides. They eat the soy leaves, but the real damage comes after they eat as they transmit viruses. Eddie told me, "Once that leaf gets black, that's it. . . . It's devastating." I asked about the effectiveness of insecticide, and he explained:

> The worst part about it is there's no one insecticide that's dedicated to the whitefly. . . . The effectiveness of applications on whitefly is very low. You're spending expensive chemicals, spending lots of money, you're getting very low effectiveness. . . . The deal is this: you don't want to let it get to be where it's a big problem. You see it, get it right away. If you

wait three, four, five days—here—that's deadly. Once it gets to be a big problem, you're just not going to beat it.

During my first research period in 2012, the whitefly did not come up in a single conversation; but when I returned in 2014 it was a major issue for all farmers I interviewed in Bahia. Eddie noted that their main insect control was using residual insecticides, which require moisture to be effective. Two dry years in Western Bahia had rendered their most effective line of defense useless.

This was not the first time the whitefly had threatened the Brazilian soy crop. A 1973 report warned of large whitefly populations in the soy fields of Paraná and São Paulo as well as an increased incidence of related viruses. The whole soy crop was affected, and high whitefly numbers were blamed on the great extension of the cultivation of soybeans, long planting seasons, and a long, hot summer. The authors of the report recommended restricting the cropping season, researching whitefly control strategies, and breeding virus-resistant plants (A. S. Costa, Costa, and Sauer 1973). The whitefly continued to run amok and, still, the only effective treatment is integrated pest management—using diverse cropping rotations and biological control (Togni et al. 2019). In 2007 the Bahia state government instituted a *vazio sanitário* (clean waiting period, or quarantine), a period during which all soy plants must be removed. This was primarily intended to control soy rust, but it would also help with whitefly by removing host plants. At the time of my research, in Western Bahia this quarantine period ran from August 15 to October 15 (though the dates are subject to change) with the cost of an infraction at 15,000 reais (according to Ian). None of these solutions appeal to flexible farmers who choose rotations based on market prices, have little patience for biological control, and who do not want to remove soy plants.

"Emergent ecologies," Eben Kirksey writes, "describes parasitic invasions that destroyed established communities while simultaneously opening up new possibilities for flourishing" (Kirksey 2015, 4). But who here is the parasite? The soy rust fungus? The whitefly? The soybean? The farmer? Bruce Braun (2015) describes capital itself as a parasite. "Parasites are key players in emergent ecologies" (Kirksey 2015, 4) and represent biological or social freeloaders—a description that might suit all of the above. Capital, farmer, soybean plant, soybean fungus, and whitefly are world forming. They are also all nomads—crossing biospheres, national borders, and fence lines with ease, colonizing space while there is profit in that endeavor and continuing on in search of something else when resources and opportunity become scarce. Weeds slip through the careful plans of flexible farmers, but not uniformly. Soybean rust demonstrates that flexible farmers can indeed adapt quickly to agronomic problems, and the whitefly shows that they can't fix everything without changing the fundamental ways they farm.

This nomadism contrasts directly with the ways Indigenous and quilombolo communities engage with Cerrado land. For example, the Indigenous Canela of the Cerrado, in the state of Maranhão, classify soil in oppositional and complementary pairs: "weak soil" and "good soil," "very soft soil" and "hard clay," and so on. These soil pairs inscribe meaning on the soil and prescribe agricultural use but avoid the discourse or practice of improvement according to a single rubric of fertility. Midwestern farmers often speak of "putting on fertility" instead of "putting on fertilizer"; fertility is a clearly defined goal, and all soils are said to be fertile or infertile for specific cash crops. The Canela, on the other hand, listen to the soil and work with it (T. Miller 2019). The frame of improvement and putting on fertility contrasts with agroecologically inspired narratives of remediation, healing, and restoration of the land or feeding the soil (Penniman and Washington 2018).

Making Good Farmers: Care and Emergent Agroecologies

Much of this discussion has centered on soil as the primary concern of soy farmers in Western Bahia, but the fear of loss of yield is also extremely important to them. Ane Gracia (2017) notes in her ethnography of soy in Bahia that planting is done daquele jeito or by any means necessary, but harvest is done with care so as not to lose even a single bean. US farmers hailing from a more temperate climate were struck by the intensity of pest pressure in Brazil—from the tiny whitefly to the microscopic soy rust. Keeping labor, value, images, politics, and material effects in conversation allows us to see these connections and disconnections as social worlds. The soil, insects, weeds, and fungi of the Cerrado make farming difficult and expensive. Focusing on this encounter decenters capital and power; this is one aspect of friction—that local life impedes development. The other side of friction is that it provides the traction necessary to accelerate development.

While complaining about the difficult growing conditions in Brazil, farmers often turned this around to say that when they return to the United States to farm, they will return as experts in soil and pest management. The skill gained in learning to develop, build, and construct soil changes the soil, but it also changes the farmer. Many spoke of their eventual return to the United States after they could afford to purchase land or to take over their family's farm. When I asked what practices they would bring back, many focused on the business practices of hiring, the managerial aspects of farming, and keeping tidy records of accounting and business transactions. Others also brought up soil management techniques they had adopted in Brazil. The fickle and needy soils of the Cerrado had taught them the importance of consistent soil testing, extensive fertilizer applications, minimizing tillage, and keeping track of pH levels of the soil. The advanced soil management techniques that make Cerrado soils productive for industrial farming are not agronomically necessary practices on the comparatively fertile soils of the US Midwest, but such techniques and practices could give farmers a competitive advantage over neighboring farmers by reducing costs, increasing yields, and reducing erosion.

Frank spoke of becoming a better farmer in Brazil and bringing Brazilian farming practices back to the United States. If he came back to Missouri, "I would inoculate soy, add manganese, keep an office, be attentive to paperwork, hire workers, bring Brazilian workers up, pay closer attention to soils." In his view, this training made him a better farmer, but he could not bring all of these farming practices back up North. Agronomic differences between Missouri and Western Bahia meant that he could not translate farming practices directly between the sites—Western Bahia called for specific attention to the soil, depended on different seeds and even different crops, and had much higher insect pressure—but he could take back with him a Brazilian approach to farming: "It would change my farming practices too. . . . When I first came here was the first year of soybean rust. We've never talked about putting fungicide on soybeans. Soybean rust hit so hard here, everyone had to think about it. And suddenly we figured out we probably should be using these fungicides even if you don't have rust."

This meant more attention to soil testing, an understanding of controlling fungal plant diseases, and an agronomically and economically informed approach to insect and pest management. Eddie similarly described a process of learning, not imposition:

> A lot of guys who come here, I've seen them come and go. They think they're going to bring the United States to Brazil. That doesn't work. What you've got to do is do a little bit of both. You've got to get a guy who knows what he doesn't know and nothing else. You bring your know-how because you can't get too far on the other side. You can't be too much saying, "Well I know more than the other guy," and just farm the way you want to, because there are things here that are different that you need to learn. On the other hand, you can't get too far on the other side saying, "I need to learn from the Brazilians," because a lot of the Brazilians that are doing this are learning, too. Agriculture in this place is different than Paraná. It's different than Rio Grande do Sul, and it's even different than Mato Grosso. Bahia has its own little characteristics you need to learn just like I'm sure Iowa does or Nebraska does or South Dakota does.

Eddie and his father, as well as many US farmers, had arrived in Brazil with agronomic, business, and life plans, but they found that they had to adapt to the realities of farming in Brazil, or return to the United States unsuccessful. When Eddie arrived, they "realized pretty quick there is no way that's going to happen.... We completely changed what we were thinking. And I have no regrets, but you've got to learn."

Much like Eddie, Dennis too recognized the need to adapt to the way Brazilians farm and to adapt to the Cerrado. He listed micronutrient fertilization, pH management, and fungicide application as practices he had adopted in order to adjust to the complications of farming in Brazil and to the "weakness" of the soils:

> It's a lot more difficult to farm here. The level of technology that is applied at the agronomic level is much higher in terms of just balancing the soil [pH], micronutrients, and then we're doing multiple applications of chemical, of fungicide. We're doing foliar fertilization. We're doing stuff that here the top-end guys are experimenting with and it's a fact of business in Brazil that you have to do it. . . . Here the soils are so weak that you have to spoon-feed the soil. You can't afford to just throw fertilizer on it. And then you're dealing with issues of fungicide, so it's a lot more complicated to farm here.

He was unwilling to give up the idea that Americans brought something special and different to the region. The ecology of Soylandia has been transformed, and indeed broad swaths of the Cerrado are unrecognizable as anything besides monocultures of soy and cotton. Despite that destruction and simplification, to paraphrase Marx, "people make Soylandia, but they do not make it as they please." Flexible farmers adapt to the soils and pests of the Cerrado by adopting new farming practices and even values of farming.

Midwestern family farmers managed soil fertilization, pests, and climate using local workers and expertise—even with technically more difficult cotton fields. As one farmer said, "It's a dream to farm in Brazil; the difficult side is in the city." By this, he meant seed selection, tillage, harvesting, and all the agronomic aspects of farming are simple and easy, but the challenging issues correspond with business in town and the government officials there: complying with worker and environmental protections and foreign land laws; managing investors and business partners; and negotiating with workers and agricultural input dealers.

US farmers intended to treat the Cerrado as a kind of blank slate on which to create their farms; instead, they had to engage. The Cerrado's resilience to farming calls for constant upkeep; the so-called wasteland is active, not passive. The very premise of the wasteland discourse is discounted by the historical reality and current existence of agroecological and agroforestry livelihoods mastered by

Indigenous and quilombolo communities in the river valleys of the region. These communities, like those studied by Theresa Miller (2019), show that while intensive fertilization is necessary to coax industrial crops out of the Cerrado soils, it is not necessary to produce plentiful, healthy food. The encounter between the farmers and the Cerrado created changing practices. Farmers adapted fertilization, tillage, seed selection, and pest management to Cerrado agroecology and Brazilian environmental regulations. Their values changed as they used the differences between US and Cerrado soils as evidence of deficit and claimed a role as developers and producers of value. They became valued as transformers of wasteland to valued farmland. This elevated farming from mere livelihood to "hero" work. Their contribution to the Brazil Model fine-tuned it and prepared it for export to the United States. Finally, their work with the land altered it in permanent ways but also in ways that require constant maintenance.

Soy production has left significant changes on the Cerrado but not without near-constant pesticide and fertilizer use. This change (Cerrado to farmland) is not static. It calls for constant work to maintain the Cerrado, while the resilient Cerrado is always working to reclaim itself. The positive agency of things—farmers, seeds, soils, plants—restricts any model from being perfectly implemented as planned. Soil, weeds, pests, and weather get in the way of flexible farming. The farmers are enrolled in the project of making disparate plants, soils, and organisms into tamable, replicable, and profitable pieces of Soylandia. While farmers and their workers clear land, plant crops, and kill weeds and pests, new ecologies emerge and farmers themselves change the way they engage with the environment. That farmers, farmworkers, soils, plants, and assorted weedy characters emerge together does not mean that this assembly is sustainable, mutually beneficial, or in simple terms, good. The generativity of industrial agriculture reproduces and sustains itself in all of its destructive glory, but it is nevertheless generative. This is one paradox of flexible farming in the Cerrado.

Degradation and destruction of the Cerrado by soy farmers is well documented; so what I address here is how ecologies emerge out of the rubble of industrial farming and how farmers themselves emerge out of it. This perspective captures a more realistic picture of the material realities of industrial farming: even highly capitalized, technified, and chemical-intensive farms need to reconcile with the material realities of climate, soil, and pests; and these encounters have ample space for weediness—for pests, diseases, and erosion that wreak havoc on meticulously planned fields. The ecologies of these places are not eliminated; they fight back. More significantly, however, this perspective captures elements of hope and despair. That weeds and other life can survive and even thrive under industrial agriculture gives us hope for their survival, and it shows spaces of powerlessness for the powerful. Unfortunately, this perspective also suggests that these farmers are adapting new advanced practices; carrying them back to the United States (as we will see later) signals deeper states of despair. This flexibility is a key aspect of flexible farming: adapting farming practices quickly, without holding on to culturally significant practices and without pursuing innovation for its own sake. Farmers are transforming the Cerrado into soy fields; they are also developing practices and models to transform other grasslands into soy fields. Their impact is both limited in the Cerrado and not limited to the Cerrado.

Flexible farmers try to alienate their farms from ecological life, but despite their intentions they have to engage deeply with life in the Cerrado. The result is both an emergent ecology of industrial agriculture in the tropical Cerrado and an emergent farmer equipped with new skills, expertise, and know-how. Their dependence on farmworkers, farm managers, and agronomists made this transition possible, but the farmers also learned how to farm in a new way. Not only have they bought this land; they have been trained to be better farmers.

VALUE AND COMMUNITY IN SOYLANDIA

My first interview of US farmers in Western Bahia was with a Minnesota-born agricultural consultant who once owned and operated a soy farm in Brazil. He specialized in leading tours and consulting for Americans interested in buying land in Brazil. He began our interview with a warning to stay away from the US farmers in Western Bahia. He encouraged me to study Mennonite farmers in Goiás, Brazilian agronomists in Mozambique, and Brazilian farmers in South Sudan—anyone but US farmers in Bahia. Mennonites from Ohio and Georgia, he said, stick to their religion; collectively buy and sell; integrate themselves into the local culture; and avoid the most technologically advanced techniques. They might not be financially sustainable, but they are "more effective than the fucking apes of Western Bahia." US farmers are "entrepreneurial, business first, Republican, George Bush type farmers," and "they don't go to birthday parties, soccer games, churches, and don't integrate at all with the community." He went on to identify specific farmers as "criminal," "Brazilianized," or finally "getting their shit together." He said that research with them would be difficult because they are secretive, miserable because they are unpleasant to be around, and uninteresting because they do whatever the market calls for. "A lot of the [North American] farmers in Western Bahia," he told me, "are just assholes. There are criminals as well as fantastic farmers."[1]

I took this early interview seriously. It challenged both the underlying propositions for the research (that the farmers would create or re-create new values, relations, and communities in a new place) and the methodological basis (that I could get them to talk to me). At the same time, the consultant's turn to themes of value, morality, identity, and (lack of) community deepened my interest in this group. He told me it would not be possible to study farming practices with this community because they did not do the work. So who did? What is work like on a transnational farm? He told me that they do whatever will generate the most profit and that aesthetics, culture, and community had little influence over their farming. So what does a farming community without values or relationships look like? In this section I argue that they have become flexible farmers, decoupled from place, but different. They manage farmworkers, work in an office, and place importance on clean clothing, clean trucks, and living in a city; for them, this defines good farming and community.

People-Making in the Cerrado

Midwestern farmers in Brazil possess highly technified machinery, operate within market-driven institutions, and engage in a global commodity market of soy. It may be attractive, then, to view them as "capital personified" (Marx and Engels 1978, 257).[2] However, research on large-scale farmers throughout Latin America indicates that farmers hold ethical and social values of work in balance as they defend their own work, often balancing agrarian and industrial regimes of value. Economic anthropologists and geographers remind us that the economy is more than markets (Gudeman 2001), work is more than wage labor (Gibson-Graham 2006), and value is more than capitalist value (Graeber 2001).

Value has been conceptualized anthropologically in three ways: as a system of values (for example family values, progressive values, or conservative values); as a maximized economic payoff; and linguistically as the meaning of symbols. David Graeber's (2001) theory of anthropological value collapses these meanings into one unified theory of value. Action is the subject of value realization and contestation and the product of that negotiation. Value, as the importance of action, is subject to legitimation as actors defend their know-how and their work, thus entailing a process of "people-making" (Graeber 2013). He writes that "we have to place ourselves back in that original tradition: one that understands human beings as projects of mutual creation, value as the way such projects become meaningful to the actors, and the worlds we inhabit as emerging from those projects rather than the other way around" (Graeber 2013, 238). Actions both establish one's status as a legitimate social actor and remake actors as they tie emerging actions to articulations of the self and community. Value and action are cocreative in that changing forms of work or action redefine socially valued forms of work and action while social constraints around what is considered legitimate, honorable, or valuable action constrain and define permissible behavior.

Farmwork emerges out of the material realities of production—political economy and agroecology—but also out of social imaginations of what constitutes good and legitimate work.

The embodied struggles of elites defy liberal, rational calculations and emerge in other studies of elite landholders. Ranchers in Acre, Brazil, for example, connect their migration from southern Brazil to family legacies of migration from Europe and to nationalist discourses on taming, colonizing, and developing Amazonia. They also defend their work as contributing to national food security (Hoelle 2015). Brazilian landholders and soy producers in Bolivia also make claims on their work as development or improvement. In the words of one farmer, "We came with money, we put in technology, it was really a win-win relationship. We all win, the Brazilians won, Bolivia won, and the Bolivian producer won" (Mackey 2011, 20). Soy producers in Bolivia juxtapose themselves against the Morales government as moral compasses of capitalism (Valdivia 2010). Gaucho farmers in Santarém, Brazil, explain their move to the Center-West as a response to high land prices in the South and increasing land concentration in Mato Grosso, but they also highlight family histories of migration and farming (Adams 2010).

Boundaries and practices of communities change, especially for migrant communities. Minkoff-Zern's (2012) work with migrant Triqui and Mixteco peoples in California shows how practices and identities shift within the community to fit their adopted social and ecological environment. Rather than replicate Indigenous farming practices, they adapted planting and irrigation practices to fit the local landscape and agroecology, and they integrated farming practices learned while working as farm laborers. Intermixing through work on industrial farms and in their own community garden, the distinct ethnic groups began to forge a new pan-Oaxacan identity based on solidarity over difference. While continuing to change, communities (re)produce both internal difference and collective difference from outsiders.[3] Communities also fight. They fight among themselves over shared meanings, stewardship of the land, and belonging; and they fight as a collectivity against outsiders (Colloredo-Mansfeld 2009) as they work toward personal and collective visions of progress for, stewardship of, and production of the community.

Value is social and as such is negotiated and renegotiated. Like migrant Triqui and Mixteco farmers in California or Holdeman Mennonites in Rio Verde, Goiás (Ofstehage 2018c), US farmers in Western Bahia have created a new community in a new place. But where those communities build on collective identities, collective good, and collective futures, the American community in Luís Eduardo has created a community centered on individuality and competition. In order to understand the emergence of this community I turn to the concept of "figured worlds." Figured worlds are "socially and culturally constructed realm[s] of interpretation in which particular characters and actors are recognized, significance is assigned to certain acts, and particular outcomes are valued over others" (Holland et al. 2001, 52). In chapter 4 we saw how an emergent community creates value out of transnational farming; in this chapter we will see the way these values shape community interactions. Figured worlds are particularly useful in understanding the elements that pull emergent communities together into what William Westermeyer calls "collectively constructed systems of meaning against which events, developments, self, and others are interpreted" (Westermeyer 2019, 9). Figured worlds are organized and reproduced socially through cooperation and conflict. Changing meanings and norms of practice make up collective figured worlds in which practices are shared, disputed, forgotten, and emergent. And the generation of figured worlds challenges, builds on, and integrates wider narratives of value and meaning. The US farmers have formed a (mostly) common set of values (e.g., bravado, competition, individualism) built around hypermasculinity, whiteness, and heteronormativity. Even in conflict, they have created a figured world made up of individuals, not collectivities. In Brazil, I observed conflicts on multiple levels in the transnational farmer community. These conflicts arose in part from the flexible farming aspect of their transplanted, new community. Not only were they severed from home communities and institutions; they were concomitantly thrown into direct competition for farmland and financing.

Transnational farmers have removed themselves from their home communities. Yet their migration is far different from that of farmworkers migrating to the United States who risk their lives to migrate and confront violent opposition in their adopted homelands and workplaces (Holmes 2013). Instead, their migration is a privileged one, and perhaps for this reason they have found little need to form communities of solidarity. They face opposition from the Brazilian state in the form of bureaucracy, but their main opposition is other US farmers. Competing as such, they have created a sense of antagonism, competition, and disregard within their new community. This is not altogether surprising; farmers in the US Midwest compete for productive farmland, pitting neighbor against neighbor as they attempt to balance accumulation and farm survival (M. Bell 2010).[4] The community of farmers in Luís Eduardo compete for farmland but also for investors and investor capital. Further, they exist in a community with little visible presence of elders, institutions, and family; this relative autonomy gives them space to set their own rules.

Together, changes in work and practice in Brazil have reconfigured the community's valuation of land and labor and have also created new figured worlds of practice. Young, white men with access to capital, relocated far from community, family, and rooted social networks, and set in a place they imagine to be the

Wild West create an environment rife with privilege, capital, freedom, and power. Additionally, these farmers are in competition for land and capital. Altogether, they have created a community built largely on antagonism.

US farmers in Western Bahia tell a story in which they are both culprits and victims of capitalist expansion. They escape the crisis of industrial agriculture on the North American Prairie by reinforcing and contributing to the expansion of industrial agriculture on the Brazilian Cerrado. Crisis does not lead inevitably to the contraction of capital, but to its creative and improvised expansion. This movement of farmers from sites of crisis to commodity frontiers says a lot about how land grabs take place and what motivates the farmers, yet it does not adequately address the multiple human and nonhuman encounters.

In a LinkedIn manifesto on good farming in Brazil, Jacob Iowa writes that his farm upholds high business and ethical standards. Corruption, bribes, and kickbacks, he writes, are commonplace in Brazil; and ethical standards are failing among transnational farmers in Brazil, government politicians and bureaucrats, and Brazilian farmers. This claim of upholding good business ethics and accurate accounting sheets was extremely common among US farmers. When I asked how they would farm in the United States if they returned, all of them said that they would enact a more managerial role and spend their time in the office rather than the field. They often explained this decision in terms of commodified labor. Why work in the field, when you can hire cheap farm labor and earn more per hour in the office? Indeed, North American farmers in Bahia spend 50–60 percent of their working day in the office, and the remaining time is spent checking in on workers. The rare minutes spent in a tractor are only to impress visiting agricultural tourists or farm investors.

As North Americans' work has become reoriented away from the field and toward the office, so have their valuations of that work. Having detached themselves from farmwork and the farm itself, they have come to place greater value on economic efficiency (seeing their work in terms of capital cost-benefit) and on being good managers of labor and regulations. This change has not been limited to their sense of value; in fact, it is an integral part in the formation or disaggregation of their community. Farmers like Ian often framed their work and business as progressive and forward-thinking, in distinction to the romantic and naive way farming is done "back home." They argue that farming is a business, not a lifestyle; thus, a good farmer is one who efficiently and profitably manages the business. However, the concept of a good farmer in Luís Eduardo moves beyond local gossip on yields and straight rows.

Management and worker relations also have an effect on how the farmers see themselves in relation to previous generations of farmers. Ian felt this especially in relation to older generations of his family. His grandfather sees the Brazil farm as part of the family legacy, and his father and uncle think the family is better off working together on a large family farm; but Ian wanted to manage the Brazilian farm differently from their Illinois farm:

> What made the [Illinois] farm grow and prosper when they were my age is different than it is now. . . . They had to work a lot of hours and do it in a tractor; I mean they had to be out there doing physical labor; and now with the size the [Brazilian] farm's grown to, it's a disadvantage to have that feeling that you need to be out in the tractor every day; because you need to be managing people because you've got all these employees; and you put yourself in a tractor, you reduce yourself to one person instead of multiplying.

His grandfather, he told me, sees the farm as a legacy that the grandchildren will continue; his father and uncle see it the same way. But Ian expressed his frustration with their more conservative mindset, saying that while the older generations understand the importance of Ian's management work, "they don't enjoy that work, managing people." Yet Ian had to do that work, and he could not "just do that for free, just for fun." What was difficult for the older generations, according to Ian, was the connection between labor and ownership—the idea that everybody will just work together on family land—but that was not how Ian wanted to manage the farm. The generational differences in ideas of good work and good farming extended to their ideas of what the farm was to the family—whether a business or a continuation of farming traditions and the site of family reproduction. The Brazilian farm was under Ian's management, and he could implement his own vision, but he also hoped to change how the Illinois farm worked. In Illinois they did not measure performance metrics or adjust production to fit market trends, and according to him you have to make a decision:

> If you run this thing like a business, 'cause that's what the competitors are doing, you have to make that decision: is this a lifestyle or a business? If it's a lifestyle, well there's enough land, we can run it like this hippie [he trails off] . . . and there will be enough money; but if you want to be a business and you want to be able to grow and bring in new generations in the future, then you can't run it like a lifestyle.

Flexible farming was the rational business choice for Ian, but he had lost his passion for tractor driving and turning the dirt:

> I drove the tractors and I understand the agronomic side; I can do all those things, but I decided my time is better spent on the management side. And there's importance to knowing that other side so you can hire

other people to do it, but you have to be able to question what they're doing. . . . I've probably spent no more than five days a year in a tractor now. I don't have a passion for tractor driving like my uncle and dad do. What really makes them feel good is to go out and turn the dirt and stuff; I don't get the feeling that they do.

Ian's father echoed this difference, saying that one of the things he thought about a lot was "not being in the tractor and not doing the real physical work." The shift was difficult for him because "I have to work"—a telling juxtaposition of office work with fieldwork. For John Illinois—whether on the family's farm in Brazil or their farm in Illinois—work is in a tractor, not an office." He struggled with adopting the managerial frame every day, but, he reflected, it is "how it needs to be"; you "have to adopt that frame." You have to learn to manage labor.

The Good Farmer as Businessperson

When I asked what practices they would take with them if they happened to farm in the United States, farmers often reported this style of farm management and a shift toward office work as the most important. Dennis implemented a "North American" style of farming because local business practices are "backward." While conceding that Brazilians knew how to coax production from the Cerrado in one moment, he pointed to their lack of business and accounting acumen in the next:

> What I bring to the company is more of the management, cost control, financial management, sales; the company does the marketing, the way we use a more North American style I guess you would say. I do believe that they're backward; at least in [Tocantins] they want to use everything in terms of how many sacks per hectare this is going to cost, or how much they need to get in return in sacks per hectare—a lot of things in sacks per hectare. And that's really a backward way to work. We tend to ignore that and just focus on bottom line, return on investment, in terms of managing companies.

I often asked farmers to comment on how they have contributed to Brazil. I expected them to speak on farming practices or farming know-how, but surprisingly they focused instead on proficiency at paying bills on time, managing accounts, and maintaining business relationships—a source of pride for US farmers in Western Bahia. Jacob saw his family contributing to the community "just from the fact that we pay our bills on time and conduct ourselves in a serious businesslike manner. I don't know, maybe that sounds pretty bad, but there is a lot of, I don't know how I can put it, shenanigans. You always have to be looking over your shoulder. There's always somebody trying to, seems like trying to take advantage of you, trying to get the best of you."

For Ian too, the role of Americans is to bring some degree of rationality or business principles to Brazil. When I asked if he saw a role for himself in improving the region, he said yes, at least originally. "Originally, yes, I thought about contribution to society, but then I thought that everything is already set up for workers. We wanted to provide good housing and jobs. . . . If we treat them well, they'll treat us well. But that's not how it turned out—everyone is for themselves. There's no give and take, so I decided to just run the business and let things take care of themselves."

Eddie saw his work in Brazil as a job, managing 50 employees generally, another 20 indirect employees, 30 investors, and lender banks. "I've got over 100 people that are looking for answers every day, generally." Unlike southern Brazil, he said, where farmers "love their land and would never leave it," farmers in Western Bahia "haven't had enough time really to put those roots down." He related to both ways of farming, noting that farming in Brazil is high pressure, but his family has roots in the United States: "My grandfather got into farming and he loved it, because he wanted to do it. It was a dream of his. My dad grew up with it. From his teens on he helped build the farm, and then—here I am. I think when I'm done with this, I'd love to get back to the family kind of farming." Eddie holds two visions of farming in balance: farming in Brazil, which is temporary, profit-driven, and managerial; and farming in Upstate New York, which would involve family, long-term commitments, and joy.

When I asked Eddie what good farming looked like, he described a neighboring Brazilian farm in comparison with US farms. The Brazilian neighbor was "more capitalized, and they do things the right way from a business perspective. They farm well because . . . generally, if you're well capitalized and do things right on the business side, it follows through on the farm. . . . If you pay your bills and you're a good farm, you're well-respected." In the United States, he explained, things were the other way around: "If you do things well in the field, it follows through to your business."

Jacob similarly framed good farming as good business and good management; for him, it is "no different from any business or industry. . . . It comes down to people. It's no different here; it's just that the sample pool that you have to pull from are uneducated and illiterate and unskilled; and it creates more of a management problem, and you have more turnover." To meet this challenge, he works closely with their human resources department to make sure that they "do things right, according to the labor department; and to help find the right people." Once they have the right people, his work becomes about timing: "to have everything well programmed out, and then execute on it so you're planting at the right time, and spraying at the right time, and putting your fertilizer on at the right time. Otherwise, you can start to lose yield potential." Despite his frequent complaints of an unskilled Brazilian workforce, he depends heavily on Brazilian workers, and he prefers it that way:

> You really need to have the local manager managing a lot of that day-to-day stuff. . . . I could try and find some Americans to come down and help run things on the farm more, but I would have a hard time . . . finding people that can really adapt to the culture, be among the workers and learn the language, and stay around here for a long period of time; so I strongly prefer having a local manager and training those types of guys.

Cosmopolitan Rural Masculinity

In a community made up almost exclusively of men, the movement of a farmer from a tractor to an office, and the transformation of good farming—from straight crop rows to balanced accounting sheets—are implicitly about masculinity. Rural masculinity evolves with economic, technological, and cultural changes. Masculinity in farming communities is socially mediated and changes with the agricultural economy. Flexible farming is even further removed from work, plants, and soils than midcentury mechanized US farming. In Western Bahia, soy farmers performed a distinct kind of rural masculinity based on business aesthetics and cleanliness. They performed this masculinity for the Brazilian business community, for their workers, and for US investors.

Despite embracing managerial models of farming, US farmers struggled to look the part of farm owners in Brazil. Too often they wore work clothes instead of business clothes. Frank explained that it was a learning process for him: "[João, a farmworker] had the same attitude about my truck. You know, we were on a dirt road. And they would always say, 'Can we wash your truck for you?' And I was like, 'No, I want people to see that I'm working.' It's like, 'Ugh. No,' you know. If your truck's dirty that makes us look bad. People think, 'That guy must be broke if his truck's dirty.'"[5]

Frank did not like how much of Brazilian culture is "for show," but João emphasized that Frank represented the farm and the farmworkers. The workers, according to Frank, wanted to be proud to wear the shirt: "*Vestir a camisa*, as they say here. Like, we would say, 'Ride for the brand.' Here, they say they 'work for the shirt.'"

In America, he explained, he would drive a tractor maybe 250 hours per year, and a combine for maybe 250 hours per year. "That's a hell of a lot. . . . Compare that to a Brazilian guy who would be my age, then a tractor guy for twenty years. He would drive in a month what I would drive in a year." Hiring a specialized tractor driver, I suggested, might also provide more skilled fieldwork. He demurred, perhaps offended at my suggestion, and said "maybe. . . . But then there's the flipside of it. Maybe I can drive a tractor just as good as he can. He's much cheaper than I am. And then there's the other side: The things I need to do in town, at the bank, on the internet, with my Google Drive, he doesn't know how to do at all." He continued, "[My father] still did it [tractor driving] or had me do it. . . . We do that because we feel good at it, real comfortable, because we know that we're doing something and you can see what you're getting done, as opposed to doing your financial statements—it doesn't seem like farming."

"Tractor driving is a profession in Brazil; farmers can only really hope to be as good, not better, and labor is cheap enough that it never pays to drive the tractor when there's other work to do." But as he, his father, and even his workers say, tractor driving is not a luxury he can afford:

> You know in America, whether you drive the tractor or have your hired man do it, you and the hired man might have similar value per hour. But down here, if it's manual labor and you're out there doing it yourself, even your workers are going to look at you funny. They're going to be like, "Look, your job is to make sure we get paid, to make sure there's food here, to make sure there's diesel. Why are you here pulling wrenches?"

Workers critiqued Frank's clothing as well as the way he worked on the farm. According to him, the farmworkers were surprised that he knew how to fix things and that he was willing to get dirty. Clean clothes, a clean pickup, and keeping up appearances was demanded by workers, but Frank also agreed that image matters, especially in terms of financing and reputation. It made a difference. "If I were to go back and farm now," he told me, "I would be certain I'm paying more attention to image than I did before." I pushed Frank to tell me more, and his answer suggested that he continued to struggle with what he saw as evidence of the importance of appearance and his belief that appearance shouldn't matter. The best farmer in the region, he said, was never in newspaper articles or television interviews, but frequently produces high corn and soybean yields in the middle of the "gaucho graveyard; he's farming where no one has any right to farm." Meanwhile, some farmers in the best farming areas have gone bankrupt, "driving their Land Rovers in town, going to all the parties; and they were in the fat farm magazines, and not taking care of their work."

"Keep Yourself and Your Things Clean"

Frank connected clean farm sites, not fields, to business opportunities. "If you're big, and you have an office in town, and it's the newest and was designed by such and such architect . . . all of the multinationals and the banks run to finance that guy. He's the guy. A visitor's coming to town, who does the farmers' association take you to? That guy." Frank expressed frustration with a Brazilian overemphasis on image while, characteristically of our conversations, also conceding that he would be a better farmer if he placed more focus on image.

> In Tocantins [a bordering state to Bahia] . . . this (farmer) is so broke he's about to go inside out, but he just built a brand new headquarters for his farm, and transplanted palm trees to this plant, went out and found full-sized palm trees to plant—they're going to die. From what I know about a palm tree, they're not going to make it. But, it had to look beautiful. Because then everybody will say, 'Ah, that's the guy. That's the guy you want to do business with.' . . . An image matters a lot, more than I would have thought in America. If I were to go back and farm now [in the United States], I would be certain I'm paying more attention to image than I did before.

To "keep yourself and your things clean" in Brazil presents a standard of quality that attracts business partners, Frank said. "There will be a farmer who's broke, but he has a palm tree–lined driveway, and a gardener, and green grass. And that guy gets respect, and the people want to go there and do business with him. As opposed to some simple guy who has money and pays his bills, but his place looks like a junkyard."

The difference in focusing on clean rows and clean landscapes can be attributed to investor interests, work roles, and whiteness, but the theme is consistent: a clean field is a sign of a good farmer. The field, however, is not the only site of concern for US farmers in Brazil. As representatives of the farm and as managers of capital, their own body, dress, and vehicles also need to be tidy.

On a farm visit, while we cleaned his pickup, Ian repeated a joke told to him by one of his farm managers—"Brazilian farmers look rich, but they're poor and American farmers look poor, but they're rich." Brazilian farm owners presented themselves as businesspeople with clean clothing and polished pickups to indicate that they did not need to stoop to farmwork and the accompanying close encounters with soil, oil, dust, and rain. US farmers, on the other hand, tended to disregard this and, while rarely working in a tractor, did get out of their pickups when they needed to. Further, many US farmers continued to wear work clothing that would not be out of place in their home communities of Illinois or

Iowa—button-down shirts, jeans, boots, and a seed company hat. In other words, they look like they cannot afford not to do the work.

In a conversation with Frank about what he would carry back with him if he moved back to the United States to farm, he focused on the image of the farmer that he would carry with him. That image was tied to clean pickups, "Because I would want to present a certain business image. But I would still drive a truck. It would be a very nice truck, and I would keep it clean. I wouldn't be afraid to get it dirty, but I'd then clean it, I guess."

The importance of clean shirts and clean pickups was something Frank had learned from experience in Brazil and something on which his workers lectured him. One longtime worker said that "it was fine that I work, but when I leave [the farm], I needed to clean up. Because if I went to town and had dirt on my clothes, that made the farm look bad."

Ane Gracia's ethnography of farmworkers on Luís Eduardo soy farms sheds light on Wendell's request. In her work, local farmworkers spoke similarly of gaucho farm owners in Luís Eduardo Magalhães: "The boss is like us. The boss is like us, he dirtied his hands in the soil to build this place" (Gracia 2017, 37). In Gracia's interviews, workers expressed respect for their bosses for building the farm, clearing the Cerrado, and doing hard work early on, regardless of the office-bound nature of their current work. The bosses' children who often did office work in the city, on the other hand, were not respected as bosses, nor as workers. Frank described a process of learning about how to dress from his farmworkers, a style he now performs and even evangelizes. He connected this image of the clean farmer with success.

How the transnational farmers in Brazil see themselves and their clothing differs from the perception of Brazilian prospective business partners, US-based investors, and farmworkers who look to transnational farmers' clean and tidy presentation to assess their mastery over the farm as a business. The aesthetic differences reflect the changes in rural masculinity in which farming skill, land stewardship, and farmwork lose significance in the face of business-oriented measures of success and masculinity (S. E. Bell, Hullinger, and Brislen 2015). US farmers in Brazil have not just reoriented their work around the office to complete paperwork, communicate with investors, and manage their large farms; they have reoriented their ideas of good farming around a different aesthetic of farming.

Valuing and Working the Farm

Despite the family farmers' warm embrace of farm management as modeled by their Brazilian farmer neighbors, some do find ways to distinguish themselves from Brazilians. They do this not by claiming they are better farmers, but rather that they are better managers. It is common in Brazil to quote prices for land, machinery, and high-expense items in units of sacks of soy.[6] Thus, if the market price of soy changes, so does the price of the asset in question. Upon payment, the buyer can provide the listed amount of soybeans or the cash value of the soy. Some North Americans interpret this as bartering, and they interpret bartering as something backward and unwelcome in business. They claim, then, that they are indeed better at managing farms than farmers under the Brazil Model. That they point to forms of payment as the major difference between US and Brazilian farmers shows how little difference exists between US large-scale industrial soybean farmers and Brazilian large-scale industrial soybean farmers.

Frank joked that his fellow migrants repeat a long-standing Brazilian joke: "They say Brazil is great except for the Brazilians." Farmers point to stories of North Americans who came to Brazil as fully competent farmers but who quickly went bankrupt due to worker conflicts, misunderstanding of labor or environmental regulations, or simply because they failed to adjust to the way things were done in Brazil. Patience, they said, is the key trait (next to rationality) of a successful farmer in Brazil. The North Americans' recognition of the difficult process of becoming good Brazilian farmers, dismissive as it may be, reveals the importance of understanding the lived-in realities of Soylandia.

FIGURE 28.   The land court in Piauí.

North American farmers bring with them collective and personal meanings of land, production, and good farming that are mobilized to legitimize and even celebrate their work in Brazil. The ethnographic data I have presented shows that North American farmers in Brazil are working for more than economic profit, and that their work is unfolding in relation with (not domination over) land, workers, the political economy, and crisis. They are, in other words, doing care-work. They are doing the maintenance work necessary to keep their workforce productive (if not happy) and their investors happy (if not productive). North American farmers remain neither fully autonomous in their engagement with soy production nor powerless against the forces of agrarian change. Rather, they are semiautonomous as their work emerges out of an entanglement of regulations, expertise, meanings of work and land, worker relations, and the political economy. For North Americans, then, producing soybeans in Brazil has many faces: it is the end of the US family farm and its continuation; an escape from the conditions of production in the United States and their reproduction; and a production for the market and the making of people.

A Community Out of Place

E. E. Evans-Pritchard (1976) infamously made an ethnographic breakthrough in his study of witchcraft among the Azande of Central Africa by goading two rival witches to prove to him that one was superior to the other, giving up their secrets in the process. I did not purposefully use this tactic, but I did find that pot stirring among US farmers in Western Bahia provided valuable insights. In my first interview with Ian Illinois, he asked me if I had spoken to Frank Missouri and told me that Frank had "filed a lawsuit against every single person he's done business with here. He's big into conspiracy theories and contacts investors to tell them that farmers are doing a bad job. He takes a picture of a bad part of the field and reports back voluntarily. He's done this with Ian, Iowegian Farms, Ted Brudside. . . . He's a 'pot stirrer.'" When I first spoke to Frank, he asked me if I had spoken to Ian. He told me that when he lost much of his investment and all of his savings ("every penny I ever fucking had"), he warned other farmers against working with his business partner. Instead of responding with "Thanks for the tip. That's good advice," other farmers painted him as nosy and laughed at him behind his back.

Land-grabbing, transnational farming, and industrial farming conjure up images of community destruction, displacement, and dispossession. It may be strange to think of transnational farmers as community members, yet US farmers are creating a community in Luís Eduardo. Following my work in Luís Eduardo,

I conducted a comparative ethnographic study in Rio Verde, Goiás, where a community of Holdeman Mennonites had thrived producing soybeans since 1968 (Ofstehage 2018c). A chance encounter with an American there painted a vivid picture of Luís Eduardo. While sitting in the Rio Verde bus station, over the sound of dubbed Scooby Doo, I heard the familiar sound of Midwesterners struggling with Portuguese. An older white couple was waiting with a Brazilian guide; they boarded my bus for Brasilia. On the bus we chatted briefly, and we agreed to talk at lunch. At lunch I learned that it was her first time in Brazil, but that he had been here often since the 1970s. They were retired farmers from Iowa and current investors in a US-owned farm in Mato Grosso. The man comes to Brazil annually to work and check in on his investment in Mato Grosso but was familiar with US farmers in Western Bahia as well. For her part, the woman said she worries about the Amazon and thinks soy development is a threat that should be better managed. Her husband interjected to say "but he is a farmer," with a nod to me—as if to say, we both understand that, in farming, production takes precedence over nature.

As we ate—far from Luís Eduardo—we discussed familiar names from Western Bahia. Most of our conversation covered which US farmers are good (few), which are bad (most), and which are crooks (many). When I mentioned Jacob he responded, "Eeesh!—80 percent of what he says is BS. Is he still there?" He was surprised that no one had killed Eddie yet. Frank is good; Ted Burdside, who I will reintroduce in this chapter, is "a smooth, sharp talker" who will tell you "you'd have to be stupid not to invest, with how good agriculture is in Brazil; how cheap land and labor are; there's no downside." At the time of this conversation, I had been working with the Mennonites in Rio Verde for a few months and had already gotten used to their friendly conversations and welcoming homes. I had nearly forgotten the constant state of tension and distrust that exists in the US farming community of Luís Eduardo Magalhães; this conversation brought me back there, throwing the contrast into sharp relief for me.

Competition and violence between landowners is normal in rural Brazil and rural America. Here, it is intensified because they are not just fighting for land in Brazil, they are fighting for funding, legitimacy, and attention in the United States. Many also give the impression that they have become this way because they have been living on the lawless Brazilian frontier and that they would not act the same way at home.

"He Doesn't Know What He's Doing"

I was first introduced to an undercurrent of antagonism within the community at a birthday party for one of Ian's farm managers in Luís Eduardo Magalhães.

After some Americans left, a farmer pulled me aside and let me know that they referred to the one who had left early as "the retard" because of his social behavior and the fact that "he doesn't know what he's doing." However, he praised the farmer's dad as a sharp guy who managed to extricate himself from a working relationship with another US farmer—one who "took royalty money under the table for land deals" and then organized a machinery cooperative but operated it as a fraudulent scheme.

The role of antagonism within the community appeared in lawsuits and Thanksgiving celebrations as well as in everyday conversation. I heard numerous offhand ethical comments about farmers being too "greedy and self-centered" or "too nosy in another's business" by reporting back to investors in the United States on the relative progress in farm operations. I even heard numerous allegations that one farmer's girlfriend was a lesbian. One of my longest recorded interviews was an extended explanation of the immorality of another farmer. Not all comments on other farmers were negative, but even positive comments had an edge to them, as if to say that good farmers were the exception. For example, Frank commended one group for their ethical work: "Soy Brazil [Dennis's farm] is doing good work, not all done for ego; coming from a different place. They have long-term goals." Yet the overarching feeling and atmosphere was of competition, mutual dislike, and distrust.

The reputation of a hard-fighting community in Luís Eduardo drew Dennis away and toward Tocantins where farmers "have the mentality that the more people that open up soybean farms, the more people to make money; the more support services, grain elevators, and we see that happening now." The farming community in Tocantins, according to Dennis, is supportive, open with information ("though they lie about their yields just like Iowan farmers"), and helpful. "They loan machinery; and we have neighbors that help each other out; you know, that kind of thing." In Tocantins, he feels his farm blends in—that you could drive by and you would not know whether it was an American or Brazilian farm. Dennis intentionally avoided moving to Luís Eduardo in Western Bahia. He liked the topography and support services of Western Bahia, but the issue was the Americans. "I have been a farmer all my life; I know what it's like to be young and competitive after all that, and you go [to Luís Eduardo] and it's like that times ten." He had thought about socializing with other Americans, but he was wary: "I just don't like the feel [in Luís Eduardo] at all. There's too many young guys. . . . There's some guys that get over there and they just go crazy. . . . In Luís Eduardo they let their competitive nature come out and it seems like there's just too much of that going on."

He came back to their youth later in the interview and pointed to the lack of older farmers as a reason for this competitive nature: "You don't have a lot of maturity [in Luís Eduardo]. . . . [In Illinois] you have a few young guys but most of them are older."

Others pointed to competition for investment as the main driver of discord. Frank supported this connection between competition for investors and antagonism. "At home [in Missouri], the fight if you're farming is to get more land. You're always trying to bid more, to rent more. . . . Here, there's so much land. If you get outbid for something, you let it go. There is a fight for investors—for media attention to feed their ego." But he had not expected this when he came down. He had spoken to a German with experience in the area who warned him against moving to Luís Eduardo: "Well, what if you don't live in Luís Eduardo? It's all cloak and dagger," but he dismissed the man and moved anyway.

At many of our interviews in Barreiras, Frank spoke of why he lived there instead of Luís Eduardo. "When I'm here, this is home. I sit down with people and we talk about things people talk about. When I'm in Luís Eduardo, we sit down, and we talk about money. With the Americans, you're going to talk about money and how stupid all your employees are—the 'little brown fuckers' is what they call them. You're going to talk about how much money you're making, how much money that guy has, what that airplane cost, how much we're going to spend in Vegas."

That antiworker sentiments and capitalocentrism dominated conversations in Luís Eduardo should not come as a surprise. As we saw in chapter 4, Americans in Brazil spend their days managing workers and finances; they judge each other and themselves by how profitably they manage their businesses; and they have created a figured world centered on opposition and competition.

To this point, Frank described the case of Sarah and Leon Oster who were introduced in chapter 1. Leon and his family began farming soon after arriving in Brazil, though he later regretted his fast pace in purchasing, clearing, and planting the farm. At the time of his move, soybean prices had increased from 6.00 USD to 13.00 USD and the housing boom had crashed in Idaho. Land value in Western Bahia is quoted in "sacks of soy" instead of reais or dollars, so an increase in soy price translates directly to an increase in land value. Increasing farmland values in Brazil and a lower value for his home and farmland sales in Idaho greatly reduced his starting capital. According to Frank, Leon trusted the wrong people:

> When Leon and Sarah Oster arrived in Luís Eduardo, Ted agreed to sell them a tractor. Leon paid and Ted Burdside said he'd deliver when he was done planting. [Ted] planted late and didn't get the tractor to Leon until it was much too late to plant. The late planting ruined the year for [Leon]. Leon had only 400 hectares [and so] could have planted in a few

days, but Ted didn't care, kept the tractor. [He] removed the dual tires too. [Leon] went bankrupt because of the domino effect of planting late and losing the crop. When they were planning to come down, Betty told Sarah how great it was down in Luís Eduardo, then told her it was awful after she arrived. Nobody was friendly, they made fun of Leon behind his back, especially Ted.

Leon confirmed this story. He added that the prior season had produced a bumper crop and soy prices were high, so many area farmers bought new farm machinery, leading to a shortage of tractors and his desperation for finding one. Leon described the encounter as a perplexing affair. In the beginning Ted was helpful: "he helped [Leon] rent [his] first house, he set up a post office box, stuff like that," but then "he was getting too busy for [Leon]." As Frank recounted, Ted agreed to sell the small, well-used tractor but "needed to use it until his beans were planted." Leon finally had access to the tractor in January, a full two and a half months after most farmers had planted their soybeans. Of Ted, Leon remembered him being a "little farmer. . . . He just had his family farm and then he landed his first big farm," but now "he would be hard to find . . . when people are trying to hunt him down [for various lawsuits]." At the time, Frank provided an Excel file of lawsuits including two labor cases in Brazil, forty-one civil and criminal cases in Brazil, and one lawsuit filed in the United States by some of his investors (as outlined in chapter 1). Ever compassionate, Leon said that Ted just got caught up in "chasing the money and not planting the crop. . . . It's enticing. You can go to Brazil, and you can rent 10,000 acres at a time all in one chunk. There's nowhere else in the world that you can do that. That's exciting—or it can be exciting, especially when you're in your twenties, to be able to go to Brazil."

Difficulties in securing farm machinery, and according to Leon, weather and paperwork issues, delayed his first year's planting beyond an acceptable growing year length; and soon after starting the farm Leon went bankrupt and had to return to the United States. Though he does not own a farm today, he hopes to either purchase a farm or engage in farming as a farmworker in order to return to agricultural work. In interviews he joked that "we went—[he laughs]. We joke around. We came down with six suitcases, and some money. Left with six suitcases." But the nature of these difficulties is striking in that it is, or at least is perceived to be, an intentional sabotage of an agrarian dream.

The incident between Leon and Ted was often on Frank's mind during our conversations. Frank explained his feelings toward Ted Burdside: "[Ted] hired thugs to beat workers; the third one finally confessed to stealing a light bar from a tractor. The thugs were civil police. The worker is now in jail and [Ted] brags about it. [Ted says] 'They were fucking thieves.'" Frank claims Ted hired publicity interns to get interviews and publicity and started doing local philanthropy for children to gain attention. "A lawyer that was reviewing the books to prepare to go public found gross fraud. She reported this and was fired. She reported this to the investors, sued Ted for the firing, and can now collect his property—if she could find it."

Suing the Competitors

Not surprisingly, farmer conflicts have made their way to courtrooms in the United States and Brazil. In one prominent and often-discussed case of disquiet among the community, a farmer once located in Luís Eduardo Magalhães is being sued by investors who are predominantly friends, family, neighbors, and acquaintances. Thirty-four plaintiffs allege that the farmer misrepresented costs and returns in making an investment pitch by providing low estimates for rental contracts, materials, and fertilizer. A lawsuit for one farm lays out individual investments of between $50,000 and $500,000 with expectations of 26 percent returns on investment. In other pitches he calculated projected returns of 25–40 percent and possible returns of 50–60 percent. While soliciting a total $5 to $10 million, the farmer raised only $1.3 million. He did not communicate this to investors. In investment pitches, the farmer identified the perceived risks to investment as political risk, currency fluctuations, and weather but then countered by arguing that Brazil is stable and pro-agriculture, maintains controls over inflation, and weather is not a factor in production. The plaintiffs allege that this was without a full accounting of the costs of production and the risks of farming in Brazil.

After the first year of production, the investors received high returns on their investment, though the plaintiffs believe that payments were made from new investment monies, not profit from actual farm operations. Investors in the second call for investment were paid in turn, the plaintiffs argue, by a third call for investment instead of from profits from farm operations. The plaintiffs contend that these investment cycles essentially amounted to a pyramid scheme, caged in misinformation about profits, costs, risks, and production. The case was recently settled out of court, and the defendant has agreed to pay settlements to the plaintiffs. In defense of Ted, Ian told me he thinks Ted was "certainly a poor manager, that lost all the money, but not fraudulent. . . . He tried to do too much with not enough money and got too big too fast. He raised 20 million dollars and lost every penny of that, plus he still owes 5 or 10 million down here that they'll never get." This lawsuit shows the growing antagonism and distrust within the community of farmers and investors, the shift toward legal means of settling internal disputes, and the primacy of capital in creating and dissolving community connections.

Wild West

On a trip back from Frank's farm in Piauí, much of our discussion was centered on conflict: "A lot of Americans construct an idea that Brazil is lawless, Wild West, and act accordingly." He held resentment toward other US farmers who laugh at him and say he is "stupid" or "naive" and just does not understand "how it's done" or is "too much of a 'pussy' to do things how they're done in Brazil."

Frank's struggle over land and assets on the Piauí farm continued and work still had not begun on the farm. Because assets were tied up, there was no money to pay for inputs or wages. The workers, Fernando and Luís, accepted cows as payment with the promise that they would be paid when possible. They also had a garden and food paid for by Frank. Much of the work is just to keep the cattle and horse alive and, presumably, to keep possession of the farm. Currently, a Brazilian landowner, a Brazilian farm manager, and another US landowner were all suing each other over land disputes at and near the Piauí farm. Frank was working to get the name of one of the Americans, Flint, removed from the legal documents and to remove him completely as manager of the farm. Until then, he had little control over finances. Frank had thought of creating a new company and leaving everything else, just in order to gain rights over their accounts again, although that would mean losing the old ones. He referred to Flint's father as a *grilageiro* (land-grabber) who was on the wrong side of a land war. "Americans screw each other over here—no cooperatives, no hanging out; it's not like other immigrant communities." He feels more a part of the Brazilian community, with the English-language school that he manages, going to weddings and funerals, and trying to treat workers well. He "expected more community with other farmers here." The local agrarian judge later ruled against all parties in the suit, finding that the original seller did not have legal rights to sell the land. In Frank's words, Flint had sold the Belgian landowner "a pig in a poke."

I once asked Frank what he thought of the following quote about English migrants in Brazil in the nineteenth century: "Whenever I hear a foreigner complain that he has failed in Brazil, and rail against the people and their institutions, it is proof positive to me that the country has every right to complain of him—in fact that he is a 'ne'er do well,' that he drinks, or is an idler, he is incorrigibly dishonest; or finally, to be charitable, that he is an impossible man" (Freyre 2011, 126). He thought it fit this group well. Frank had indeed worked to integrate himself into the local community through his English-language school and by making friend with Brazilians throughout town. On another level, part of Frank's frequent discourse about crooks within the American community in Luis Eduardo was a rejection of their insular individuality.

Thanksgiving in the Cerrado

The American community in Luís Eduardo had few nonwork gatherings and few nonwork spaces. There are no Midwest-style farmers' cooperatives in which to gather; no American-attended churches in which to worship together; and no diner where one would regularly expect to find a group of Americans eating around a shared table. Their community is centered on work—much of it online and focused outward toward investors. Thanksgiving 2014 found me in the unenviable position of choosing between two competing invitations. One was from Frank who hosted an annual Thanksgiving celebration in his capacity as director of the English-language school. This was a moment for children and parents to take part in a celebration of US cultural traditions, to receive certificates of achievement, and to meet English teachers. The second came from Ian who hosted several other US farmers and their (mostly Brazilian) partners at his home. I chose the second—partially to introduce myself to some farmers I had not yet been able to reach, and partially to finally see how they interacted together. Until that moment I had never seen more than one US farmer in a single place. It was an unusual slice of midwestern-style normalcy in Soylandia.

When I arrive late, the small house is busy. Betty and Ian are there, along with Matt Jenson (who owns 1,500 acres near Luís Eduardo) and his brother Miles and friend Andy; John Wright (Ian's chief operating officer) and his Brazilian girlfriend; Eric and his Brazilian girlfriend; and Ian's kids. Adam Bender arrives around 5:30. Most of our conversation is about planting. Matt is renting land in Tocantins from Wilson Funk of Rio Verde, and people are curious about that. When Adam arrives, they ask a lot of questions about the harvest in Indiana, where his family operates a mixed-use farm. They have land here and in Indiana, and he comes and goes from Brazil often. Alongside football, the farmers discuss global farmland investments. Adam recently took a trip to West Africa as part of an Indiana leadership board, and says, "It's a dump." Things are "really bad there" and there is not much "serious agriculture."

I was really interested to see who was and was not invited. A lot of people I might have expected to see were not there. This gathering has been held since their first year here—first at a church, then at Ted Burdside's house, and now at Ian's. There were a lot of fond memories of Ted as host—for his participation in a foot race or for trying to throw a football over his house (he did).

The women have done most of the cooking, and they bring out food, beer, and dessert. The group happens to be segregated by both gender and nationality, as most partners are Brazilian. The women, for the most part, stay in the kitchen while the American men sit in front of the television in the living room. We eat buffet style. There is cheesy green bean casserole, a potato dish, chicken, something made with pecans, and sweet potatoes. Turkey is unavailable, but they have "very large chickens." For dessert there are both pumpkin and cherry pies (Betty brought down both cans from the United States), a chocolate dessert, *maracuja* (passionfruit mousse—the only really Brazilian dish), and Ian's birthday cake. More than anything, Thanksgiving in the Cerrado gave me an impression of overwhelming normalcy during my fieldwork; money was discussed, but not extensively; it was mostly just joking, small talk, eating full plates of food, and watching American football. The striking thing was the absence of broader social groups—a few brought girlfriends or spouses, but no older generations of parents, aunts and uncles, or grandparents; and besides Ian's children, none of a younger generation.

Encounters with the Brazilian Community

The American community in Luís Eduardo primarily interacted with each other and with a limited number of Brazilians. Frank Missouri lived a different kind of lifestyle in nearby Barreiras. He critiqued many of his fellow Americans as having no respect for Brazil or Brazilians, calling them "commodity traders, not farmers" who consider that "a good deal is to fuck somebody over—a zero-sum game." A 2005 farmers' association strike brought this outlook into focus for him. According to Frank, Eli—an American who has been farming in Bahia since the 1980s but declined to be interviewed for my research—was active in the strike and Frank himself reluctantly participated, but few other Americans did. On a drive out to his farm, Ian brought up the same protests to me, saying the farmers were demanding a better exchange rate and that the protest was stupid and pointless.

Few Americans are involved in any way with the farmer associations. Jacob remembered going to a meeting and feeling that he was better off sending his human resources manager in his place the next time. Eddie reported attending a few meetings and feeling that "they didn't make a foreigner feel welcome so I dropped it." Eddie, who may be more integrated into Brazilian society than many other farmers, continued, saying that he respects farmer associations and partnerships with Brazilians, but that one must "trust and verify." "I think at certain times, you've got to make some leaps—calculated leaps, but make some leaps. That's part of Brazilian culture. It's a whole different conversation, but if you trust too much in what the Brazilians are telling you, you could fall into a trap, and you need to be on your toes and take calculated risks."

Unmoored

Young, white men alone in the Cerrado created a figured world built on competition and expectations that "anything goes" on the frontier. Without arbitra-
tion from elders, they settle disagreements through lawsuits, social exclusion, and
rumor-spreading. Flexible farming means a closer engagement with capital and
finance, placing farmers in direct competition. Without a strong local social net-
work, this community of mostly single, privileged young men had little social
infrastructure to check their behavior; narratives of the Wild West only encouraged them. Left alone and unmoored, changes in practices, community, value,
and identity were accelerated. As farmwork was mechanized and outsourced, it
lost its importance as a measure of a good farmer; just as midwestern farmers now say that "Roundup Ready beans make a good farmer lazy and a lazy
farmer good." More important now is the management of investors, contracts,
and workers. This shift is reflected in how farmers value a good farmer: he is now
a farmer who makes money, creates returns on investment for financiers, and
wins negotiations.

This disconnection may suggest that the farmers have not coalesced around a
figured world and have rejected the formation of a community; yet I argue that
they have in fact formed a figured world, but it is one defined by individuality, greed, and entrepreneurship. Despite attempts by Frank and others to create
a close-knit community, they remain divided and antagonistic but also linked
together. Dennis repeatedly listed this antagonism as a reason for buying a farm
in Tocantins instead of Bahia. A host of factors contributed to this antagonism,
including power, demeanors, and privilege; but the two main factors were a shift
toward business-first values and competition for investors. First, as we saw in the
chapter 4, the values of transnational farming and farming throughout Soylandia
are focused on efficiency and business management. Among this community,
this has come at the cost of valuing cooperation and solidarity. Second, while
competition is common in many farming communities, competition here is centered on individuals. In order to convince a potential investor to invest, a farmer
must show that the idea of farming in Brazil is profitable, that he or she is the best
qualified to manage that investment, and that another farmer with a similar pitch
is not qualified. In Luís Eduardo the community is reconstituted on a foundation
of mistrust, blame, and competition.

THE AFTERMATH

"In our case, yeah, the endgame is probably closer than it ever has been for us." Sitting in his Luís Eduardo office, Eddie complained about rising input costs, increasingly intractable pest problems, chronic drought, and increasing government regulation in Brazil. He was looking for a way out—"a good ending." They had turned down a lucrative offer for the farm three years earlier. We wanted to be here. I don't know if we'd do the same thing today." For Eddie, it is hard to imagine leaving Brazil and impossible to imagine continuing farming. Very few of the community members have long-term plans in the region; many have sold their farms and others are just waiting for the right offer. Stories do not end, they transition, and that is even more the case with the mobility of flexible farmers. Flexible farming is as much about entering Soylandia smoothly as it is about exiting profitably. This chapter shows how transnational farmers parlay their farms into a future in Brazil or a return to the United States.

Economic and Ecological Collapse

In that last conversation I had with Eddie, he seemed resigned. Disrupted weather and price volatility made farming—especially investor-dependent farming—difficult. At the same time, the continued regulation of foreign landholding in Brazil limited the farm's ability to expand, and interests from larger agribusiness buyers such as SLC Agricola provided an easy and profitable way out. Volatility, more than anything, gave Eddie problems:

> For me, if you're talking about exchange rates or interest rates or a lot of these economic factors—I don't really care if they're good or bad—frankly. Because, generally, I can make a case that anything is good or I can make a case that anything is bad, but what I don't want is volatility. And we have a lot of volatility, which is what's been happening. Boy, it's really hard to plan, to budget, and to do things in a fashion that you need to do them to make money in this place.

The US farmers were initially drawn to Brazil by perfect soy growing conditions, but they have learned that seasons can be unpredictable. Although only one recognized climate change, all of them saw a fall in precipitation, unpredictable rainfall patterns, and hotter dry seasons.[1] "We planted in dust three times," Eddie told me. "Once it worked out really well. Twice it didn't." When they had first arrived in Brazil, they depended on long, general, soaking rains; more recently it would rain less and be more scattered. "Every year is a different year" is a common refrain for farmers, he told me; but in the last few years growing conditions had been strangely erratic and difficult.

In our last conversation, Eddie gave me the impression that he was no longer complaining about the day-to-day management of the farm and instead was fed up with the entire endeavor and was plotting his next step. I asked him if he was on his way out.

> I would say this: I think the bigger you get, the more problems you have here. When I talk to a lot of large, Brazilian farmers—guys who are in my position—like me, they are all thinking the same thing: "I've got to move on to something else shortly. This is too much stress." Where they go from here, I don't know, but I do think there are a lot in this area that feel like that. That could be just because we've had a couple bad years in a row here. I don't know.

He pointed to the risks they faced in Brazil. First, the risk-reward was at an "all-time low" as profits had fallen in recent years and operating expenses continued to rise. Increasingly inconsistent rainfall, rising production costs, and a government seemingly unfriendly to agribusiness made him question not just the continued viability of his farm but farming in Brazil in general. He was not sure whether the early years of clearing Cerrado and staking land claims was easier or harder than managing the farm in 2014: "Just for me to look at operating a hectare of soybeans in this day and age . . . I mean, when you take into account the weather that's happened, you take into account the prices, take into account the cost of . . . I think you say to yourself, 'Boy, I don't know if it really makes sense in 2014 to come here and buy some land as an American.'"

When they arrived, Eddie said, the upside was much higher; land and production costs were cheaper compared to the United States. But now, land prices were rising quickly, labor costs were much higher, and climate change was putting their yields at risk. "I think in fifteen years—or definitely in the last six or seven—that advantage that Brazil had enjoyed, especially in this region here, I think is gone." Starting out, they paid employees a minimum wage of R$80 month; "Today, on the farm, with labor convention the way it is, R$900." Costs were rising as well: "I called a diesel company last month and I said I want a load of fuel. 'Yeah, okay, R$2.35.' Okay. I call him a few weeks later: 'R$2.39.' Okay. I call him next time: 'R$2.50.' Next month it is going to be R$2.70. Whoa!"

Increasing land values, and the promise of speculative profit, helped the family ride out the difficult years, but enforcement of foreign land laws had made land acquisition difficult. As a Brazilian citizen, Eddie himself could purchase land, but not his company: "We're foreign owned. And that's obviously a huge . . . We can't even really lease the land." Regulations and the paperwork and bureaucrats that came with it had gotten worse—he gestured to a mountain of loose sheets of paper: "Now it's this size. . . . That stack of paper over there, half of that is regulation stuff. . . . You know, it's tough. . . . I can't concentrate—it makes it hard to focus on what you've got to focus on to be a successful farm." So Eddie was thinking of getting out of farming in Brazil. "Boy, it's awful hard to make money. It's flat out hard to make money with the costs the way they are, the political environment the way it is—it's tough. It's tough."

These conversations at the end of my fieldwork were imbued with a sadness that I had not expected to see in comparatively powerful, privileged men. For Eddie, moving on seemed inevitable, but not easy:

> I'm married to a Brazilian—I've got two kids that are [dual citizens]— I have a lot of connections here. My dad is married to a Brazilian. He has two [dual citizenship children]. So, I think I'm always going to be in Brazil in some form or fashion. There's no way I'm going to escape that—not that I want to. I will say this: from a business perspective, in the fifteen years I've been here, this is probably the worst I've felt about where Brazil is going and where I am right now. It's hard to do things right now. . . . Ten years ago, fifteen years ago, we started all these things; and it was hard, but you had so much upside, and everyone wanted you here. It was a welcoming feeling, and everyone worked with you.

The economic and environmental landscape of Brazil further pushed the family and investors to get out while they could: "For us, you know, we've got a lot safer places to invest, a lot easier places to invest. . . . And then there's some major . . . I think there's a currency risk. I personally think the economy in Brazil is overheated and going to get worse, and I think they're headed for trouble here, and I'd prefer not to be here when it pops."

Two years before my interview with Eddie, Caleb Indiana doubted their future of farming in Brazil as well. Brazil, he told me, was not "remarkably profitable as in the States" in terms of production. Much of the profitability for the Carters and other US farms in Soylandia came from land speculation. Yet the expected land appreciation in Roraima had never materialized. In 2003 they were farming in Mato Grosso and looking for other places to invest. They toured Tocantins and Mapitoba, but they chose Roraima for its well-developed infrastructure: "paved roads to the farm, electricity to the farm, no cleaning out [of Amazon forest], just savannah." The region had been reporting good crop yields, and they expected they could sell the land to Venezuela after it was developed.[2] Land was "really cheap" (R\$40 per hectare in 2000 and R\$100 per hectare in 2003). They wanted to get into the region while land was still cheap and their investors were interested, so they formed an investment company and bought land in Roraima. But during the time they were planning this move, the farmland value rose again, from R\$100 per hectare in 2003 to R\$800–1,000 per hectare in 2004, but they still felt they got the land at a good price.

Unfortunately 2004 and 2005 were "horrible years in Brazil; we lost all of our operating capital, we had to go and get loans at the bank to stay in business. We didn't have to sell land, but we lost a lot of money." Soon after, according to Caleb, investors began to lose interest in Brazilian agriculture and "nobody was looking for new regions [to invest in]." Geopolitical conflict between Brazil and Venezuela reduced the prospect of selling land later on, and farmers and investors "got cold feet about farming in Roraima." The investors who had formed the investment company with the Indiana family fired Caleb's dad Brad as manager. This is the risk of flexible farming. It depends on both farm production and land speculation: if farm production is lower than expected, the farm is in trouble; if land speculating falls through, the farm fails.

By 2010, still managing the farm in Mato Grosso along with property in Roraima, the investment partners began advertising the Mato Grosso farm for sale. It quickly sold for 30 percent over their target price. The land was bought in physical sacks of soy instead of cash. Luckily for them, after they had received the grain for the agreed price, the market price for soy increased and they closed with a considerable amount of money. For tax reasons, they decided it would be better to reinvest the money in Roraima, "so that's how the farming operation up here got started. Last year we built a shed and bought a bunch of lime and fertilizer and we've got ground ready." Their luck changed again. The next year they only planted 100 hectares due to flooding, and they lost 40 percent of their yield to mid-season drought.

At the time of our interview, they intended to stick with their plan in Roraima. They would start with 300 hectares and double their production area every year. That year they planted 500 of the 700 hectares they had planned for, had to replant 250 hectares of that, and intended to re-replant an additional 100 later on. "So, at the end of the year, we're probably only gonna harvest about 400 hectares, and our yields are gonna be low, and most of the money we were gonna spend on 700 hectares we've already spent on replant—on just this 400. If we get back 50 percent, it will be a victory; it's a very bad year."

Hearing this in an interview was difficult. Caleb told their story painfully. Even if I could not relate to land speculation woes, I deeply understood the anguish of drought, flooding, and failed crops. Unsure and unprepared to address the emotions of the interview, I asked if they had had bad luck or if there was anything they could have done differently. Of course, he had thought about that before. He spoke about machinery issues ("our planter's fifteen years old"), planting times and depth, and corporate reorganization, but he thought they could keep going at least for a few more seasons:

> We have a lot more land than we can get to with our machinery, with our capital, and our time. . . . If we were to bring everything that's under our management we'd be strapped. I think we could still do it at an efficient level, but at some point in time—and this is where Brazil's going to—you have to move to a corporation-style farming, where you have employees and you just have to change your management structure.

This was not their own decision. The flexibility afforded through flexible land, crops, and land does not extend to capital, financing, and investors. While farmers are able to quickly change production strategies and work arrangements, they cannot do so without agreement from investors. The future of the farm depended on investors:

> So we're at a little bit of a crossroads. Some of the investors are getting older, some want out; do we get everybody else out and just have our own family farm operation? Do we sell the whole thing? If we get a good price, and everybody retires, I [could] find a day job. We're at a crossroads, especially after the last four years. Or do we try to develop all this land and then sell it? . . . Maybe not this year but . . . or not sell out but do some kind of merger. . . . I think that, even in Brazil, a structural change: either families are gonna become companies, or companies are gonna buy out family farms or you're gonna split. These guys that are

real big farmers, like 50,000 acres, 100,000 acres—are they gonna split up the farms for their kids and nephews? Or are they gonna try and keep it together and do a single operation? We're going through that, but I think a lot of people will in the next five-ten years.

Bringing Soylandia Home and Making Home in Soylandia

Upon contacting Frank before my return trip and the beginning of my primary research, I was informed that many farmers were no longer in the area. Some had sold their farms, others had lost control of their farms to investors, still others were reportedly evading lawsuits. I was an ethnographer with a disappearing community. Research with this group of transnational farmers had always been tricky as they moved easily across borders and never settled in place for long. Yet, now, several farmers had disappeared from the site altogether. I had expected that I could conduct this research in place, at a physical site, despite the fact that farmers themselves were not grounded in Luís Eduardo. The well-financed, technologically advanced family farmers of Bahia were returning to the United States or had seemingly disappeared after less than ten years. But the small-scale, "backward" Mennonites, with firm roots in Rio Verde, were still grounded after more than forty years (Ofstehage 2018a). This chapter returns to the question of how to make sense of a community of farmers that seems to be disappearing from the Bahia landscape and the Luís Eduardo community simultaneously thriving in terms of capital and technology. I propose that this disintegration of the community is not a failure but a transitory step for flexible farmers in between one endeavor and other. Their continued movement shows how their investments come under threat and how they are prepared to quickly move on.

In my first interview with Dennis Tocantins in Illinois, he listed landownership regulations for foreign owners as one of the main limitations for them. There have been restrictions on foreign ownership since they first arrived, including requiring a visa for landowners, limitations on buying land near borders, and having to set up a Brazilian *limitada* (limited liability company). In 2010 the administration of the Brazilian president Luís (Lula) Ignacio da Silva placed stronger limits on foreign landownership. While this restriction did not affect existing ownership, it did severely limit farm expansion of foreign-owned farms:

> A couple of years ago they issued a new rule that if you operate on more than 51 percent foreign capital, your company is not a Brazilian company; it's a foreign company. So now we have to abide by the original

rules. They say we're grandfathered in, but we're barely over the limit. They are very confusing limits; it's by county, [but] that's supposed to be the limit nationwide, so technically we can't buy any more land. I would guess that all the groups [in Luís Eduardo] would be limited from buying any more land. You would need written permission from, literally, the Senate.

Farmers saw this new land law as both a threat to their business plan and as unnecessary because there is little difference between sulistas and foreigners. "It's not even an issue," Ian told me. This new land rule put Dennis's land speculation strategy at risk, while bad growing conditions damaged their agricultural production. After making a large machinery purchase in 2013, Dennis operated 600 hectares of land owned by the investment group, and another 1,800 hectares of rented land. They were facing greater insect pressure, persistent problems with soybean rust, and got caught in a drought. Expecting 50 bushels per acre, they yielded 30–40. By the completion of my research in 2014, he had sold his farm in Tocantins. A brochure advertising the sale of land, farm machinery, and other farm assets by a US farmer in Tocantins displays this financialization of the farm. There is no description of the topography, climate, and soils of the farm. Rather, the brochure focuses on industry background, shared production investments, investment performance, machinery assets, and returns on equity investments. Not until the last notes does the reader learn about production history, and then only in terms of yield averages. And again, the decision to sell was not Dennis's alone:

> We started trying to sell the company about a year ago—year and a half ago. The board basically sat down and talked about it and decided we couldn't afford to lose that kind of money . . . so we went ahead and decided to get out. Unfortunately, it's not a very easy process to get out. We tried to sell. . . . Our goal was to sell the entire company— the *fazenda*, the *limitada*, the whole thing. We thought we had a pretty good buying proposition because by [selling the farm along with the *limitada*) you avoid the problems with Brazilian land laws. . . . You hand over the LLC and [the buyer has] everything they need in Brazil.

One thing Dennis regretted was not having a clearer "exit strategy" for the Brazilian farm. Another problem, surprisingly, was that the farm was too small to garner serious interest from many larger farms. "We were hoping that we'd grown to the point where it was big enough that someone would pick it up—and we walk away, and one way or another with all our cash, and the business continues on." At the time of my research the farm was still in limbo, between deals that had been made but not yet followed through on.

Dennis listed an inefficient workforce, specifically naming Brazilian accountants, of which three would be needed to do the work of one US accountant; an antibusiness government in which "[Dilma (then Brazilian president from the Workers' Party)] is probably not very short of communist; she has catered to a very socialist party that doesn't believe that there needs to be profit for companies." From his perspective, the Workers' Party holds companies responsible for providing jobs but does not take responsibility for helping companies stay profitable.

Landownership is where he would focus his business strategy if he did it again. "I would probably come in and clear land and buy it cheap there, and then try to pull out of it year two, and move and do that—keep doing that." But this strategy depends on the desires of the investors and the board of the company. "We sold the business on this certain model—the model of buy, develop, hold, and operate—and while they would accept us maybe selling some property and then reinvesting, if we would have just done a wholesale and roll everything out every two to three years . . . I'm not sure whether our investors would have been supportive of [transitioning away from production toward speculation] at all."

Finally, like Eddie, Dennis was simply exhausted. "Honestly it just . . . I've been here twelve years. That's a lot, and I'm tired. I'm tired. I'm tired." Yet he held out hope for another farming venture. Dennis was happy to put investor relations behind him in his new adventure. He had tried "farming a normal US farm" and a large farm in Brazil, and now he was not interested in "making a big splash" anymore. He just wanted to do something he enjoyed. But he also thought his work in Brazil had prepared him for contributing to his daughter's small CSA (community-supported agriculture) farm. Production techniques, he said, were his daughter's thing; there is not a lot of crossover, but what he adds is his knowledge of marketing and business:

> One of the reasons we've been able to keep our membership in our company happy is that we've had a really open-door policy. They call me any time. I mean, literally you get called at 8:30–9 o'clock at night and you're sitting on the couch watching TV. I remember calls. . . . You know, you have a discussion about what's going on. And so, I've kept them very informed and been very open; and when things weren't going right I would tell them that things weren't going right, you know, so that there was never any big surprises.

Dennis continues to manage his farmland real estate business in Illinois. He has also gotten involved in his daughter's small Illinois farm. As a community-supported farm, his daughter focuses on creating connections with her customers using newsletters and electronic communication. I asked him if his experience in

Brazil would be useful on a small, diversified Illinois farm. He said no, at least not in terms of production techniques ("Honestly, that's really her thing. I don't step into that too much because the kind of production I've done is so different that there's a lot of the times not a lot of crossover"). But he does offer suggestions and "sometimes she listens—sometimes she doesn't." Most of these suggestions extend from his open-door policy with investors which translates well to her task of creating a community of reliable customers.

Ian was planning to keep the farm in Western Bahia, though not necessarily with him there. In 2012, when I asked him about his plans for the future, he said he wanted to get better before he got bigger. He would like to have it in a place where if he left, the workers and managers would be able to pick everything up. He had worked on outlining a mission and vision for this purpose. He wanted everything in place so people would do whatever he wanted them to but without his input. When I visited the next year, they were operating under the same plan as before, not expanding but focusing on managing the land they had. Meanwhile, the family was expanding the Illinois farm to suit the need to accommodate the six families who wanted to get involved: his father, uncle, two cousins, Ian, and his sister. None had expressed any interest in working on or taking over the Brazil farm. They all wanted to be involved in the Illinois farm where they were expanding the pig operation. Regardless of the future of the Illinois family farm, Ian saw the future of farming in Brazil thus:

> Now, I think farms based here in these frontier areas of Brazil are run more like I knew it than it is in the US; they're bigger in size on average, and the owners simply can't . . . it's impossible for them to be out doing all the labor, like they are at home. So really I think in a way the Brazilian farmers are better prepared than the US farmer for the way I think agriculture's gonna head in the next ten, twenty years. We see hogs, dairy, poultry all integrating, all becoming much bigger; I think we'll see the same thing in this row-crop agriculture. I think these larger Brazilian farmers are looking at this like a business; and looking at the margins; and understanding the business better; and trying to take advantage in that.

And Ian was uniquely qualified to bring that model back to Illinois:

> The advantage I have now, back in the US [is that] there's not many people like me that have had this experience of large, very large scale with lots of employees and lots of money moving around and trying to manage risk. So many people at home, they don't even figure up the numbers to see if they've made money or not; so how are you gonna know how much you can pay to rent a farm if you don't know . . . ?

His dad agreed. He told me that their work in Brazil had taught them to soil test more frequently, to hire more workers, and to "think a little more about not being in the tractor and not doing the real physical work; I think about it, but it's a real shift for me 'cause I have to work."

Frank's plans were the most in flux. By 2014 he had been managing a farm in Piauí for a Belgian investor for two years. Frank wanted to take part or full ownership of the farm if the land titling could be finalized, but he expected to go home to Missouri at some point as well. But he said "If I were to go home, I'm still going to be coming to Brazil all the time. It's in me now." He also hoped to open ten new English-language schools in Barreiras—he had dreamed of opening thirty. The rancor and ill-will of the American community actually kept him around to an extent; he listed staying around to collect on bills owed and to collect as cases "wind through the court system." He hoped to collect over R$300,000. In Missouri his dad and uncle were ready to retire, and were hoping Frank would take over the 1,500 acres in neighboring counties. The last time he visited Missouri his dad "very much saw me coming home and being a hired hand, which after you've been out on your own is a little hard. Everybody has trouble going back to the farm—to reintegrate." He had considered trying to manage farms in Brazil and the United States but dismissed the idea as having too much potential for going wrong. One thing that kept him in Brazil, and part of the original pull for him, was to make a seemingly broken system work. He had discovered the "map of the mine field" and took pride in being able to survive in a difficult community and political environment. For the last five years he had focused on "helping other people not suffer what I did; or help[ing] people get out of bad situations," and he wanted to continue that work. Speaking of people he was helping, he said:

> You're an innocent little lamb, and the lion grabs you by the neck and shakes you around a few times. You know, they were in a spot where their Brazilian partner really knew what he was doing, and they really— like I did—thought they were being a good partner and thought it was a partnership. [But] the slowness of the Brazilian legal system is something that the evildoers count on—that you will eventually get sick of it, or that they can do evil things and get away with it because justice may not catch up with them until after they're dead.

It may be easy to dismiss Frank's framing of local Bahians as lions and transnational farmers and landowners as innocent lambs, but Frank was speaking as a victim of bad land deals and a friend of people who had lost land, capital, and machinery to deals that had gone wrong.

The Iowa family have lost control of their farm, but Jacob remains in Brasilia. After not returning any profit to investors in the early years, they turned to a New York investment bank for expansion and "capitalization" soon after the economic crisis hit and the fund was spent. They then turned to a London agricultural investment company seeking to invest $250 million in production agriculture. The company bought out the farm's partners and later grouped the investment with other agricultural investments and went public. At the time of my research, Paul was chief executive officer of the company; Jacob was chief operating officer; and they were both board members, while a London agricultural investment company is the sole shareholder.

The Iowa family had sold options to BMX, a publicly traded company, who owned a 70 percent share of their farm. BMX then sold the farm, and they had no choice in the sale because they had a minority stake. Jacob now works in Brasilia as a consultant. A year earlier I had asked his father about his future and how they fit into the legacy of the family farm. His statement made clear that the Brazilian farm itself was not an enduring aspect of the family or even of his son's occupation but that it had opened up possibilities that were otherwise closed to them. It allowed the family to capitalize on Brazilian agricultural growth and to provide Jacob with agribusiness credentials:

> Legacy of farm? If you're a farmer and you have that type of mentality, you just think in a particular way. I don't know if I can describe the legacy part of it. When I told him I was going to start a farm, he was shocked; he never saw me in that way. I understand business and have experience with the international side. Then Jacob—he is in a unique situation. There aren't many people with his experience. If he wanted to do something else he could do anything. Cargill would be knocking at his door. At the same time, I anticipate that he might come home and take over here. He has adapted well. One investor said that his biggest surprise was Jacob. He was either going to succeed or go down in fire. He's culturally and business-wise adapted there.

Moving On

The aftermath of failed forays into Brazilian soybean production elicited talk of new opportunities but also of great sadness. Leon, after going bankrupt in Brazil, "sold everything. So I had no equipment, no farm, no nothing. When I came back to the US, I had some debt, and six suitcases." He went on to work for his father-in-law in Alaska for a summer, then worked on a big potato farm in Washington for four years, then moved to North Dakota for a year, and at the time of our last interview was living in Colorado.

> I would love to farm again, but I don't ever see the capital cost. Starting from scratch, how will it ever happen? . . . When I bought my [Idaho] farm the first time it was $1,700 an acre, and now I'm seeing farms that are out now it's like $8,000 to $9,000 an acre. It's just crazy. And then equipment—I could probably buy the same equipment for mostly the same price. But land, and the availability of land, are just . . . I was pretty depressed there for probably about four years, five years.

Still, he told me he would "farm 40 acres if I could . . . we just miss—we like doing it. Yeah. I'll want to do it until I'm dead." He regretted not living in Brazil for a year to better understand the economics and dynamics of buying land and farming there; he also suspects his family would have been better off having stayed on their Idaho farm.

The disintegration of the American community and their gradual movement away from soybean production portends a renewed crisis in Brazilian soybean production. But this is not how the sector is portrayed. An interview with a Foreign Agricultural Service (USDA-FAS) functionary in Brasília revealed a narrative of continued growth and progress in Brazil. Government incentives to encourage agricultural development and migration from the coast to the interior worked but not without some difficulties. The financial cost of these programs was high; many farms failed because they did not know how to grow crops in the Cerrado, and commodity prices were low. Farmers had to be bailed out in the 1980s and were asking for help again in 2005–2006. "So," said the functionary, "there's costs of developing Brazil." But the last five years (2007–2012) had been favorable; farmers had been paid good prices, and good production weather improved yields. This allowed many farms to pay down loans, but it also increased farmland values to the point that "it's not as easy for the American farmer to come down and farm anymore." But, he said, expansion was still expected:

> Luís Eduardo Magalhães was just a gas station in 1983; now 70,000 people and big, boom metropolis, just because of agriculture; this is the plateau region and the rains are good the closer you are to the state line. . . . Some of the savanna has lots of trees but this was basically grassland, very easy to clear—and start planting. . . . These guys started going up to Piauí. This area is still an area of expansion.

A later interview with another functionary at the FAS office in the US Embassy in Brasília presented a less rosy outlook. Thirty-five percent of costs are transportation, she told me; but while the government stalled infrastructure plans, firms are building railroads and ports by themselves, and the Transnordestino (a highway to connect several northeast and center-west Brazilian states) should help get crops from Mapitoba to Recife—even if that will be years ahead. Global commodity prices had been falling for two years, weather had wiped out crops in Mato Grosso and Bahia, gas prices were high, the exchange rate was worsening, and "bureaucracy is always bad."

We are left to make sense of these competing narratives. FAS tells a story of progress and near unlimited opportunity. Family farmers in Bahia narrate a stagnating situation in Bahia leading them to go bankrupt, sell out, or simply maintain their current situation. In terms of stability, the situation is chaotic; but in terms of flexible farming, while it is perhaps a hassle, it is also a welcome opportunity to sell land at a profit and then either buy cheaper land elsewhere, return to farm in the United States, or apply the skills learned in Brazil to consulting work. The farmers, having fled crisis in the United States, are repeating that process again in Brazil. But while many of the American farmers have left and others are plotting their exit, Soylandia will remain.

The Brazilian adventure has ended for many of the US farmers, but Soylandia, as both a territory and a dream, remains intact and even consolidated. The fate of US farms after the flight of their owners back to the United States is likely to be consolidated as part of a Brazilian-owned farm in the region or to be purchased by one of the larger farmland investment firms such as SLC Agricola or TIAA-CREF. The harsh lesson in this is that the farmers themselves are also replaceable parts in Soylandia. While the story of North Americans in Brazil is in many ways spectacular, their actual role in developing farmland, creating agricultural operations, and implementing innovative business practices is not special.

CONCLUSION

Welcome to Soylandia

In the introduction, I presented three welcomes to Soylandia. First, this book is about how US farmers were welcomed into the agroecology, society, and government of soy production in Brazil. Second, it is an invitation for readers to hear that story through detailed ethnography. And third, it is about how the rest of the world is becoming like Soylandia. So, what does this mean for the rest of the world?

The Soylandia model is already being implemented and expanded. This model of a technological packet and cheap lands exists elsewhere—the Argentinean Pampas, for example (Zorzoli 2022).[1] In Brazil, the government of Jair Bolsonaro has reduced foreign landownership restrictions; relaxed enforcement of environmental protections for the Cerrado and Amazonia; and called for an opening up of indigenous land for development. President Bolsonaro himself commented, "Onde tem uma terra indígena, tem uma riqueza embaixo dela. Temos que mudar isso daí" (Where there is indigenous land, there is wealth underneath it. We need to change this situation) (Dolzan 2017). Colonists in crisp T-shirts and suede loafers implement flexible uses of land, labor, and crops to expand the soy frontier. In the words of one Brazilian farmer in Mato Grosso, "We took a state that was worthless, a land that was worthless and we tamed it with technology and new methods of fertilization" (Harris 2021).

In the United States the average farm size has doubled in twenty years, and larger farms have been realizing better financial returns by using capital and labor much more intensely. Consolidation of farms has occurred alongside increasing farm specialization and, like the farmers in this ethnography, many large corporate farms are in fact family farms. Ninety percent of farms with over $1 million in sales in 2015 were family farms, though they were heavily dependent on custom work (similar to Brazilian *erceirização,* which is hiring nonfarm employees to spray pesticides, harvest grain, etc.) and hired farmworkers. Remarkably, the Brazil Model has made its way back to the United States. In 2002 a South Dakotan farmer with farmland in Brazil was featured in a story for the magazine *Top Producer.* In the article he recited his mantra, "I must grow to compete globally." The author defines his strategy as the "Brazilian model in which he's doubled in size several times over from 400 acres in 1987 to 10,000 plus in 2002." He is willing to travel up to forty miles from his home base to access farmland. This distancing strategy has helped him enlarge his holdings since, according to his observation, "local competition for land is political," thus he had had difficulty renting in his region due to being seen as "too aggressive." He makes expansion possible by owning equipment but paying employees to operate it and doing his own custom work when he is free.

Other farmers are finding ways to buy and sell land anonymously in order to aggressively acquire land without social ramifications. For example, in 2020 an Illinois-based farm management and real estate company with ties to Ian Illinois's farm in Bahia moved six farmland auctions in response to the COVID-19 pandemic.[2] The auctions were made virtual in order to keep people safe, but customers preferred the online auction because it bestowed anonymity. Their website states that "the virtual platform allows bidders to compete against a friend or neighbor without the social pressure of being together in the same room bidding at a traditional auction. Bidders are known only by their bidding number so there are no potential hard feelings. Everyone is anonymous except, eventually, the winning bidder." The company does not expect the virtual auctions to replace in-person auctions, but interest in them is growing.

A US farmer in Brazil with a blog wrote an entry on the news about opening up Mozambique land for soy production. He calls it an honorable goal that would help Mozambique. However, he states:

> What has been done in the Cerrado of Brazil over the last 30 years is a cake walk compared to the journey that awaits new pioneers to Mozambique. The differences include little things like the hundreds of thousands of undetonated land mines that still pollute various areas of Mozambique. I have punctured fuel tanks and tires with sticks and small trees in Brazil, but I have never hit a land mine. Without even touching on government, the AIDS epidemic, and no basic public infrastructure in your children's lifetime, Brazilians will be foreigners in Mozambique. Even the continental Portuguese with strong African tribal accents will be a

challenge. The most interesting implication of this invitation reflects on American agriculture. This offer brings into question the wisdom of paying $10,000 an acre for land that grows 45 bushel soybeans in the United States when Mozambique is renting ground for under $6 an acre. Mozambique is a lot closer to China than Chicago.

The US farmer/blogger points to both the ongoing global pursuit of cheap, productive farmland—fine-tuned by US farmers in the Brazilian Cerrado—and the need for such farmland buyers to reckon with culture, land, war, and infrastructure. His closing reference to markets in China and almost impossibly cheap land in Mozambique suggests that, in his opinion, these opportunities will generate new solutions to these new problems and farmers will make it work.

The same agricultural magazines that first garnered the interest of US farmers in Brazil are now demonstrating how US farmers can implement the Brazil Model at home. An article in *Farm Futures* includes a text box on "how farmers tamed Brazil's hinterlands" and an image of a Brazilian farmer in front of blue skies, seemingly endless fields of cotton, and shiny machinery. He is white, older, smiling, and wears a clean shirt. There are also photos of "dirty" workers standing in front of a field, buses to transport workers, and portable restrooms—all set across from ads for Mycogen seeds and Verdict Herbicide (Thompson 2014). These images give the reader a visual reference to what this model would look like on the ground. Informed by a Brazilian farmer who owns 79,000 acres of Mato Grosso farmland spread over five farms, the article lists the "Secrets of the Brazilian mega-farmers: Management tips from your toughest neighbors":

1. See the target.
2. If at first you don't succeed, innovate.
3. Spot opportunities and act.
4. Know the numbers.
5. No family baggage.
6. Keep investing in your resources.

In sum, the article calls for less sentimentality in farm decisions. The author quotes a Brazilian farmer who advises US farmers to take lessons from Soylandia. "One big difference between the big Brazilian farmers and the big US farmer," the Brazilian farmer says, "is the relative lack of sentimentality on the part of the big Brazilian producer." The author explains, "The Brazilian mega-farmer often doesn't even live on the farm. He lives in town and commutes to the farm. The Brazilians in expansion areas like Mato Grosso and the Mapito region of Brazil will often deny it, but [according to the Brazilian farmers] 'if someone comes along someday with enough money, [the Brazilian farmer] will sell the place in a minute.'" This lack of sentimentality is "one of the first things Americans note when they visit the area," says the writer, who has assisted with purchases and investments in agricultural production in Brazil.

Soylandia is a model for agriculture without sentimentality, connection, or care; yet what I have tried to show here is that, despite this hope for a disconnected farm unit, life and farming are vibrant and defy total control. Despite that disconnection between the model and reality, advocates continue to propose Soylandia as the future of farming. Whether Soylandia or a million little soylandias come to fruition, they will continue to unfold not in the abstract but in fields, boardrooms, farm offices, agribusiness cities, pickups, and airplanes.

Carol Warrior (2017) likens flexibility to slime molds or the blob creature in its ambiguity, fungibility, and mobility. Characters in films and everyday outdoorspeople may find the molds disgusting, disconcerting, and sometimes beyond recognition, but their flexibility makes them powerful. Unfortunately, this same flexibility makes capital insidious. Farmers in this story use capital and mobility to respond to crisis, to expand the frontier of soybean cultivation, and to become transnational farmers; at the same time, they are rooted in place by friction that limits the impact of capital and movility. The friction of pest infestations, government regulations, and soil infertility presents challenges that leads some of the farmers to fail. The same friction leads some to become so well-streamlined as to allow the farmers to manage them from thousands of miles away. This is the generative power of flexibility. The generativity of soy monocrops is ugly, but not just destructive. Unfortunately, much of what is generated is productive of further agricultural expansion, environmental degradation, and community dispossession. From this work on the frontier of Soylandia and at the frontier of what family farming can look like, models of future agriculture are being perfected.

Soylandia is a territory, a prescription, and a dream. One could find some hope in the flexibility of farmers. While we were chatting in his pickup, Frank once mentioned that, although he thinks antigenetic modification rhetoric is nonsense, he also thinks farmer resistance to it is nonsense. "Let's put a label on it," he told me, and consumers can choose to pay above-market price for non-GMO food if they want to. Similarly, one could argue that a farmer would not need to be convinced that climate change is real in order to implement no-tillage and plant cover crops to reduce greenhouse gas emissions; rather, the availability of carbon credits for the implementation of such practices might be enough. Still, the disconnection implicit in Soylandia and flexible farming is deeply concerning. In her work on farmland markets, Madeleine Fairbairn sees the financial sector interest in farmland as a wakeup call. Land, she reminds us, "is too vital—to the pride of farmers, to the cultural identity of indigenous peoples, to the food security of rural communities—to be casually surrendered to wealthy institutions for whom it serves as just one more weapon in an investment arsenal" (Fairbairn 2020, 147). The lesson of Soylandia is that it is not just the farmland that is being rendered as a market asset and stripped of other meanings and uses. The farmworkers and farm owners alike are made into replaceable cogs; the crops are planted with little consideration for nutrition, sustainability, or cultural significance; and other life, including traditional communities and local flora and fauna, are ignored or destroyed. Soylandia can be implemented nearly anywhere with nearly any crop, but the pesky realities of flexible farming make the complete taming of workers, crops, and land nearly impossible. Both aspects of Soylandia, whether within the demarcated borders or out in the wild, merit deep attention in order to notice where soil, people, and plants are being made flexible and where they are resisting.

Science fiction interprets the present and imagines the future, sometimes as utopia and sometimes as dystopia. In *The Word for World Is Forest*, Ursula Le Guin wrote about a planet that the indigenous population called "Athshe" and colonizers from Earth called "New Tahiti." The forested planet was cleared and converted to massive soy fields, and its indigenous population became farmworkers. Reviews of the book were generally positive, but many critics claimed the Earth colonizers were cartoonishly villainous. Yet much of the story sounds familiar. Captain Davidson, the antihero, complains of having to follow environmental regulations to reduce erosion: "You had to leave a lot of trees standing where you planned to put farms." But he still could not see why a soybean farm needed to waste a lot of space on trees if the land was managed really scientifically. "It wasn't like that in Ohio; if you wanted corn you grew corn, and no space wasted on trees and stuff. But then Earth was a tamed planet and New Tahiti wasn't. That's what he was here for: to tame it" (Le Guin 2017, 3). Again echoing some of the US farmers in Brazil, in a debate with a logging foreman Captain Davidson complained about the work ethic of the locals: "I can't get enough work out of 'em in the mill to make up for their keep. Or for their being such a damn headache. They just don't work" (18). Even Frank's statement that many US farmers called their workers "little brown fuckers" is mirrored in Le Guin's reference to "little green fellers" and "little green men." The world of Soylandia this book has documented is in many ways eerily close to Le Guin's dystopian vision. To know what the future holds is impossible, but a goal of science fiction and of ethnography can be to find ways to ward against futures we detest.

AFTERWORD

Fixed Farming

This vision of Soylandia is not inevitable, nor is flexible farming.[1] My scattered references throughout this book to my fieldwork with a colony of Holdeman Mennonites in Rio Verde, Goiás, point to another pathway. Decades before the flexible farmers arrived in Western Bahia, Mennonite colonists were driven by a sense of cultural crisis (as well as increasing farmland values in the United States) to find cheap farmland in Brazil. In the United States, military enlistment through the Vietnam War draft threatened their pacifism and a prominent Supreme Court decision raised fears of losing autonomy over their children's educational curriculum. The increasing ubiquity of color television even brought worldly influences into their homes and threatened their cultural norms.[2] In 1968 nine Mennonites toured rural Brazil in search of arable farmland. Guided by happenstance and a portentous omen, they purchased 10,000 hectares of native Cerrado land from a single landowner and founded a colony on the outskirts of Rio Verde, Goiás. These colonists used their experience of growing crops in Georgia's red clay soils (similar to Cerrado latosols) to become early soy pioneers in Goiás. They planted rice to build the soil, added soil amendments to raise the pH and increase soil fertility, and then adopted a rotation of corn and soybeans. Today they practice a style of farming centered on family, community, and religion. Unlike many soy-producing Mennonite colonies that dominate agricultural landscapes in Latin America, this community has less access to technology, capital, and land than their neighboring farmers.

Work in the Mennonite colony was not flexible. Families lived on their farms and accounted for the vast majority of the farmwork. The little labor that was hired consisted of community members who lived in the colony. In the colony, good work was that which contributed to the family and community. One colonist told me that "what's important [for men] is providing for the family. . . . If you don't provide for your family you're worse than an infidel." Good farmers provide for their family, but they do not place profit ahead of family. Those who were perceived to be placing technology, profit, or prestige ahead of family were first chastised and later, if they persisted, shunned by the community. They often challenged other farmers in the region—questioning how one could be a farmer without "actually farming." They joked about Brazilian and American farmers being "hitched to the satellite" (dependent on GPS technology and self-guided tractors) and falling asleep at the tractor wheel. Workers in the colony were family members; the work itself was deeply meaningful; and the work consisted mostly of fieldwork, not office work.

Land in the colony was not flexible. There were gently undulating hills (not the flat landscapes of Western Bahia), diverse soils, and varied microclimates. This landscape diversity led the farmers to plant more diversified crops. Soybean grew well on some fields while other fields were better suited for hay or pasture. Land was purposefully distanced from land markets in the colony through two social mechanisms. First, those who sold land outside of the colony—that is, to non-Mennonite Brazilians or Americans—would be chastised. Second, and more harshly, those who accumulated land in excess of what was needed to sustain a family would be shunned and excommunicated from the colony and the church. Both mechanisms had been in regular use and a new community of excommunicated Mennonites was emerging in Tocantins at the time of my research. These protections for community (but not collective) land kept landholding in the community to 30–250 hectares per family and maintained both the land base of the community and land distribution. Speculative farmland acquisition was disruptive and unwelcome in the Mennonite community.

Crops in the colony were not flexible. Despite the dominance, and profitability, of sugar cane in the area, the tall grass was absent from Mennonite farms. It required too much labor, cost too much, and ruined their soil. The crops were diverse, differentiated, suited to field conditions, and suited to farmer preferences. Herbert Funk, an affable third-generation farmer in the colony, owned ten hectares of land, previously planted to soy, but at the time of my research he had planted hay for dairy cows because he was "not much of a soy person." He sold his surplus hay to a county-managed horse-riding program for children, to a farmers' syndicate, and to private horse owners. He did this despite his father's warning that hay was a luxury crop without productive ends because, in his words, he was just cutting the hay, not riding horses. Other farmers had livestock on the farm so that their children could raise animals and build character. Changes to farming practices were deliberate. Farmers in the colony had adopted *safrinha* (a second crop in the growing year), hybrid seed (and later genetically modified seed), and no-tillage ten years after the neighboring Brazilian farmers had demonstrated the ability of these practices to increase productivity (in the case of safrinha and hybrid seeds) and reduce disastrous soil erosion (in the case of no-tillage).

The Mennonite colony was experiencing its own issues with farming in Brazil. They too were exiting agriculture, but primarily due to a shrinking land base that can no longer sustain families. Those who sold land to outsiders moved back to the United States, much like many flexible farmers, but the younger generations of Mennonites in the colony (second and third generation) stayed in Brazil. Some young colonists purchased land in Mato Grosso to start a new colony where land was cheaper and the soil was more fertile. Many stayed in Rio Verde and found work outside of agriculture. Dirt working (building earthen dams and foundations) was a common occupation. The colony had built and managed a printing press for religious literature; held services at two churches in the colony and one in the city; and maintained a busy, noisy school. Even if their agricultural future was in doubt, they seemed to be committed to staying. "Aftermath" may not even be an appropriate term for the colony. The colonists' intention in coming to Brazil was not to return profit or even to be farmers—it was to create a community where they were exempt from military service, free to teach their children what they wanted to, and autonomous from worldliness.

The Mennonite colony provides a counterexample to flexible farming. They connect to the land, work, and crops where flexible farmers alienate, but they too perceive the Cerrado as a wasteland. They employ similar, if less intensive, soil and pest management techniques, and like flexible farmers they have pushed the soybean frontier a little further. The colony is not a model of sustainability nor an ideal community, but I return to them here to underpin the idea that other engagements with soy and Soylandia are possible.

Appendix

RESEARCH METHODS

Finding Transnational Farmers: Field Methods

I worked in Luís Eduardo Magalhães, Bahia, to conduct research with US farmers about their hopes and plans as soy farmers. This included documenting the industrialization of a farming landscape as well as the emerging diversity of farming lifeways within the corporate world of soy. I worked with farmers and farmworkers in the fields and observed office work to understand everyday farming techniques and business practices. I observed who was doing what on these farms and how they were doing it. Using my experience growing up on a South Dakota soybean farm and a formal agronomy education, I reflected on the differences and the hybridization of US and Brazilian farming styles. In my field notes I recorded my observations regarding what practices were utilized, how they were performed, who performed them, what machinery was used, and what reasons farmers and farmworkers provided for these practices. Using my agronomy training, I paid particular attention to tillage practices, pest management, seed selection, and the construction of conservation structures—including terraces, grassed waterways, and riparian buffers. The everyday practices of planting and harvesting in the field or ordering fertilizer, and office work (such as ordering inputs, making contracts, and developing plans) all provided ethnographic insights at the site where structures of agrarian change are situated in actor knowledge, skills, and values.

Along with recording these everyday farming practices, I also studied how farmers frame practices as ethical matters. Semistructured interviews ascertained the relative importance or value given to different practices. I recorded offhand remarks made by landowners, managers, and farmworkers that indicated their distaste or preference for certain kinds of work, landscape aesthetics, or other ethical statements in order to observe the everyday ethics of farming. This often meant long pickup rides from Luís Eduardo to farms near the escarpment that separates Bahia from Tocantins—rides that offered time for questions I had prepared for months to ask, questions I had never thought to ask, and most importantly time for patient listening. I then compared these offhand statements with official discourse such as mission statements or labor contracts in order to locate the site of everyday ethics.

I observed farmers' participation in social events such as farm shows, Thanksgiving dinners, and birthday parties to document social relations. I took note of who talks to whom, how groups form, who mixes between groups, and how rituals and speech acts differ between groups. This work enabled an analysis of spheres of cooperation, conflict, and avoidance between farmers, farmworkers, farm managers, and other actors. Semistructured interviews explored perspectives on labor and environmental regulations and on political engagement in Brazil. While farmers went in and out of the country, I was based in Luís Eduardo; even when they were in Brazil they shuffled between farm in the countryside, home in the city, and excursions elsewhere. In order to understand social relations, I supplemented in-person research with a digital situational analysis in which I identified digital communication such as investor reports, farming update emails, farm websites, farmer blogs, Facebook interactions, and Skype conversations. This enabled me to better understand the digital work that is necessary to operate a transnational farm and how digital engagement allows farmers to connect with communities back home, investors, and potential investors. I used investor reports, farm plans, loan applications, and other business documents to corroborate interview data, tell corporate histories, and show changing farm plans. I also incorporated farmer blogs to understand how farmers present their work to the public and to friends and family. I composed self-reflective journal entries in which I critically analyzed my own discomfort with the justifications for and effects of large-scale soy farming in Brazil, due to my own family connection to soy farming.

I analyzed visions of success and good farming by conducting career-history interviews that capture farmers' lives before moving, the process of choosing to move, the move itself, and the process of founding a farm in Brazil. Career histories revealed sites of difference and sameness as well as sites of entanglement between seemingly disparate actors and processes. These interviews established short-term and long-term goals of migration, and they placed the migration and work within a frame of crisis or a frame of profit accumulation.

My position and research topic limited the voices that appear in my research and this monograph. Women's voices are lacking in this research. This is primarily because most US-owned farms are operated by single men who may have a romantic partner, but usually not one involved in the farm. This is interesting in itself in the way it separates this lifestyle from the traditional view of a farm family as a family unit. It is also interesting in terms of who stays and who goes in migration flows. In conducting participant observation and extensive interviews with large-scale landowners, I found my avenues for research with farmworkers and local communities limited. My identity as a white man from North America researching white male farmers from North America marked these interactions as risky business for the precarious position of farmworkers. As a result of these limitations, this ethnography became an ethnography of whiteness and masculinity (particularly chapters 1, 2, and 4).

Finally, a short note on definitions. The notion of the family farm is broadly defined by the United States Department of Agriculture (USDA) as any farm where the majority of the business is owned by the operator and individuals related to the operator. By contrast, the Programa Nacional de Fortalecimento da Agricultura Familiar of Brazil defines the family farm in terms of who performs labor, where the majority of income is coming from, who owns the land, and how much land is owned (BNDES n.d.). The colloquial idea of a family farm has evolved in both the United States and Brazil, becoming in both cases a purer form of a unit of economic production. US farmers in this ethnography came primarily from the Midwest, but not all of them. Most operate their farms as a satellite of their family farm, but not all are family farmers. Some may even question if they are farmers at all, based on their dependence on outside capital and hired labor. While recognizing differences in the definition of a family farm, I make some generalizations for clarity of prose. I refer to this group—made up of mostly young, educated, white men who migrated from (mostly) the US Midwest between 1985 and 2005—as midwestern family farmers, while also recognizing the possible arguments against my use of "midwestern," "family," and "farmers." I do this to reflect the fact that farmers often returned to their roots, to make connections to their agrarian family histories clear, and because they referred to themselves as farmers and to their families as farm families. While recognizing challenges to their self-identifications, I will use the terms they use to describe themselves.

On Studying Up

This monograph builds on the emerging study of the generation of capitalism by asking several questions: What are the practices, relations, and values of transnational industrial agriculture? What new social and material arrangements are generated from this emergent livelihood strategy? Studying up provides rich ethnographic material on an ethnographically understudied group—elites—but requires a modified ethnographic toolkit (Nader 1972). As shown in other ethnographies of elite farmers of Brazil, participant observation can be modified or refocused to better capture the daily lives of elites. Jeffrey Hoelle (2015) observed cattle auctions to identify and analyze social interactions between ranchers and ranch hands, and the meanings assigned to bulls, clothing, and behavior, while Ryan Adams (2010) attended social events, shared rides with soy farmers, attended birthday parties, and spent time with them at tractor supply stores and nearby beaches. Likewise, my research with large-scale soy farmers followed the nature of their work and was, therefore, conducted as much in the pickup truck and the office as in the field.

Transitioning from my earlier research on small-scale Bolivian quinoa farmers to transnational soy farmers in Brazil was difficult. Midwestern family farmers in Bahia offered skeptical yet open invitations to interview them and visit their farms. I wholeheartedly appreciate these gestures. My presence there was always as an aloof outsider at best and a member of the cultural and political opposition at worst. I worked to keep my political opinions on global warming, genetically modified crops, the Movimento dos Trabalhadores Rurais Sem Terra (landless workers' movement, MST), and large-scale farming in general to myself, but when an interlocutor asked my opinion, I gave it. I held these opinions close for two reasons; one practical and the other ethnographic. First, I was already marked as an outsider and a nosy intellectual. To put my political opinions into the open would further distance me from my interlocutors. Second, my research was designed to ask why these farmers were there and why they farmed the way they did. I was there to challenge scholarly perceptions of transnational farming and industrial soy production as well as my own.

There were times when conflict was unavoidable—for example, a heated conversation about the social construction of race or the legitimacy of climate change evidence. There is also the common prelude to a potentially controversial subject: "I don't know if you're a liberal, but . . ." which I heard often.[1] One tool in my ethnographic kit that aided in my search for common ground was agronomic knowledge and farming experience. I often referred to agronomic principles while discussing tillage practices, pest pressure, or farming technology and I often related my research or the on-the-ground realities I was seeing to my own childhood farming experiences. This, more than anything, gave me a measure of legitimacy as a researcher and an expert to be taken seriously.

Like most ethnographers, I was plagued by questions about what I was doing in Brazil and why I was there. I also had moments of sheer exhaustion with the constant requirement of being ready with a comment or question and of having to be careful not to say the wrong thing. It was moments of mischaracterization, misinterpreted statements, and slips that often elicited the most interesting comments—for example, the joy of smelling 2,4-D or the expressions of simultaneous empathy for the Landless Workers' Movement and the subsequent dismissal of them as drug-addicted bums.

On Conducting Transnational Research

Transnational ethnography requires practical and logistical adjustments. Communities are unbounded and social interaction is often digital. I adjusted by traveling frequently, Skyping, and reading online postings by farmers. I also took the opportunity to engage in participant observation of that transnational community by taking an ethnographic approach to the internet.

Ethnography of transnational communities challenges a foundational ethnographic concept of "being there." Transnational communities are not confined to a singular "there," as transnational characters move back and forth; maintain frequent lines of communication across borders; and dwell, work, and play in disparate places. Researchers can capture this reality by attending reconfigurations of community. Where members reunite for celebrations, periods of mourning, or business-related tasks, I propose a different kind of participant observation. It would include the ethnographer's attempts to address the challenges of transnational community research as a means of researching the new modalities of social relations within these communities. Without reliable face-to-face connections, transnational ethnography can utilize Skype calls, public blogs, Facebook posts, and chain emails as ethnographic data. These become elements of participant observation into how transnational characters maintain vibrant communities.

Halfway through a Skype call with a farmer who had gone bankrupt in Brazil and had returned to the United States, a solution to the problem and an opportunity to do some interesting research struck me. Why not approach the interview and the experience of using Skype as participant observation? From that point on, I approached Skype interviews as a chance to capture how farmers communicate with family and friends and to observe what technology they use or are comfortable with. Participant observation then becomes a matter of seeing how they present themselves and how they communicate. This is especially important because this is likely one of the main ways that investors keep track or how new investors would do research on a company.

This community is rarely together in person, but it has vibrant virtual communities. Almost all have Skype and are at least comfortable with using it. One day, working with a farmer in his office, the only sound breaking the silence was the frequent "ting" of an incoming or outgoing Skype message. Communication is kept alive through other means as well. Some farmers publish blogs, directed toward family and friends, in which they discuss themes as diverse as Brazilian farming policy, currency markets, local diet, and daily farming life. Others operate more business-like blogs for agricultural journals, in which they focus on the issues that can inform US farmers about the goings-on in Brazil. Still others even have Instagram feeds or farm Facebook pages to publish pictures and daily reflections. A less public route is to publish informal newsletters that are distributed to family, friends, colleagues, and investors. These often show the progress on the farm, farmwork, landscapes (ideal and not), and agronomic factors (pests, evidence of erosion, evidence of drought, etc.).

Each of these methods of communication—Instagram, Skype, Facebook, email, and newsletters—provided a dual function for me as a researcher. Each conveys information in raw form as well as information on the social lives of farmers. Blogs and newsletters keep farmers involved in social networks (whether networks of farmers spread throughout Brazil or kin networks). They allow farmers to maintain personas in absentia (as good neighbors or farmers or entrepreneurs) through their selective portrayal of farmwork, farm landscapes, and general farm life. Investor reports maintain their persona as a good businessperson and a good farmer by focusing more squarely on the financial and managerial aspects of farming in Brazil. These reports have multiple functions, ranging from business transparency to relieving investors' worries to courting new investors.

In-person participant observation was also a tremendously important part of my research. I rode along with farmers as they surveyed their fields and their field hands. I helped them check seed depth during planting and worked on planters when they were not functioning right. I spent time in their offices as much as possible to see the stacks of paperwork. I even accompanied them to the local court to deliver paperwork. These observations showed me how US farmers learn to produce soybeans in a different agroecology and, for that matter, a different hemisphere; how they manage different (and from their perspective intrusive) environmental and labor regulations; how they learn to manage farmworkers; and how they create and adopt new values of work. However, the observation of everyday agricultural and business practices depends on one important thing: being there.

Glossary of Portuguese Words

Bancada Ruralista—Powerful faction within the National Congress allied with the interests of commercial agribusiness

bandeirante—Literally flag carriers—slavers, explorers, and adventurers of colonial Brazil

campo Cerrado—Dense stands of small trees in the Cerrado environment

Cerrado—A vast tropical savanna in Brazil

churrascaria—Brazilian barbecue

comunidades geraizeiras—People living in the *gerais*

confederados—Members of the Confederacy of the US South who migrated to Brazil in the nineteenth century

daquele jeito—By any means necessary

desbravadores—Trailblazers

estatuto do trabalhador—Rural worker statute

fazenda—Large plantation farm in Brazil, similar to *hacienda* in Spanish

fechos de gerais—Land held in common on the plateaus of the Brazilian Cerrado

fechos de pasto—Mixed farming and animal husbandry in the valleys of the Brazilian Cerrado

feijoada—Stew of beans and beef or pork, served with rice

gaucho—Generally, a person from Rio Grande do Sul

gerais—Common land of the Cerrado, used for pasture, foraging, and ceremony

geraizeiros—People living in the *gerais*

grileiro or grilageiro—Land-grabber

grilagem—Land-grabbing

invasores—Invaders

lanchonete—Diners, often roadside, in which customers usually pay for plates by the pound

laranja—A joint partnership with a citizen who acts as a figurehead but holds little real power on the farm

limitada—Limited liability company

maracuja—Passionfruit mousse

pioneiros—Pioneers

quilombolas—Afro-Brazilian residents of a *quilombo* settlement

quinuero—Quinoa farmer

ribeirinhos—People living near the rivers in the valley

ruralista—Rural caucus

safrinha—A second crop in the growing year (corn after soybeans in Goiás, soybeans after soybeans in Mato Grosso, and a cover crop after soybeans in Western Bahia)

senhores—Bosses, used to refer to plantation owners

sesmeiros—Portuguese land colonizers

soldados rasos—Crazy soldiers

sulistas—Brazilians from the southern states of Paraná, Santa Catarina, and Rio Grande do Sul

terceirização—Outsourcing

terra de cultura—Extremely fertile loamy soil

terra preta—Black soil

terra vermelha—Red soil

Transnordestino—Major highway project to connect states of the Brazilian Center-West

tranquilo—Easygoing

vazio agricola—Agricultural abyss

vazio sanitário—Quarantine, a state-defined continuous period when no live crop plants (soybean or cotton) can be maintained in a given area

vestir a camisa—Literally, "wear the shirt," meaning being proud to be part of a team

Notes

INTRODUCTION

1. All farm names and research subject names are pseudonyms. Farmers and farms will appear in each chapter of the book and one can follow their individual stories as much as their collective story. To facilitate that, I have given them surnames that represent their home states in the United States (e.g., Ian Illinois, Jacob Iowa, Paul Iowa, Eddie Upstate, Kurt Indiana, and Frank Missouri). Dennis Tocantins is an exception; in order to avoid having two farmers with the same surname (Illinois), I will demarcate Dennis by his home state in Brazil. Farm profiles also appear in chapter 1 to clarify. The reader can also follow individual farmer's stories by referring to their entries in the index. *Fazenda* is the Portuguese word for a large farm, comparable to *hacienda* in Spanish.

2. Jorge Filho's dissertation is the first of many dissertations and master's theses by Brazilian scholars I reference in this book. In my research I have been introduced to a wealth of empirically rich and beautifully written work by young Brazilian scholars; much of this work has never been published in peer-reviewed journals, let alone high-impact English language journals. I highly recommend the reader pursue these references and read this generative and enlightening work.

3. Susanna Hecht (Hecht 2005; Hecht and Rajão 2020) and Gustavo Oliveira (Oliveira 2016; 2018) explore this territory and highlight both the structural aspects that create the shape of Soylandia and the local cultural, economic, and ecological realities that shape the heterogeneity of the space.

4. For more on agricultural financialization, see Ouma 2016, Sommerville and Magnan 2015, and Fairbairn 2015.

5. For more on sacrifice zones, see Heaberlin and Shattuck 2023, Carrillo and Ispen 2021, Edelman 2021, Valdivia 2015, and Ofstehage, Wolford, and Borras 2022. Pereira et al. 2017 provides an analysis of the term in relation to the Brazilian Cerrado. For more on funder and environmentalists' preferences for conservation funding for high-carbon, charismatic ecoregions over less charismatic but highly biodiverse ecoregions, see Qin et al. 2023.

6. See Deleuze and Guattari 1987 for more on deterritoriality, V. Turner 2017 for more on liminality, and Arce and Long 2000 for more recent work on cosmopolitan space. One could argue that the transnational soybean farm resembles the cosmopolitan airport discussed by Arce and Long more than the family farm of the popular imagination.

7. Rheas are large, emu-like grassland birds native to Brazil that are reaching vulnerable status, according to the IUCN (International Union for Conservation of Nature). US farmers call them emus.

8. For ethnographic work with the farmworkers at soy farms in Western Bahia, see Gracia 2017.

9. For more works on the episodic expansion of agricultural territory in Brazil, see S. J. Stein 1986, Hutchinson 1957, Shirley 1971, Rogers 2010, and Johnson 1971.

10. Plantations are a model for inserting capital into agriculture while also creating racialized workforces, alienating people and plants from the land, and replacing grounded ecosystems and communities with extractive cash crop agriculture. Yet plantations remain rooted in the land and contain social connection and social reproduction, even if they are

exploitative and extractive. Flexible farming is a clear demonstration of the possibilities of the plantation and what scholars call the Plantationocene (Chao et al. 2023; Wolford 2021), one function of which is displacement of people, plants, soil, and microbes. This alienation and relocation is not a seamless grafting together of disparate things but a process of translation and mutual becoming. Flexible farming adaptations generate new ideas for progress, for good work, even for valued or wasteland landscapes. The flexible farm is under constant threat from disease outbreak, soil degradation, worker unrest, and climate change; it nurtures weeds, plant diseases, and worker mobilization (Ofstehage 2021b). The power of the plantation or flexible farm and its weaknesses are at the heart of this work. This book aims not only to assess how transnational farming works today but to ask what this says about the future of farming.

11. See Rissing and Jones 2022 for more on the multiple values of landscapes. Gracia captures the value attributed to the soy landscape by most soy farm owners:

> The land that was worked to build the region as a producer of soy acquires the meaning of land as a space to be exploited, land as a commodity from which to obtain surplus value. Land is just a space, a place that has to be exploited and developed in order to obtain wealth. Land only becomes a productive space, using technology to develop it. The land becomes the physical space where this technology works to create a product to be sold, the technology becomes more important than the land. People no longer work the land, they work the technology, making the land just a space where the technology works, creating an "open-air factory," the land as part of the factory's production process. (Gracia 2017, 85; my translation).

12. Much like their Brazilian counterparts (Almeida 2017).

13. Flexible farming is inversely related to the phenomena of flexibility *in* farming (Aase, Chaudhary, and Vetaas 2010) in that flexible communities find resilience by abandoning their base of place and land rather than by using flexibility to maintain these.

14. In Youjin Chung's ethnography of farmland deals in Tanzania, she quotes an agricultural engineer who describes bringing African farmers "out of their caves and [into] the modern world" through an outgrower program (2024, 40).

1. BRAZIL IS "THE BIG ANSWER TO A LOT OF QUESTIONS"

1. In this chapter I will introduce the primary characters in the ethnography. We will be hearing from them throughout the book and it is good to keep their names in mind.

2. I use "acres," "alqueires," and "hectares" to describe area; my use of each term is determined by how each source referred to land, whether using the US measure (acres) or the Brazilian measures (hectares or alqueires). For reference, a hectare is equal to 2.56 acres and a Goiás alqueire is 4.84 hectares. I also use Brazilian reais, US dollars, and sacks of soy in reference to monetary value. A sack of soy is equivalent to the market value of 60 kilograms of soybeans in US dollars. The Brazilian real conversion to US dollars fluctuated widely during my research, between 1 USD = 2.6 Brazilian reais to 1 USD = 4 Brazilian reais.

3. In the context of rural Maranhão, *gaucho* can either identify a person born in the Brazilian state of Rio Grande do Sul or more broadly as any outsider. *Pioneiros* include small-scale producers who introduced new ways of doing agriculture in the region. *Soldados rasos* are a subset of pioneiros responsible for the initial *limpando a terra* (clearing of the land). Together, pioneiros and soldados rasos cleared the way for large-scale producers to enter the region (Gaspar and Andrade 2014).

4. Part of the *boi*, *bala*, and *biblia* (cattle, bullets, and bibles) lobbies.

5. Thanks to Glenda Ofstehage for this insight.

6. On its face, the US agricultural economy is strong for family farmers. In 2011, 96 percent of US farm entities were family farms and their production accounted for 87 percent of US crop production by value (MacDonald, Korb, and Hoppe 2013). However, the loosely defined "family farm," "any farm where the majority of the [agricultural] business is owned by the operator and individuals related to the operator, including relatives who do not live with the operator" (Hoppe 2014, 56), belies the vast difference in small, medium, and large-scale farms. The US agricultural sector had a net income of $118 billion in 2011. Large and very large-scale family farms accounted for only 2 percent of total farms while accounting for 35 percent of the value of production; midsize family farms accounted for 5.7 percent of total farms and 24.8 percent of the value of production; and small-scale, sales-based farms accounted for 31.5 percent of total farms and only 11.9 percent of the value of production (Hoppe 2014). Small-scale farmers are facing great challenges, and this is particularly true for young and beginning farmers. Like all farmers, they face the everyday agronomic difficulties of weather, soil health, and pest management, but their biggest concerns, as mentioned earlier, are capital, land access, and health care. The financialization of farming has limited their access to land and their opportunities to farm profitably or to farm at all.

7. A saying attributed to President Nixon's secretary of agriculture, Earl Butz, "Get big or get out" is now a common refrain in farming circles.

8. As of 2012, average farmland prices in Illinois exceeded $10,000 per acre.

9. A land manager described the process of land formalization and consolidation as follows:

> You've got to go identify the property. You have to identify it in a region that is fertile and largely fallow. You have to then understand if there are any people who are going to hold out and that kind of thing. And you start building in the center and you build out toward the edges and you keep going until you think you've got the appropriate size. In Russia, very often the people who are living on that 2.7-hectare farm don't even understand what they have. They are not educated people; they have a piece of paper that says they own the land. Well, when we look at the piece of paper, we realize that that's not what it really says. It doesn't have, you know, the fourteen stamps, the three seals, the eight signatures, and that kind of thing. So what has taken us the most time is having people actually go out and help that farmer register his or her own land so that then they can sell it to us, which we have to go re-register. . . . There is the proverbial sixty-three thousand pages of documents that are needed just to get one farm put together." (Fairbairn 2020, 94)

10. See Madeleine Fairbairn (2020) for a deeper ethnographic engagement with investment pitches.

11. Audaciously, they projected hiring a US agronomist/farm manager despite extensive differences between US and Brazilian soils, pests, and climate.

12. In the context of the trial, this evidence was used as a counterclaim to state that the defendants were responsible for any negligent misrepresentations of the investment opportunity because they themselves had introduced the opportunity to their friends and families.

2. WASTELANDSCAPES AND SACRIFICE ZONES

1. A study of frontier development by Mairon G. Bastos Lima and Laura Kmoch (2021) points to a four-stage process of state abandonment, selective support for local development beneficiaries, disregard for potential harms of development, and later imposition of nonthreatening sustainability programs to legitimize development.

2. Improvement of wastelands is often connected to biblical themes of ruination and salvation for soil and soul. Wasteland "resists notions of proper or appropriate use," and its redemption offers material and spiritual rewards (Palma 2014, 3).

3. Many of the endemic species of the Cerrado have not yet been evaluated for conservation status. As of 2022, only 15 percent of the plants had been evaluated (Oliveira Santana and Simon 2022).

4. Modern characterizations of the bandeirantes fall into two general categories: as merciless hunters of Indigenous people and as heroes, at various times compared to Spanish conquistadors, Americans in the Wild West, the Dutch in the East Indies, and the English in Australia (L. Oliveira 1993).

5. For Eduardo Gudynas (2008), the Brazil Model of farming entails monocultures, strong commodification, and export-oriented production. Genetically modified seed, no-tillage farming, precision fertilizer and pesticide application, and cutting-edge farm machinery serve as a technological package while the farm itself is packaged as a hierarchically organized and highly capitalized business operated by "rural managers, most of them with university-level education, living in cities, and specialized in business management" (515). The transformation of business organization and practices is also reflected in a neoliberal hegemony in which large-scale soybean farmers come to see themselves as pioneers and heroes of market-oriented export agriculture, while looking to the market as legitimation of their work (Peine 2010).

6. Translations from Bezerra and Gonzaga 2019 are mine. Original: "geração de empregos e para a nossa produção, que é de fundamental importância para o Brasil, principalmente para o povo do Estado do Tocantins, da Bahia, do Maranhão e do Piauí."

7. Original: "Há ali milhares e milhares de alqueires, de hectares, que precisam da industrialização. E qual é o mecanismo para essa industrialização? É o dinheiro. É preciso que as pessoas de todo o Brasil venham para o nosso Estado, a fim de investir e agregar valor a essa produção importante que é o agronegócio, que é a agricultura."

8. Original: "É preciso que o Governo volte a permitir que qualquer pessoa, estrangeira ou não, que queira comprar sua terra aqui tenha o direito de comprá-la e de produzir nela."

9. Original: "É o agronegócio que está empregando, é o agronegócio que está gerando mão de obra, é o agronegócio que está trazendo dividendos para estes quatro Estados por meio do Matopiba e do Brasil todo."

10. Throughout the research process, Embrapa agronomists, North Carolina State University soil scientists, Brazilian farmers, and Mennonite farmers expressed some degree of ownership of this model.

11. Some southerners migrated collectively—for example, the Associacão do Benfica, which formed from a movement of former farmworkers, their families, and other locals attracted to the movement. In 1986 they organized 1,280 families to purchase 56,000 hectares in Western Bahia. Of this group, thirteen communities survive today. As others have stated, they faced low soil fertility, insufficient water, and from their perspective little state support (B. de C. D. Moura and Lavoratti 2012).

12. "A gentleman from nearby once came asking for my signature on a paper, to prove my customary right. God didn't let me do it, otherwise I don't even know where I would be today. I figured they wanted to take my land. . . . I have seen these evictions happen, grabbers coming in a caravan to expropriate people who lived on this land for 100 years. To be dragged, tossed onto a truck, someone who worked to tame the land, without the right even to take their things." "Land here? No way it had any value. My brothers themselves sold their lands, and they did it for 'peanuts'. Nowadays, they have nothing with which to buy one of these plots." "My grandfather, my father and I lived there on the plateaus, and then a few years ago they brought this soy project and pushed us to the valleys. Nobody

cared whether that was our land. They came with documents and sent us out" (Russo Lopes, Bastos Lima, and Reis 2021, 9).

13. "They moved us out of the plateaus, where we had our cattle grazing freely." "Then we came to the valleys close to the water. But now some small rivers are even disappearing during the dry season. This is not normal"; "[This stream] never dried, and now it's been three months that it's been dry. Soy arrived about three years ago and about two years ago the water started dwindling. Each day that passes, they deforest more. Nobody here has water anymore" (Russo Lopes, Bastos Lima, and Reis 2021, 9).

14. "Unfortunately, to produce food, I need to deforest. I am here producing food, food for the world" (Russo Lopes, Bastos Lima, and Reis 2021, 11).

15. Sometimes, as in Rudi Colloredo-Mansfeld's (1999) drawing sessions during his fieldwork in Ecuador, this became a moment where I as ethnographer was silent and static and community members approached me to ask their own questions.

16. White settlers of South Dakota, for example, framed the space as wasteland—yet here it was in relation to the relative scarcity of agricultural production. Edith Eudora Hohl, an emigrant from St. Louis to Lyman County, South Dakota, wrote in her 1938 book *Land of the Burnt Thigh* that "one had to begin at the beginning" in this "desolate, forgottonland," this "wasteland." "It would take slow, back-breaking labor and time . . . to make the prairie bloom" (Biolsi 2018, 22). After settling the area, she staked a claim on transformation of waste to value. "The plains which had stretched to the horizon that spring untouched by a plow, unoccupied by white men, were now unrecognizable. A hundred thousand acres of fertile waste land had been haltered . . . never had a raw primitive land seen such progress in so short a time" (22). In *Conquest of Arid America* the writer William Smythe expresses Ms. Hohl's racial undertones explicitly. His work is a manifesto for both Western expansion and scientific farming practices. His hope was to convert wasteland to farmland and expand Western civilization. All that was needed was "millions of sturdy men and stout-hearted women to conquer the waste places and to work for themselves" (Smythe 1905, 258). He dreamt of an "America, under the powerful dominance of the ancient Saxon spirit, engaged in the conquest of its waste-places and the making of new forms of civilization worthy of the race, the place, and the age" (309).

17. A common refrain of US farmers was that Western Bahia was the Wild West—a place without prior claims, ready to be developed and fought for by any means necessary. Farmers did not recognize prior local communities because their impact on the land was less obvious and not productive in their eyes. This allowed farmers to reject accusations of land-grabbing or dispossession because they believed they were only really improving the land. Likewise, without obvious markers of economic action in the area that would be recognizable to outsiders, they could claim they were job creators who brought work to the area. For example, sulistas (from the Brazilian South) in Santarém claim to be responsible producers. One large-scale farmer defended their work: "In every group there are people who are dangerous or disrespectful, but those of us in Santarém who are farming this way are responsible. We preserve and we respect nature. We provide jobs and opportunities in a place where there were none" (Adams 2015, 91). The economics of land use also defines the Cerrado as wasteland. Brazilian farmers in Rondonia claimed to be pioneers, founders, and adventurers; they took pride in transforming forest to land and open land to farm land, all while continuing farming and migration histories (Cordeiro 2018). Southern Brazilians did the same in Western Bahia, although while claiming to generate wealth they did so by deforesting the land, dispossessing communities, and exploiting the workers (Haesbaert 1998). Brazilian farmers in Bolivia also produce a hegemony of productivism and extractivism while claiming to bring development, modernity, technology, know-how, and capital to that country (Valdivia 2010).

18. The Chinese government labels Tibet as a wasteland in reference to labor practices and landscape features. Land without agriculture was regarded by state bureaucrats as empty, and the state policy was to "attack the grasslands" and wage war against the earth (Yeh 2013, 64). What existed was seen as waste, barbaric, empty. Labeling the landscape as waste was a veiled labeling of Tibetans as wasteful, lazy, and uncivilized. The Chinese state offered transformation of the land as well as the people.

19. This is despite the identification of the Cerrado as a biodiversity hotspot and a conservation priority (Mittermeier et al. 2004; Myers et al. 2000).

20. Eloy et al. find that these traditional land-use practices have been excluded from Forest Law legislation due to (1) strong opposition to any use of cattle or fire on sensitive biomes despite long-term use of fire to manage the Cerrado (Welch 2014; Welch et al. 2013); (2) the weakness of traditional populations and family farmers in policy setting; and (3) support from agribusiness for these measures as an acceptable cost of business and as a way of legitimizing their sustainability and environmentalist discourse compared to slash-and-burn Indigenous communities (Eloy et al. 2016).

21. For example, Nicholas Kawa's (2016) work on "terra preta do indio" in Amazonia connects soil chemistry, the fallout from the US Civil War, pre-Colombian Indigenous populations, and Caboclo communities today. "Terra preta do indio" (black Indian earth) has higher pH, more stable organic matter, and higher concentration of plant-available phosphorous and other nutrients than the predominant soils of the region. This fertile soil is what soil scientists call an anthropogenic soil; it was created by human hands. Indigenous communities added biochar to the soil; this transformed it slowly from red soil, with few plant-available nutrients, to black soil high in organic matter and high in plant-available nutrients. Today local groups call farming in the black Amazonian earth *uma batalha* (a battle) in comparison with red Amazonian soils. Terra preta soils allow cultivation of crops with higher nutrient demands, but they also demand greater labor because of increased weed and pest pressure. The burden of tilling black soils blurs the common distinction of fertile/infertile or productive/unproductive soil. Soil becomes burdensome when it is overly fertile and thus attracts unwanted insects and plants, which calls for greater labor. Kawa suggests seeing soil as a "collaborative engagement with this diversity of lifeforms" (Kawa 2016, 71). This view may help move us beyond deficit models of soil quality in which difference is equated with lack, and quality is based on suitability for industrial row crop monocultures.

22. For example, white settler colonialists in the United States not only socially constructed arid landscape of the Southwest as worthless and fit only for savage, violent, backward people but they also restricted shepherding, destroyed peach orchards in blatant attempts to make them into wasteland, and discredited and disallowed environmentally appropriate livelihoods. Their final blow was the actual making of toxic landscapes through the expansion of uranium mines and spills (Voyles 2015).

23. For white settlers in the Dakotas, land was claimed by damming rivers and plowing soil on Indigenous peoples' land where their ancestors are buried: "Because Native people remain barriers to capitalist development, their bodies needed to be removed—both from beneath and atop the soil—therefore eliminating their rightful relationship with the land" (Estes 2019, 47).

3. WORKING SOYLANDIA

1. For the most part, the farmers' framing of local farmworkers mirrored capitalists' views of Betsimisaraka workers in Madagascar who "came late to the job, quit without notice, absented themselves for days after being paid, took no pride in their tasks, were lazy, vulgar, and learned slowly," according to elites, reflecting that "land, labor, and

unequal relations of power are interlocked (Sodikoff 2012, 53, 72). Similarly, ethnic Chinese tie land use, land, and laziness to backwardness (Yeh 2013).

2. Despite many complaints about Brazilian regulations and the relative strength of the union of rural workers, few US farmers participate in negotiations between farmer and rural workers' union negotiations. Most avoid political involvement altogether. For example, while many Brazilian and some US farmers supported a national farmers' protest in June 2005, several US farmers openly derided the protest during interviews.

3. Frank also remembered the case of "Fazenda Kansas" in which a commodity broker bought land sight unseen for $25 and brought in neighbors.

> They didn't check anything, just started farming. Their first year was rice, which did really badly; the third year they brought me in. They need[ed] to save the farm. . . . I needed to see irrigation work; they promised that the irrigation guy had bought into the project and was committed. Turned out he sold them all bad parts, had very little pressure, could not even keep up with evapotranspiration. Needed a lot of money to make it work. During that first year IBAMA showed up and said they had to stop and leave the area—it was a federal nature reserve. He called one of the main investors and turns out it was the second time they had been notified by IBAMA, nobody had informed him though. So the investor knew irrigation didn't work, knew IBAMA was on their case. Several of the other farms had some land in federally reserved spaces too.

4. Brazilian agribusiness is particularly creative in their use of Instagram, Facebook, and other venues to glamorize large-scale agriculture. The rise of agronejo music is a stunning example of the glamorization of agriculture in Brazil (Marshall 2022).

5. Eddie remembered one instance when an investor suggested replacing a small, inexpensive part of the discs, which are used for chopping crop stubble. Eddie highlighted that while the farm was "spending millions and millions of dollars in fertilizer and seed and chemicals and sprayers," this 2,000 reais expense paid immediate dividends in improved chopping.

4. FLEXIBLE FARMING AND THE WEEDINESS OF SOYLANDIA

1. This nomenclature of clean fields is shared by Brazilian farmers nearby and Argentinian farmers in the Gran Chaco (Zorzoli 2022).

2. For more perspectives on social science engagements with soil, see Krzywoszynska and Marchesi 2020, VanWinkle and Friedman 2017, Lyons 2020, Marchesi 2016, and Goldstein 2016.

3. This also differs from soy farmers, even elite soy farmers in India who prefer manure and other nonsynthetic fertilizers and a soil-building approach described by Richa Kumar:

> Soil fertility was understood not as the addition of specific external nutrients such as DAP or urea (nitrogen). Upper-caste farmers added chemical fertilizers to these plots, yet the results were poor. Fertility referred to the intrinsic strength of the soil, which could only be nourished over the long term through two processes: manure and mud.
>
> Every year in the summer cart loads of animal manure were spread on the fields to improve the fertility by upper-caste farmers and those from economically better-off *adivasi* households. This was done in spite of using chemical fertilizers such as DAP for soyabean and urea for wheat.
>
> Similarly, mud from the bed of the village pond or other low-lying areas, which dried up in the summer, was added to improve soil fertility. It was also useful in levelling parts of the field that were low lying and tended to get waterlogged.

> Suraj Jat had put 1,000 trolleys of mud in some of his fields from the village pond in the summer of 2006. Suraj recalled that his father used to put cow dung (*gobar ki khad*) and plough into the field a green crop of jute (*san ki hari khad*). The next year's output of soyabean used to be very good and weeds would also be negligible. (Kumar 2016, 135)

4. However, many resist the adoption of no-tillage due to preferences for "clean field" aesthetics, spring planting timing, and avoiding overuse of herbicides (Kawa 2021).

5. Serena Stein and Jessie Luna describe a similar feeling among Mozambican farmers:

> Pesticides clung to Lino's clothing after a long day on the farm, giving him a cheiro de sucesso, or the "smell of success," as he called it. . . . The chemical cheiro wafting from his shirt, skin, and hair was the sensorial evidence of an industrious spirit. The cheiro tied the danger of exposure to values of sacrifice, which played an important role in the emerging ideal of masculinity for these young farmers. That is, Lino demonstrated his knowledge of the risks of handling pesticides. His children were not to accompany him to the fields when he was spraying. He instructed them to wash his tomatoes thoroughly to remove the residues before eating. Yet, in his spraying demonstrations for his laborers, Lino did not wear protective gear. Soaked in the acrid smell and sticky residues, with knowledge of the potential harms of exposure, he exhibited a drive toward modernity, at whatever cost. (S. Stein and Luna 2021, 99)

6. Control of fungi in the soil enabled year-round, massive scales of monocultures of industrial strawberries, intensive and abusive use of migrant farm labor, control not only of land but also of soil, and cheap strawberries (Guthman 2019).

7. I speak of weeds as referenced by farmers and agronomists; but understanding that the division of plants as crops and weeds is problematic (T. VanWinkle 2018).

5. VALUE AND COMMUNITY IN SOYLANDIA

1. I found that, for the most part, they were generous with their time, open during interviews, and willing to address difficult questions. I believe the consultant's experience with them led him to characterize them as such, but I had a professional if not warm relationship with most of the farmers. It was not joyful, but neither was it miserable.

2. The (dis)connection between economy and market is an enduring question of social science. In *Economic and Philosophic Manuscripts of 1844*, Marx argues that capital estranges workers from nature, society, and even their own body and work. "With the increasing value of the world of things proceeds in direct proportion the devaluation of the world of men. Labor produces not only commodities; it produces itself and the worker as a commodity" (Marx and Engels 1978, 71). The feminist economic anthropologist Sylvia Yanagisako (2002) warns against assuming political classes share common interests; kinship, gender, and family, she argues, are underaddressed by Marx but crucial in the structuring of capitalist action. The family farm is often juxtaposed against multinational corporations and capital, but these family farms (like the family firms analyzed by Yanagisako) reproduce themselves by engaging with capital. Consequently, both the worker and the capitalist are estranged from society, nature, and themselves.

3. Alberto Arce (2009) illustrates the production of difference within communities and in relation to the market. In a small Guatemalan village, coffee producers fracture along lines of class, gender, and value as they pursue market alternatives that support their household and personal needs. While women pursue a coffee roasting and direct trade relationship with consumers in the United States, their husbands decry their distraction

from work in the house. At the same time, men disagree over their visions of progress for the community and the market alternatives that would support these visions.

4. This antagonism is not new to rural US communities. Kathryn Dudley (2003) found an entrenchment of the entrepreneurial self and a disintegration of rural communities into antagonistic networks of blame, resentment, and perceived injustices. One Minnesota farmer recounted resentfully the failure of justice during the 1980s farm crisis: "I know guys that had big debt write-offs in the '80s. Who had to pay that debt write-off? I did! Through higher interest rates. . . . You're subsidizing the guy that's competing against you!" (Dudley 1996, 52). Responsibility, justice, and praise are expressed in individual terms in response to individual actions or inaction. Thus the market, government, and agribusiness are located at the periphery of debates of value, merit, and justice; and individuals are placed at the center. Dudley finds that, in postcrisis Minnesota, individuality is not contrary to community, but constitutive of it.

5. Serena Stein and Jessie Luna offer a striking contrast among soy farmers in Mozambique who make sure to return home "dirtied with soil, sweat, and chemicals as material evidence of [their] dedication to farming" (2021, 99).

6. The term "sack of soy" refers to the market value of 60 kilograms of soybeans. One also has the option of delivering literal sacks of soy as payment. A search for "sacks of soy" on Google Scholar on February 2, 2018, returned fourteen results (one of which is my own discussion of the term in a published paper). Even a search for the Portuguese term *saco de soja* returned only 108 results. It is not a widely used term in agricultural studies or markets, yet it is part of common speech in Brazil. The term was first introduced to me in an interview with Caleb Carter, who proposed I make it part of my study: "I'd just like to put a bug in your ear; I'd be interested if you talk to people who've invested in Brazilian agriculture, I'm guessing they'll give you information in dollars. If you talk to people who are operating in Brazil I'm guessing they will tell you sacks, hectares, and that type of thing and if that seems like it's not a big piece of information I think it's huge. Because of the way they measure success, the way they measure results, the way they measure stuff." True to his lead, most US farmers responded poorly to "sacks of soy" and rarely used the term, in fact more often using it as an example of the backwardness of Brazilian farmers.

6. THE AFTERMATH

1. Studies show that decreasing and erratic precipitation in the Cerrado is correlated with deforestation in the Amazon (Coe et al. 2017).

2. It is unclear whether he meant the Venezuelan state, Venezuelan businesses, or Venezuelan farmers.

CONCLUSION

1. Argentinian farmers in the Pampas take advantage of extremely cheap land to profit from even low production on marginal lands and from the speculative profit of "rehabilitating" land and selling it for far more than they purchased it for (Zorzoli 2022).

2. In Ian's words:

> They're the first or second largest farm management company in the Midwest, half a million acres under management. A lot of their clients are heirs, people who inherit the land who don't know anything about it. So [the company] manages the land, collects the money and makes sure the land is being taken care of and charge a management fee for doing that. And down here, they set up a fund in the US that their clients invested in and then they set up the farm. They

operate a similar system as in the US. They hired me to farm it for them and then they collect a management fee for it—make sure I'm doing a good job. We've farmed land for them back in the US for thirty years so that's how we, that's how they got started here 'cause we were here, and they approached us.

AFTERWORD

1. As Ane Gracia notes in her ethnography, "The temporalities produced by soy can be understood and experienced in different ways that relate the people who live them within a social dynamic. This exercise of looking in depth at reality, at soy, at people, is a necessary analysis to understand these many realities" (Gracia 2017, 173).

2. To the Mennonites, "worldly" connoted non-Mennonite people, ideas, and ways of life.

APPENDIX

1. In my research with Mennonites the phrase was "I don't know if you're an atheist, but ..."

References

Aase, Tor Halfdan, Ram P. Chaudhary, and Ole R. Vetaas. 2010. "Farming Flexibility and Food Security under Climatic Uncertainty: Manang, Nepal Himalaya." *Area* 42 (2): 228–38.

Abdala, Guilherme C., Linda S. Caldas, Michael Haridasan, and George Eiten. 1998. "Above and Belowground Organic Matter and Root:Shoot Ratio in a Cerrado in Central Brazil." *Brazilian Journal of Ecology* 2 (1): 11–23.

Adams, Ryan. 2010. "Elite Landowners in Santarém: Ranchers, Gaúchos, and the Arrival of Soybeans in the Amazon." PhD diss., Indiana University Bloomington.

———. 2015. "An Emerging Alliance of Ranchers and Farmers in the Brazilian Amazon." *Tipití: Journal of the Society for the Anthropology of Lowland South America* 13 (1): 63–78.

Ag Brazil. 2012. "Ag Brazil: Services." Ag Brazil. Accessed May 12, 2012. http://www.agbrazil.com/agbrazil_services.htm.

Alcântara, Denilson Moreira de, and Guiomar Inez Germani. 2010. "As Comunidades de Fundo e Fecho de Pasto na Bahia: Luta na Terra e Suas Espacializações." *Revista de Geografia* 27 (1): 40–57.

Alencar, Ane, Cassio Pereira, Isabel Castro, Alcilene Cardoso, Lucimar Souza, Rosana Costa, Antônio José Bentes, Osvaldo Stella, Andrea Azevedo, and Jarlene Gomes. 2016. *Desmatamento nos Assentamentos da Amazônia: Histórico, Tendências e Oportunidades*. Brasilia, DF: IPAM.

Almeida, Luciana. 2017. "Na Festa, no Escritório, na Cabine do Trator: Notas sobre o Comércio de Insumos Agrícolas no 'Agronegócio' da Soja." *Política & Sociedade* 16 (35): 380–402.

Altieri, Miguel. 2009. "The Ecological Impacts of Large-Scale Agrofuel Monoculture Production Systems in the Americas." *Bulletin of Science, Technology & Society* 29: 236–44.

Alves, Vicente Eudes Lemos. 2006. "Mobilização e Modernização nos Cerrados Piauienses: Formação Territorial no Império do Agronegócio." PhD diss., Universidade de São Paulo.

———. 2009. "O Mercado de Terras nos Cerrados Piauianses: Modernização e Exclusão." *Agrária, São Paulo*, no. 10–11: 73–98.

Amado, Janaína. 1990. "The Frontier in Comparative Perspective: The United States and Brazil." In *Frontier in Comparative Perspectives: The United States and Brazil*, edited by Janaína Amado, Walter Nugent, and Warren Dean, 28–55. Washington DC : Latin American Program, Wilson Center.

Anderson, J. L. 2020. "'You're a Bigger Man': Technology and Agrarian Masculinity in Postwar America." *Agricultural History* 94 (1): 1–23.

Appel, Hannah. 2012. "Offshore Work: Oil, Modularity, and the How of Capitalism in Equatorial Guinea." *American Ethnologist* 39 (4): 692–709.

———. 2019. *The Licit Life of Capitalism: US Oil in Equatorial Guinea*. Illustrated edition. Durham, NC: Duke University Press.

Araujo, Gabriel. 2020. "Brazil Senate Clears Hurdle for Foreign Ownership of Rural Land." Reuters, December 16, 2020. https://www.reuters.com/article/us-brazil-land-idUSKBN28Q2UU.

Arce, Alberto. 2009. "Living in Times of Solidarity: Fair Trade and the Fractured Life Worlds of Guatemalan Coffee Farmers." *Journal of International Development* 21 (7): 1031–41.

Arce, Alberto, and Norman Long. 2000. "Reconfiguring Modernity and Development from an Anthropological Perspective." In *Anthropology, Development and Modernities: Exploring Discourse, Counter-Tendencies and Violence*, edited by Alberto Arce and Norman Long, 1–30. London: Routledge.

Asselin, Victor. 1982. *Grilagem: Corrupção e Violência em Terras do Carajás*. Petrópolis: Vozes.

Azevedo, Andrea A., Raoni Rajão, Marcelo A. Costa, Marcelo C. C. Stabile, Marcia N. Macedo, Tiago N. P. dos Reis, Ane Alencar, Britaldo S. Soares-Filho, and Rayane Pacheco. 2017. "Limits of Brazil's Forest Code as a Means to End Illegal Deforestation." *Proceedings of the National Academy of Sciences* 114 (29): 7653–58.

Barbosa de Jesus, Priscila, and Maria Geralda de Almeida. 2022. "Conflitos e Disputas pela Terra e pela Agua: Os Povos Geraizeiros de Correntina-BA e a Expansão do Agronegócio no Cerrado do Matopiba." *Geosaberes: Revista de Estudos Geoeducacionais* 13 (1): 40–54.

Barlett, Peggy F. 1993. *American Dreams, Rural Realities: Family Farms in Crisis*. Chapel Hill: University of North Carolina Press.

Barlett, Peggy F., and Katherine Jewsbury Conger. 2004. "Three Visions of Masculine Success on American Farms." *Men and Masculinities* 7 (2): 205–27.

Barreto, Eldo Moreira, Elizete Carvalho F. Barreto, and Isabel Figueiredo. 2017. "Comunidades Tradicionais de Fecho de Pasto e Seu Modo Próprio de Convivência com o Cerrado: História, Direitos e Desafios." Correntina, Bahia: Associação dos Pequenos Criadores do Fecho de Pasto de Clemente—ACCFC. https://ispn.org.br/comunidades-tradicionais-de-fecho-de-pasto-e-seu-modo-proprio-de-convivencia-com-o-cerrado-historia-direitos-e-desafios/.

Bastos Lima, Mairon G., and Laura Kmoch. 2021. "Neglect Paves the Way for Dispossession: The Politics of 'Last Frontiers' in Brazil and Myanmar." *World Development* 148 (December): 105681.

Batistella, Mateus, and Gustavo Souza Valladares. 2009. "Farming Expansion and Land Degradation in Western Bahia, Brazil." *Biota Neotropica* 9 (3): 61–76.

Bell, Michael. 2010. *Farming for Us All: Practical Agriculture and the Cultivation of Sustainability*. State College: Penn State University Press.

Bell, Shannon Elizabeth, Alicia Hullinger, and Lilian Brislen. 2015. "Manipulated Masculinities: Agribusiness, Deskilling, and the Rise of the Businessman-Farmer in the United States." *Rural Sociology* 80 (3): 285–313.

Bellacasa, Maria Puig de la. 2017. *Matters of Care*. Minneapolis: University of Minnesota Press.

Besky, Sarah. 2017. "Fixity: On the Inheritance and Maintenance of Tea Plantation Houses in Darjeeling, India." *American Ethnologist* 44 (4): 617–31.

Bezerra, Juscelino Eudâmidas, and Cíntia Lima Gonzaga. 2019. "O Discurso Regional do Matopiba no Poder Legislativo Federal: Práticas e Políticas." *Revista NERA*, no. 47: 46–63.

Biolsi, Thomas. 2018. *Power and Progress on the Prairie*. Minneapolis: University of Minnesota Press.

Bizerril, Marcelo X. A. 2004. "Children's Perceptions of Brazilian Cerrado Landscapes and Biodiversity." *Journal of Environmental Education* 35 (4): 47–58.

Blaikie, Piers, and Harold Brookfield. 1987. *Land Degradation and Society*. London: Methuen.

Blanc, Jacob. 2015. "Enclaves of Inequality: Brasiguaios and the Transformation of the Brazil-Paraguay Borderlands." *Journal of Peasant Studies* 42 (1): 145–58.

Blanchette, Alex. 2015. "Herding Species: Biosecurity, Posthuman Labor, and the American Industrial Pig." *Cultural Anthropology* 30 (4): 640–69.

———. 2020. *Porkopolis: American Animality, Standardized Life, and the Factory Farm*. Durham, NC: Duke University Press.

BNDES. n.d. "Requisitos para Enquadramento no Pronaf." BNDES. Accessed December 14, 2017. http://www.bndes.gov.br/wps/portal/site/home/ financiamento/produto/pronaf-requisitos.

Boadle, Anthony. 2019. "Emboldened by Bolsonaro, Armed Invaders Encroach on Brazil's Tribal Lands." Reuters, March 3, 2019. https://www.reuters.com/article/ us-brazil-indigenous-insight-idUSKCN1QK0BG.

Boaventura, Karita de Jesus, Claiton Marcio da Silva, and Sandro Dutra e Silva. 2023. "Building Soil Fertility: Embrapa and the Agronomic Development for the 'Conquest' of the Brazilian Cerrado (1975–95)." *Historia Agraria* 89:247–78.

Bobrow-Strain, Aaron. 2007. *Intimate Enemies: Landowners, Power, and Violence in Chiapas*. Durham, NC: Duke University Press.

Borlaug, Norman E., and Christopher Dowswell. 2003. "Feeding a World of Ten Billion People: A 21st Century Challenge." In *In the Wake of the Double Helix: From the Green Revolution to the Gene Revolution; Proceedings of an International Congress, University of Bologna, Italy, May 27 to 31, 2003*, edited by Roberto Tuberosa, Ronald Phillips, and Mike Gale, 3–23. Bologna: Avenue Media.

Borras, Saturnino M., Jennifer C. Franco, S. Ryan Isakson, Les Levidow, and Pietje Vervest. 2016. "The Rise of Flex Crops and Commodities: Implications for Research." *Journal of Peasant Studies* 43 (1): 93–115.

Botelho, Adielson Correia, and Maristela de Paula Andrade. 2012. "A Expansão da Silvicultura: Impactos Socioambientais em Territórios Camponeses no Leste Maranhense." In *Encontro Nacional de Geografia Agrária*, 1–13. Uberlandia, MG.

Brandão, Paulo Roberto Baqueiro. 2015. "Questões Emergentes para um (Novo) Temário da Geografia Política do Oeste Baiano." *Redes* 20 (3): 382–400.

Brannstrom, Christian, Wendy Jepson, Anthony M. Filippi, Daniel Redo, Zengwang Xu, and Srinivasan Ganesh. 2008. "Land Change in the Brazilian Savanna (Cerrado), 1986–2002: Comparative Analysis and Implications for Land-Use Policy." *Land Use Policy* 25 (4): 579–95.

Braun, Bruce. 2015. "The 2013 Antipode RGS-IBG Lecture: New Materialisms and Neoliberal Natures." *Antipode* 47 (1): 1–14.

Brumer, Anita. 2004. "Gênero e Agricultura: A Situação da Mulher na Agricultura do Rio Grande do Sul." *Revista Estudos Feministas* 12 (1): 205–27.

Buttel, Frederick H. 1989. "The US Farm Crisis and the Restructuring of American Agriculture: Domestic and International Dimensions." In *The International Farm Crisis*, edited by David Goodman and Michael Redclift, 46–83. New York: St. Martin's Press.

Cabral, Lídia, Poonam Pandey, and Xiuli Xu. 2022. "Epic Narratives of the Green Revolution in Brazil, China, and India." *Agriculture and Human Values*, no. 39: 249–67.

Calmon, Daniela. 2022. "Shifting Frontiers: The Making of Matopiba in Brazil and Global Redirected Land Use and Control Change." *Journal of Peasant Studies* 49 (2): 263–87.

Campbell, Jeremy M. 2015. *Conjuring Property: Speculation and Environmental Futures in the Brazilian Amazon*. Seattle: University of Washington Press.

Carrillo, Ian R., and Annabel Ipsen. 2021. "Worksites as Sacrifice Zones: Structural Precarity and Covid-19 in US Meatpacking." *Sociological Perspectives* 64 (5): 726–46.

Castro, Luís Felipe Perdigão de, Eva Hershaw, and Sérgio Sauer. 2018. "Estrangeirização e Internacionalização de Terras no Brasil: Oportunidades para Quem?" *Estudos Internacionais: Revista de Relações Internacionais da PUC Minas* 5 (2): 74–102.

Chaddad, Fabio. 2016. "Enabling Conditions." In *The Economics and Organization of Brazilian Agriculture*, edited by Fabio Chaddad, 19–44. San Diego, CA: Academic Press.

Chao, Sophie, Wendy Wolford, Andrew Ofstehage, Shallal Guttal, Euclides Gonçalves, and Fernanda Ayala. 2023. "The Plantationocene as Analytical Concept: A Forum for Dialogue and Reflection." *Journal of Peasant Studies* 51 (3): 541–63.

Chung, Youjin. 2024. *Sweet Deal, Bitter Landscape: Gender Politics and Liminality in Tanzania's New Enclosures*. Ithaca, NY: Cornell University Press.

Coe, Michael T., Paulo M. Brando, Linda A. Deegan, Marcia N. Macedo, Christopher Neill, and Divino V. Silvério. 2017. "The Forests of the Amazon and Cerrado Moderate Regional Climate and Are the Key to the Future." *Tropical Conservation Science* 10:1–6.

Coimbra Jr., Carlos, Nancy M. Flowers, Francisco M. Salzano, and Ricardo V. Santos, eds. 2004. *The Xavánte in Transition: Health, Ecology, and Bioanthropology in Central Brazil*. Ann Arbor: University of Michigan Press.

Colloredo-Mansfeld, Rudi. 1999. *The Native Leisure Class: Consumption and Cultural Creativity in the Andes*. Chicago: University of Chicago Press.

———. 2009. *Fighting Like a Community: Andean Civil Society in an Era of Indian Uprisings*. Chicago: University of Chicago Press.

Cordeiro, Manuela Souza Siqueira. 2018. "Pioneiros, Fundadores e Aventureiros: A Ocupação de Terras em Rondônia." *Revista de Antropologia* 61 (1): 125–46.

Correia, João Roberto, Adriana Reatto, and Silvio Tulio Spera. 2004. "Solos e Suas Relacoes com o Uso e o Manejo." In *Cerrado: Correção do Solo e Adubação*, edited by Djalma Martinao Gomes de Sousa and Edson Lobato, 29–62. 2nd ed. Brasilia, DF: Embrapa.

Correia, Joel E. 2019. "Soy States: Resource Politics, Violent Environments and Soybean Territorialization in Paraguay." *Journal of Peasant Studies* 46 (2): 316–36.

Costa, A. S., C. L. Costa, and H. F. G. Sauer. 1973. "Surto de Mosca-Branca em Culturas do Paraná e São Paulo." *Anais da Sociedade Entomologica do Brasil* 2 (1): 20–30.

Costa, Diandra Hoffmann, and Marcos Leandro Mondardo. 2013. "A Modernização da Agricultura no Oeste Baiano: Migração Sulista e Novas Territorialidades." *Revista Geonorte* 4 (12): 1347–61.

Craib, Raymond. 2022. *Adventure Capitalism: A History of Libertarian Exit, from the Era of Decolonization to the Digital Age*. Oakland, CA: PM Press.

Cronon, William. 1992. "A Place for Stories: Nature, History, and Narrative." *Journal of American History* 78 (4): 1347–76.

Cunha, Tassio Barreto. 2016. "A Produção no Oeste da Bahia Controlada por Estrangeiros e a Sua Vinculação/Subordinação ao Capital." *Revista Campo-Território* 11 (25): 5–34.

Deleuze, Gilles, and Pierre Félix Guattari. 1987. *A Thousand Plateaus: Capitalism and Schizophrenia*. Minneapolis: University of Minnesota Press.

Diniz, José Alexandre Felizola. 1984. "Modernização e Conflito na Fronteira Ocidental do Nordeste." *Revista GeoNordeste* 1 (1): 12–20.

Dolzan, Marcio. 2017. "'Não Podemos Abrir as Portas para Todo Mundo', Diz Bolsonaro em Palestra na Hebraica." *Estadão*, April 3, 2017. https://politica. estadao.com.br/noticias/geral,nao-podemos-abrir-as-portas-para-todo-mundo-diz-bolsonaro-em-palestra-na-hebraica,70001725522.

Duarte e Silva, Sandro. 2010. "A Natureza contra o Progresso: Mitos e Narrativas do 'Destino Bandeirante' na Expansão Desenvolvimentista." *Textos de Historia: Revista do Programa de Pós-Graduação em História da UnB* 17 (1): 85–106.

Dudley, Kathryn Marie. 1996. "The Problem of Community in Rural America." *Culture & Agriculture* 18 (2): 47–57.

———. 2002. *Debt and Dispossession: Farm Loss in America's Heartland*. Chicago: University of Chicago Press.

———. 2003. "The Entrepreneurial Self: Identity and Morality in a Midwestern Farming Community." In *Fighting for the Farm: Rural America Transformed*, edited by Jane Adams, 175–91. Philadelphia: University of Pennsylvania Press.

Durigan, Giselda, Cássia Beatriz Munhoz, Maria José Brito Zakia, Rafael S. Oliveira, Natashi A. L. Pilon, Raul Silva Telles do Valle, Bruno M. T. Walter, Eliane A. Honda, and Arnildo Pott. 2022. "Cerrado Wetlands: Multiple Ecosystems Deserving Legal Protection as a Unique and Irreplaceable Treasure." *Perspectives in Ecology and Conservation* 20 (3): 185–96.

Edelman, Marc. 2021. "Hollowed Out Heartland, USA: How Capital Sacrificed Communities and Paved the Way for Authoritarian Populism." *Journal of Rural Studies* 82 (February): 505–17.

Eloy, Ludivine, Catherine Aubertin, Fabiano Toni, Silvia Laine Borges Lúcio, and Marion Bosgiraud. 2016. "On the Margins of Soy Farms: Traditional Populations and Selective Environmental Policies in the Brazilian Cerrado." *Journal of Peasant Studies* 43 (2): 494–516.

Eloy, Ludivine, Isabel Belloni Schmidt, Silvia Laine Borges, Maxmiller Cardoso Ferreira, and Teomenilton A. dos Santos. 2018. "Seasonal Fire Management by Traditional Cattle Ranchers Prevents the Spread of Wildfire in the Brazilian Cerrado." *Ambio* 48:890–99.

Elson, Diane. 1979. *Value: The Representation of Labour in Capitalism*. London: Humanities Press International.

Embrapa. 2013. *Sistema Brasileiro de Classificação de Solos*. Brasilia, DF: Embrapa.

Engel-Di Mauro, Salvatore. 2014. *Ecology, Soils, and the Left: An Ecosocial Approach*. New York: Palgrave Macmillan.

Escobar, Arturo. 2007. "Worlds and Knowledges Otherwise: The Latin American Modernity/Coloniality Research Program." *Cultural Studies* 21 (2–3): 179–210.

———. 2008. *Territories of Difference: Place, Movements, Life, Redes*. Durham, NC: Duke University Press.

Estes, Nick. 2019. *Our History Is the Future: Standing Rock Versus the Dakota Access Pipeline, and the Long Tradition of Indigenous Resistance*. New York: Verso.

Evans-Pritchard, E. E. 1976. *Witchcraft, Oracles and Magic among the Azande*. London: Oxford University Press.

Fairbairn, Madeleine. 2015. "Foreignization, Financialization and Land Grab Regulation." *Journal of Agrarian Change* 15 (4): 581–91.

———. 2020. *Fields of Gold: Financing the Global Land Rush*. Ithaca, NY: Cornell University Press.

FAOSTAT. 2020. "FAOSTAT." 2020. http://www.fao.org/faostat/en/#home. Accessed March 4, 2020.

Favareto, Arilson, Louise Nakagawa, Suzana Kleeb, Paulo Seifer, and Marcos Pó. 2019. "Ha Mais Pobreza e Desigualdade do Que Bem Estar e Riqueza nos Municipios do MATOPIBA." *Revista NERA*, no. 47: 348–81.

Fearnside, Philip M. 2001. "Soybean Cultivation as a Threat to the Environment in Brazil." *Environmental Conservation* 28 (1): 23–38.

Ferreira, M. 1946. *Terras e Indios do Alto Xingu.* São Paulo: Melhoramentos.

Feuer, Reeshon. 1956. "An Exploratory Investigation of the Soils and Agricultural Potential of the Soils of the Future Federal District in the Central Plateau of Brazil." PhD diss., Cornell University.

Filho, Jorge Ney Valois Rios. 2016. "Segregação Socioespacial na Cidade do Agronegócio de Luís Eduardo Magalhães (BA)." Diss., Universidade Federal da Bahia.

Flaskerud, George. 2003. "Brazil's Soybean Production and Impact." EB-79. Fargo: North Dakota State University. https://library.ndsu.edu/ir/bitstream/ handle/10365/4906/eb030079.pdf?sequence=1&isAllowed=y.

Folha de S.Paulo. 2019. "1969: Governo Federal Anuncia Plano para Desenvolvimento do 'Vazio Agrícola.'" *Folha de S.Paulo*, November 9, 2019, sec. Banco de Dados. https://www1.folha.uol.com.br/banco-de-dados/2019/11/1969-governo-federal-anuncia-plano-para-desenvolvimento-do-vazio-agricola.shtml.

Foweraker, J. 1981. *The Struggle for Land: A Political Economy of the Pioneer Frontier in Brazil from 1930 to the Present Day.* London: Cambridge University Press.

Franco, Carvalho. 1940. *Bandeiras e Bandeirantes de São Paolo.* São Paolo: Companhia Editora Nacional.

French, John D. 2004. *Drowning in Laws: Labor Law and Brazilian Political Culture.* Chapel Hill: University of North Carolina Press.

Freyre, Gilberto. 2011. *English in Brazil: Aspects of British Influence on the Life, Landscape and Culture of Brazil.* Oxford: Boulevard Books.

Gale, Fred, Constanza Valdes, and Mark Ash. 2019. "Interdependence of China, United States, and Brazil in Soybean Trade." Washington, DC: US Department of Agriculture, Economic Research Service. https://www.ers.usda.gov/ publications/pub-details/?pubid=93389.

Garfield, Seth. 2001. *Indigenous Struggle at the Heart of Brazil: State Policy, Frontier Expansion, and the Xavante Indians, 1937–1988.* Durham, NC: Duke University Press.

Gaspar, Rafael Bezerra, and Maristela de Paula Andrade. 2014. "Gaúchos no Maranhão: Agentes, Posições Sociais e Trajetórias em Novas Fronteiras do Agronegócio." *Pós Ciências Sociais* 11 (22): 109–28.

Gibson-Graham, J. K. 2006. *A Postcapitalist Politics.* Minneapolis: University of Minnesota Press.

Gidwani, Vinay K. 2008. *Capital, Interrupted: Agrarian Development and the Politics of Work in India.* Minneapolis: University of Minnesota Press.

Godoy, Cláudia Vieira, Claudine Dinali Santos Seixas, Rafael Moreira Soares, Franscismar Correa Marcelino-Guimarães, Maurício Conrado Meyer, and Leila Maria Costamilan. 2016. "Asian Soybean Rust in Brazil: Past, Present, and Future." *Pesquisa Agropecuária Brasileira* 51 (5): 407–21.

Goldstein, Jenny E. 2016. "Knowing the Subterranean: Land Grabbing, Oil Palm, and Divergent Expertise in Indonesia's Peat Soil." *Environment and Planning A* 48 (4): 754–70.

Gordillo, Gastón R. 2014. *Rubble: The Afterlife of Destruction.* Durham, NC: Duke University Press.

Gortázar, Naiara Galarraga. 2021. "Nem um Centímetro Mais para os Indígenas e para a Biodiversidade no Brasil de Bolsonaro." *El País Brasil*, August 20, 2021, sec. Brasil. https://brasil.elpais.com/brasil/2021-08-20/nem-um-centimetro-a-mais-para-os-indigenas-e-para-a-biodiversidade-no-brasil-de-bolsonaro.html.

Gracia, Ane Sesma. 2017. "O Capital no Deserto: A Soja, as Vacas e o Dinheiro no Oeste Baiano." PhD diss., Universidad Federal da Bahia.

Graeber, David. 2001. *Toward An Anthropological Theory of Value: The False Coin of Our Own Dreams.* New York: Palgrave.

——. 2013. "It Is Value That Brings Universes into Being." *HAU: Journal of Ethnographic Theory* 3 (2): 219–43.

Graham, Laura. 2009. "The Tractor Invasion." *Cultural Survival Quarterly*, June 2009. https://www.culturalsurvival.org/publications/cultural-survival-quarterly/tractor-invasion.

Grandin, Greg. 2010. *Fordlandia: The Rise and Fall of Henry Ford's Forgotten Jungle City.* New York: Henry Holt.

Gudeman, Stephen. 2001. *The Anthropology of Economy: Community, Market, and Culture.* Malden, MA: Blackwell.

Gudynas, Eduardo. 2008. "The New Bonfire of Vanities: Soybean Cultivation and Globalization in South America." *Development* 51 (4): 512–18.

Guthman, Julie. 2019. *Wilted: Pathogens, Chemicals, and the Fragile Future of the Strawberry Industry.* Berkeley: University of California Press.

Haesbaert, Rogério. 1998. "A Noção de Rede Regional: Reflexões a Partir da Migração 'Gaúcha' no Brasil." *Revista Território* 3 (4): 55–71.

Harnack, Curtis. 2011. *Gentlemen on the Prairie: Victorians in Pioneer Iowa.* Iowa City: University of Iowa Press.

Harris, Bryan. 2021. "Brazil's New Frontier Is Transforming Its Fortunes—but at What Cost?" *Financial Times*, February 11, 2021. https://www.ft.com/content/bc8a217f-804d-4b32-b2ea-e06e08e9eb7a.

Heaberlin, Bradi, and Annie Shattuck. 2023. "Farm Stress and the Production of Rural Sacrifice Zones." *Journal of Rural Studies* 97 (January): 70–80.

Hecht, Susanna B. 2005. "Soybeans, Development and Conservation on the Amazon Frontier." *Development and Change* 36 (2): 375–404.

Hecht, Susanna B., and Charles Mann. 2008. "How Brazil Outfarmed the American Farmer." *Fortune* 157.

Hecht, Susanna, and Raoni Rajão. 2020. "From 'Green Hell' to 'Amazonia Legal': Land Use Models and the Re-Imagination of the Rainforest as a New Development Frontier." *Land Use Policy* 96 (July): 103871.

Hetherington, Kregg. 2013. "Beans before the Law: Knowledge Practices, Responsibility, and the Paraguayan Soy Boom." *Cultural Anthropology* 28 (1): 65–85.

——. 2020. *The Government of Beans: Regulating Life in the Age of Monocrops.* Durham, NC: Duke University Press.

Ho, Karen. 2009. *Liquidated: An Ethnography of Wall Street.* Durham, NC: Duke University Press.

Hoelle, Jeffrey. 2015. *Rainforest Cowboys: The Rise of Ranching and Cattle Culture in Western Amazonia.* Austin: University of Texas Press.

Holland, Dorothy, William Lachicotte Jr, Debra Skinner, and Carol Cain, eds. 2001. *Identity and Agency in Cultural Worlds.* Cambridge, MA: Harvard University Press.

Holmes, Seth. 2013. *Fresh Fruit, Broken Bodies: Migrant Farmworkers in the United States.* Berkeley: University of California Press.

Hoppe, Robert A. 2014. "Structure and Finances of U.S. Farms: Family Farm Report, 2014 Edition." Economic Information Bulletin Number 132. USDA Economic Research Service. https://www.ers.usda.gov/webdocs/publications/43913/50364_eib-132.pdf?v=.

Hosono, Akio, Carlos Magno Campos da Rocha, and Yutaka Hongo. 2016. *Development for Sustainable Agriculture: The Brazilian Cerrado*. New York: Springer.

Hunke, Philip, Eva Nora Mueller, Boris Schröder, and Peter Zeilhofer. 2015. "The Brazilian Cerrado: Assessment of Water and Soil Degradation in Catchments under Intensive Agricultural Use." *Ecohydrology* 8 (6): 1154–80.

Hutchinson, Harry. 1957. *Village and Plantation Life in Northeastern Brazil*. Seattle: University of Washington Press.

Imbirussu, Erica, Gilca Garcia de Oliveria, and Guiomar Inez Germani. 2017. "Fundos de Pasto: Community Governance of Common Resources in North-East Brazil." In *Towards Just and Sustainable Economies: The Social and Solidarity Economy North and South*, edited by Peter North and Molly Scott Cato, 155–76. Bristol, UK: Policy Press.

Izá Pereira, Lorena, Lara Buscioli, Camila Origuéla, José Sobreiro Filho, and Bernardo Fernandes. 2017. "Disputas Territoriais em Correntina–BA: Territorialização do Agronegócio, Resistência Popular e o Debate Paradigmático." *Boletim Dataluta* 118:2–9.

Janssen, Brandi. 2017. *Making Local Food Work: The Challenges and Opportunities of Today's Small Farmers*. Iowa City: University of Iowa Press.

Johnson, Allen W. 1971. *Sharecroppers of the Sertao*. Palo Alto, CA: Stanford University Press.

Kawa, Nicholas C. 2016. *Amazonia in the Anthropocene: People, Soils, Plants, Forests*. Austin: University of Texas Press.

——. 2021. "A 'Win-Win' for Soil Conservation? How Indiana Row-Crop Farmers Perceive the Benefits (and Trade-Offs) of No-Till Agriculture." *Culture, Agriculture, Food and Environment* 43 (1): 25–35.

Keller, Julie C. 2014. "'I Wanna Have My Own Damn Dairy Farm!': Women Farmers, Legibility, and Femininities in Rural Wisconsin, U.S." *Journal of Rural Social Sciences* 29 (1): 75.

Kiihl, Romeu, and E. Calvo. 2008. "A Soja no Brasil: Mais de 100 Anos de História, Quatro Décadas de Sucesso." *Agricultura Tropical: Quatro Décadas de Inovações Tecnológicas, Institucionais e Políticas*, edited by A. Albuquerque and A. Silva. Brasilia, DF: Embrapa Tecnologia da Informação.

Kirksey, Eben. 2015. *Emergent Ecologies*. Durham, NC: Duke University Press.

Klein, Herbert S., and Francisco Vidal Luna. 2018. *Feeding the World: Brazil's Transformation into a Modern Agricultural Economy*. London: Cambridge University Press.

Klink, Carlos A., and Ricardo B. Machado. 2005. "Conservation of the Brazilian Cerrado." *Conservation Biology* 19 (3): 707–13.

Kollnig, Sarah. 2019. "Industrial Chicken Meat and the Good Life in Bolivia." In *In Defense of Farmers: The Future of Agriculture in the Shadow of Corporate Power*, edited by Jane W. Gibson and Sara E. Alexander, 99–134. Lincoln: University of Nebraska Press.

Kosminsky, Ethel V. 2007. "Por uma Etnografia Feminista das Migrações Internacionais: Dos Estudos de Aculturação para os Estudos de Gênero." *Revista Estudos Feministas* 15 (3): 773–804.

Krone, Evander Eloi. 2023. "Tirar Comida da Terra para Não Se Matar no Veneno: Formas de Cooperar, Viver e de Trabalhar de Mulheres Assentadas do Vale do São Francisco." In *Cooperação, Diversidade e Criatividade: Transformações Sociomateriais em Territórios Latino-Americanos*, edited by Flávia Charão Marques and Alberto Arce, 75–105. Jundiaí: Paco e Littera.

Krzywoszynska, Anna, and Greta Marchesi. 2020. "Toward a Relational Materiality of Soils: Introduction." *Environmental Humanities* 12 (1): 190–204.

Kumar, Richa. 2016. *Rethinking Revolutions: Soyabean, Choupals, and the Changing Countryside in Central India.* New Delhi: Oxford University Press.

Lacerda, Renata. 2021. "A Cidade como Forma de Diferenciação: Famílias Pioneiras e Fundadores na Amazônia." *Wamon* 6 (1): 69–89.

Lambers, Hans, Patrícia de Britto Costa, Rafael S. Oliveira, and Fernando A. O. Silveira. 2020. "Towards More Sustainable Cropping Systems: Lessons from Native Cerrado Species." *Theoretical and Experimental Plant Physiology* 32 (3): 175–94.

Lapegna, Pablo. 2016. *Soybeans and Power: Genetically Modified Crops, Environmental Politics, and Social Movements in Argentina.* London: Oxford University Press.

Ledru, Marie-Pierre. 2002. "Late Quaternary History and Evolution of the Cerrados as Revealed by Palynological Records." In *The Cerrados of Brazil: Ecology and Natural History of Neotropical Savanna,* edited by Paolo S. Oliveira and Robert J. Marquis, 33–50. New York: Columbia University Press.

Le Guin, Ursula K. 2017. *Ursula K. Le Guin: The Hainish Novels and Stories.* Edited by Brian Attebery. Vol. 2. New York: Library of America.

Li, Tania Murray. 2014a. *Land's End: Capitalist Relations on an Indigenous Frontier.* Durham, NC: Duke University Press.

———. 2014b. "What Is Land? Assembling a Resource for Global Investment." *Transactions of the Institute of British Geographers* 39 (4): 589–602.

Liberti, Stefano, and Enrico Parenti. 2018. "Mozambique Won't Be Mato Grosso." *Le Monde Diplomatique,* June 7, 2018. https://mondediplo.com/2018/06/14mozambique.

Lima, Débora. 2019. *Terra, Trabalho e Acumulação: O Avanço da Soja na Região Matopiba.* PhD diss., Universidade Estadual de Campinas.

Lone, Stewart. 2001. *The Japanese Community in Brazil, 1908–1940.* London: Palgrave Macmillan UK.

Lopez, Mirabel Cristina Cardona. 2014. "Gaúchos em Luís Eduardo Magalhães: Os Modernizadores Tradicionalistas." Diss., Universidade Federal da Bahia.

Lyons, Kristina M. 2020. *Vital Decomposition: Soil Practitioners and Life Politics.* Durham, NC: Duke University Press.

MacDonald, James M., Penni Korb, and Robert A. Hoppe. 2013. "Farm Size and the Organization of U.S. Crop Farming." Economic Research Report 152. USDA Economic Research Service. https://www.ers.usda.gov/webdocs/publications/45108/39359_err152.pdf.

Mackey, Lee. 2011. "Legitimating Foreignization in Bolivia: Brazilian Agriculture and the Relations of Conflict and Consent in Santa Cruz." LDPI Working Paper Initiative. https://www.future-agricultures.org/wp-content/uploads/pdf-archive/Lee%20Mackey.pdf.

Mano, Ana, and Anthony Boadle. 2018. "Brazil's Wealthy Farm Belt Backs Trump-Like Presidential Candidate." Reuters, May 17, 2018. https://www.reuters.com/article/us-brazil-politics-bolsonaro-analysis-idUSKCN1II2SR.

MapBiomas. 2024. "Statistics." MapBiomas Brasil. https://brasil.mapbiomas.org/en/estatisticas/ Accessed January 4, 2024.

Marchesi, Greta. 2016. "The Blood of Heroes: Nationalist Bodies, National Soils, and the Scientific Conservation of the Federation of Colombian Coffee-Growers (1927–1946)." *Environment and Planning A: Economy and Space* 48 (4): 736–53.

Margolis, Maxine L. 1973. *The Moving Frontier: Social and Economic Change in a Southern Brazilian Community.* Gainesville: University Press of Florida.

——. 1977. "Historical Perspectives on Frontier Agriculture as an Adaptive Strategy." *American Ethnologist* 4 (1): 42–64.

Marshall, Euan. 2022. "How Agronejo Music Became an Arm of the Brazilian Far Right." Art Review. September 21, 2022. https://artreview.com/ how-agronejo-music-became-an-arm-of-the-brazilian-far-right/.

Marx, Karl. 2008. *Capital*. Oxford: Oxford University Press.

Marx, Karl, and Friedrich Engels. 1978. *The Marx-Engels Reader*. Edited by Robert C. Tucker. New York: W. W. Norton.

Maybury-Lewis, David. 1967. *Akwẽ-Shavante Society*. Oxford: Clarendon Press.

McVey, Marty, Phil Baumel, and Bob Wisner. 2000. "Brazilian Soybeans: What Is the Potential?" Iowa State University Extension and Outreach: Ag Decision Maker. 2000. http://www.extension.iastate.edu/agdm/articles/others/McVOct00.html.

Mier y Terán Giménez Cacho, Mateo. 2014. "The Political Ecology of Soybean Farming Systems in Mato Grosso, Brazil: A Cross-Scale Analysis of Farming Styles in Querência-MT." PhD thesis, University of Sussex.

——. 2016. "Soybean Agri-Food Systems Dynamics and the Diversity of Farming Styles on the Agricultural Frontier in Mato Grosso, Brazil." *Journal of Peasant Studies* 43 (2): 419–41.

Millar, Kathleen. 2018. *Reclaiming the Discarded: Life and Labor on Rio's Garbage Dump*. Durham, NC: Duke University Press.

Miller, Theresa L. 2019. *Plant Kin: A Multispecies Ethnography in Indigenous Brazil*. Austin: University of Texas Press.

Minkoff-Zern, Laura-Anne. 2012. "Pushing the Boundaries of Indigeneity and Agricultural Knowledge: Oaxacan Immigrant Gardening in California." *Agriculture and Human Values* 29 (3): 381–92.

Mittermeier, R. A., P. R. Gil, M. Hoffman, J. Pilgrim, T. Brooks, C. G. Mittermeier, J. Lamoreux, and G. A. B. Fonseca, eds. 2004. *Hotspots Revisited: Earth's Biologically Richest and Most Endangered Terrestrial Ecoregions*. Chicago: University of Chicago Press.

Mol, Annemarie, Ingunn Moser, and Jeannette Pols, eds. 2010. *Care in Practice: On Tinkering in Clinics, Homes and Farms*. New York: Columbia University Press.

Mondardo, Marcos Leandro. 2010. "A 'Territorialização' do Agronegócio Globalizado em Barreiras–BA: Migração Sulista, Reestruturação Produtiva e Contradições Sócio-Territoriais." *Revista NERA* 13 (17): 112–30.

Moraes, Maria Dione de Carvalho. 2000. "Memorias de um Sertão Desencantado: Modernização Agricola, Narrativas e Atores Sociais nos Cerrados do Sudoeste Piauiense." PhD diss., Universidade Estadual do Campinas.

Morais, Richard C. 2005. "The Great Brazilian Land Grab." *Forbes*, July 25, 2005. https://www.forbes.com/global/2005/0725/052.

Motta, Paulo E. F., Nilton Curi, and Donald P. Franzmeier. 2002. "Relation of Soils and Geomorphic Surfaces in the Brazilian Cerrado." In *The Cerrados of Brazil: Ecology and Natural History of a Neotropical Savanna*, edited by Paolo S. Oliveira and Robert J. Marquis, 13–32. New York: Columbia University Press.

Moura, Bianca de Castro Duarte, and Janes Terezinha Lavoratti. 2012. "Disparidades Socioeconômicas no Contexto Agrícola do Oeste Baiano." *Encontro Nacional de Geografia Agraria XXI*.

Moura, Jadson B., and Juliana S. R. Cabral. 2019. "Mycorrhizas in Central Savannahs: Cerrado and Caatinga." In *Mycorrhizal Fungi in South America*, edited by Marcela C. Pagano and Mónica A. Lugo, 193–202. Fungal Biology. Cham: Springer International.

Moura, Rennan Felipe Martins. 2017. "Fronteiras de Expansão da Soja no Oeste Baiano: Confrontos entre Produção Agrária e Crítica Socioambiental." PhD diss., Universidade Federal da Brasilia.

Myers, Norman, Russell A. Mittermeier, Cristina G. Mittermeier, Gustavo A. B. da Fonseca, and Jennifer Kent. 2000. "Biodiversity Hotspots for Conservation Priorities." *Nature* 403 (6772): 853–58.

Nader, Laura. 1972. "Up the Anthropologist: Perspectives Gained from Studying Up." In *Reinventing Anthropology*, edited by Dell H. Hymes, 284–311. New York: Pantheon Books.

Naylor, George. 2017. "Preface: Agricultural Parity for Land De-Commodification." In *Land Justice: Re-Imagining Land, Food, and the Commons in the United States*, edited by Justine M. Williams and Eric Holt-Giménez, xviii–xxii. Oakland, CA: Food First Books.

Nehring, Ryan. 2016. "Yield of Dreams: Marching West and the Politics of Scientific Knowledge in the Brazilian Agricultural Research Corporation (Embrapa)." *Geoforum* 77 (Supplement C): 206–17.

Nogueira, Mônica Celeida Rabelo. 2009. "Gerais a dentro e a fora: Identidade e Territorialidade entre Geraizeiros do Norte de Minas Gerais." PhD diss., Universidade Federal de Brasilia.

North Carolina Council of Churches. 2013. "'God Made a Farmer'—But What About Farmworkers?" NC Council of Churches. February 6, 2013. https://www.ncchurches.org/2013/02/god-made-a-farmer-but-what-about-farmworkers/.

Ofstehage, Andrew. 2010. "The Gift of the Middleman: An Ethnography of Quinoa Trading Networks in Los Lipez of Bolivia." Master's thesis, Wageningen University.

——. 2011. "Nusta Juira's Gift: Transforming the Market Economy through Alternative Development." *Anthropology of Work Review* 32 (2): 103–14.

——. 2012. "The Construction of an Alternative Quinoa Economy: Balancing Solidarity, Household Needs, and Profit in San Agustín, Bolivia." *Agriculture and Human Values* 29 (4): 441–54.

——. 2016. "Farming Is Easy, Becoming Brazilian Is Hard: North American Soy Farmers' Social Values of Production, Work and Land in Soylandia." *Journal of Peasant Studies* 43 (2): 442–60.

——. 2017a. "Encounters with the Brazilian Soybean Boom: Transnational Farmers and the Cerrado." In *Food, Agriculture and Social Change: The Vitality of Latin America*, edited by Stephen Sherwood, Alberto Arce, and Myriam Paredes, 60–72. London: Earthscan.

——. 2017b. "From US Farm Crisis to the Cerrado Soy Frontier: Financializing Farming and Exporting Farmers." In *Land Justice: Re-Imagining Land, Food, and the Commons in the United States*, edited by Eric Holt-Giménez and Justine Williams, 174–90. Oakland, CA: Food First Books.

——. 2018a. "Farming out of Place: Transnational Family Farmers, Flexible Farming, and the Rupture of Rural Life in Bahia, Brazil." *American Ethnologist* 45 (3): 317–29.

——. 2018b. "Financialization of Work, Value, and Social Organization among Transnational Soy Farmers in the Brazilian Cerrado." *Economic Anthropology* 5 (2): 274–85.

——. 2018c. "'When We Came There Was Nothing': Land, Work, and Value among Transnational Soybean Farmers in the Brazilian Cerrado." PhD diss., University of North Carolina.

——. 2019. "Transmission of the Brazil Model of Industrial Soybean Production: A Comparative Study of Two Migrant Farming Communities in the Brazilian Cerrado." In *In Defense of Farmers: The Future of Agriculture in the Shadow of Corporate Power*, edited by Jane W. Gibson and Sara Alexander, 289–324. Lincoln: University of Nebraska Press.

——. 2020. "Farming." *Cambridge Encyclopedia of Anthropology*. January 2020. https://www.anthroencyclopedia.com/entry/farming.

——. 2021a. "Economy and Development." In *Sage Handbook for Cultural Anthropology*, edited by Lisa Cligget and Lene Pedersen, 261–78. London: SAGE Publications.

——. 2021b. "Working the Plantationocene." *Exertions*, February 2021. https://saw.americananthro.org/pub/working-the-plantationocene/release/1.

——. 2022. "Tidy Fields and Clean Shirts: A Comparative Ethnography of Good Farming in South Dakota and Luis Eduardo Magalhães." *Culture, Agriculture, Food and Environment* 44 (1): 63–75.

——. 2023. "Making Soil in the Plantationocene." *Journal of Peasant Studies* 51 (3): 603–23.

——. 2024. "Wasteland and Paradise Garden: Building Soil in the Brazilian Cerrado." In *The Social Lives of Land*, edited by Michael Goldman, Nancy Lee Peluso, and Wendy Wolford, 168–89. Ithaca, NY: Cornell University Press.

Ofstehage, Andrew, and Ryan Nehring. 2021. "No-Till Agriculture and the Deception of Sustainability in Brazil." *International Journal of Agricultural Sustainability* 19 (3–4): 335–48.

Ofstehage, Andrew, Wendy Wolford, and Saturnino M. Borras Jr. 2022. "Contemporary Populism and the Environment." *Annual Review of Environment and Resources* 47:671–96.

Oliveira, Gustavo. 2016. "The Geopolitics of Brazilian Soybeans." *Journal of Peasant Studies* 43 (2): 348–72.

——. 2018. "Chinese Land Grabs in Brazil? Sinophobia and Foreign Investments in Brazilian Soybean Agribusiness." *Globalizations* 15 (1): 114–30.

Oliveira, Gustavo de L. T., and Mindi Schneider. 2016. "The Politics of Flexing Soybeans: China, Brazil and Global Agroindustrial Restructuring." *Journal of Peasant Studies* 43 (1): 167–94.

Oliveira, Gustavo, and Susanna Hecht. 2016. "Sacred Groves, Sacrifice Zones and Soy Production: Globalization, Intensification and Neo-Nature in South America." *Journal of Peasant Studies* 43 (2): 251–85.

Oliveira, Júlio Ernesto Souza de. 2022. "A Saga da Soja Nipo-Brasileira: Ditadura Militar e Implementação do PRODECER nos Cerrados Brasileiros (1964–1979)." PhD diss., Universidade Federal da Bahia.

Oliveira, Lucia Lippi. 1993. "Bandeirantes e Pioneiros: As Fronteiras no Brasil e nos Estado Unidos." *Revista Novos Estudos* 37 (3): 214–24.

Oliveira, R. S., L. Bezerra, E. A. Davidson, F. Pinto, C. A. Klink, D. C. Nepstad, and A. Moreira. 2005. "Deep Root Function in Soil Water Dynamics in Cerrado Savannas of Central Brazil." *Functional Ecology* 19 (4): 574–81.

Oliveira Santana, Jéssica Cauana de, and Marcelo Fragomeni Simon. 2022. "Plant Diversity Conservation in an Agricultural Frontier in the Brazilian Cerrado." *Biodiversity and Conservation* 31 (2): 667–81.

Ouma, Stefan. 2016. "From Financialization to Operations of Capital: Historicizing and Disentangling the Finance–Farmland–Nexus." *Geoforum* 72 (June): 82–93.

Palma, Vittoria Di. 2014. *Wasteland: A History*. New Haven, CT: Yale University Press.

Palmeira, Moacir, and Beatriz M. A. de Heredia. 2009. "Migrações em Áreas de Agronegócio." *TRAVESSIA—Revista do Migrante*, no. 65: 71–88.

Paredes, Myriam, Stephen Sherwood, and Alberto Arce. 2015. "La Contingencia del Cambio Social en la Agricultura y la Alimentación en América Latina." *Íconos: Revista de Ciencias Sociales* 20 (54): 11–25.

Peine, Emelie. 2010. "Corporate Mobilization on the Soybean Frontier of Mato Grosso, Brazil." In *Contesting Development: Critical Struggles for Social Change*, edited by Philip McMichael, 132–46. New York: Routledge.

——. 2021. "Chinese Investment in the Brazilian Soybean Sector: Navigating Relations of Private Governance." *Journal of Agrarian Change* 21 (1): 71–89.

Pereira, Alexia Saleme Aona de Paula, Vitor Juste dos Santos, Sabrina do Carmo Alves, Arthur Amaral e Silva, Charles Gomes da Silva, and Maria Lúcia Calijuri. 2022. "Contribution of Rural Settlements to the Deforestation Dynamics in the Legal Amazon." *Land Use Policy* 115 (April): 106039.

Penniman, Leah, and Karen Washington. 2018. *Farming While Black: Soul Fire Farm's Practical Guide to Liberation on the Land*. White River Junction, VT: Chelsea Green.

Pereira, João Baptista Borges. 2002. *Italianos no Mundo Rural Paulista*. São Paulo: Edusp.

Perry, Keisha-Khan Y. 2013. *Black Women against the Land Grab: The Fight for Racial Justice in Brazil*. Minneapolis: University of Minnesota Press.

Pinheiro, Maria Bueno, and R. Monteiro. 2010. "Contribution to the Discussions on the Origin of the Cerrado Biome: Brazilian Savanna." *Brazilian Journal of Biology* 70 (1): 95–102.

Pires, Mauro Oliveira, and Mauro Oliveira Pires. 2020. "'Cerrado': Old and New Agricultural Frontiers." *Brazilian Political Science Review* 14 (3).

Polizel, Silvia Palotti, Rita Marcia da Silva Pinto Vieira, João Pompeu, Yara da Cruz Ferreira, Eráclito Rodrigues de Sousa-Neto, Alexandre Augusto Barbosa, and Jean Pierre Henry Balbaud Ometto. 2021. "Analysing the Dynamics of Land Use in the Context of Current Conservation Policies and Land Tenure in the Cerrado—MATOPIBA Region (Brazil)." *Land Use Policy* 109 (October): 105713.

Pompeia, Caio. 2024. "*Agri-Bolsonarism*: A Movement Led by Agricultural Elites and Far-Right Politicians in Brazil. *Journal of Peasant Studies*. https://doi.org/10.108 0/03066150.2023.2301440.

Qin, Siyu, Marie Pratzer, Patrick Meyfroidt, and Tobias Kuemmerle. 2023. "Changing Determinants of International Conservation Funding Committed to Major Deforestation Regions in South America." *Biological Conservation* 288 (December): 110362.

Rausch, Lisa L., Holly K. Gibbs, Ian Schelly, Amintas Brandão Jr., Douglas C. Morton, Arnaldo Carneiro Filho, Bernardo Strassburg et al. 2019. "Soy Expansion in Brazil's Cerrado." *Conservation Letters* 12 (6): e12671.

Rede Social de Justiça e Direitos Humanos. 2018. "Imobiliárias Agrícolas Transnacionais e a Especulação com Terras na Região do MATOPIBA." Rede Social de Justiça e Direitos Humanos, GRAIN, Iner Pares, and Solidarity Sweden–Latin America. https://www.social.org.br/index.php/pub/revistas-portugues/207-imobilia-rias-agri-colas-transnacionais-e-a-especulac-a-o-com-terras-na-regia-o-do-matopiba.html.

Ribeiro, Ricardo Ferreira. 2008. "Da Amazônia para o Cerrado: As Reservas Extrativistas como Estratégias Sócioambientais de Conservação." *Sinapse Ambiental* 5 (1): 12–32.

Ricardo, Cassiano. 1956. *La Marcha Hacia el Oeste: La Influencia de la "Bandeira" en la Formación Social y Política del Brasil*. Mexico: Fondo de Cultura Económica.

Rigonato, Valney Dias. 2013. "As Representações Sociais dos Cerrados: Um Estudo de Caso no Colégio Alexandre Leal Costa, no Oeste da Bahia." *Boletim Goiano de Geografia* 33 (2): 239–58.

Riley, Mark, and Bethany Robertson. 2022. "The Virtual Good Farmer: Farmers' Use of Social Media and the (Re)Presentation of 'Good Farming.'" *Sociologia Ruralis* 62 (3): 437–58.

Rissing, Andrea, and Bradley M. Jones. 2022. "Landscapes of Value." *Economic Anthropology* 9 (2): 193–206.

Rodrigues, Roberto. 2016. "PRODECER: An Innovative International Cooperation Program." In *Development for Sustainable Agriculture*, edited by A. Hosono, C. M. C. da Rocha, and Y. Hongo, 220–34. London: Palgrave Macmillan.

Rogers, Thomas D. 2010. *The Deepest Wounds: A Labor and Environmental History of Sugar in Northeast Brazil*. Illustrated edition. Chapel Hill: University of North Carolina Press.

Rosenberg, Gabriel N. 2015. *The 4-H Harvest: Sexuality and the State in Rural America*. Philadelphia: University of Pennsylvania Press.

Russo Lopes, Gabriela, and Mairon G. Bastos Lima. 2020. "Necropolitics in the Jungle: COVID-19 and the Marginalisation of Brazil's Forest Peoples." *Bulletin of Latin American Research* 39 (S1): 92–97.

——. 2022. "Understanding Deforestation Lock-In: Insights from Land Reform Settlements in the Brazilian Amazon." *Frontiers in Forests and Global Change* 5. https://doi.org/10.3389/ffgc.2022.951290.

Russo Lopes, Gabriela, Mairon G. Bastos Lima, and Tiago N. P. dos Reis. 2021. "Maldevelopment Revisited: Inclusiveness and Social Impacts of Soy Expansion over Brazil's Cerrado in Matopiba." *World Development* 139 (March): 105316.

Sachs, Honor. 2015. *Home Rule: Households, Manhood, and National Expansion on the Eighteenth-Century Kentucky Frontier*. New Haven, CT: Yale University Press.

Sano, Edson Eyji, Luiz Alberto Dambrós, Geraldo César Oliveira, and Ricardo Seixas Brites. 2007. "Padrões de Cobertura de Solos do Estado de Goiás." In *A Encruzilhada Socioambiental: Biodiversidade, Economia e Sustentabilidade no Cerrado*, edited by Laerte Guimarães Ferreira Jr., 85–100. Goiânia: Editora UFG.

Santos, Bianca Suzy dos Reis dos. 2020. "O conflito pela Água em Correntina (BA): Narrativas e Disputas no Vale do Arrojado." PhD diss., Universidade Federal do Flurinense.

Santos, José Vicente Tavares dos. 1991. "As Novas Terras como Forma de Dominação." *Lua Nova: Revista de Cultura e Política*, no. 23: 67–82.

——. 1993. *Matuchos: Exclusão e Luta: do Sul para a Amazônia*. Petrópolis: Vozes.

Santos, Lusineide dos. 2021. "Bahia: A Grilagem e a Luta pelo Território / Bahia: The Land Grab and the Fight for the Territory." *Rede Cerrado* (blog). https://redecerrado.org.br/historiasdocerrado/en/bahia/.

Santos, Milton. 2012. *Natureza do Espaco*. São Paulo: Edusp.

Santos, Milton, and Maria Laura Silveira. 2001. *O Brasil: Territorio e Sociedade no Inicio do Seculo XXI*. Rio de Janeiro: Editora Record.

Santos, Rafael S., Martin Wiesmeier, Maurício R. Cherubin, Dener M. S. Oliveira, Jorge L. Locatelli, Marquel Holzschuh, and Carlos E. P. Cerri. 2021. "Consequences of Land-Use Change in Brazil's New Agricultural Frontier: A Soil Physical Health Assessment." *Geoderma* 400 (15): 115149.

Sauer, Sérgio, Acacio Zuniga Leite, and Nilton Luís Godoy Tubino. 2020. "Agenda Política da Terra no Governo Bolsonaro." *Revista da ANPEGE* 16 (29): 285–318.

Sauer, Sérgio, and Sergio Pereira Leite. 2012. "Agrarian Structure, Foreign Investment in Land, and Land Prices in Brazil." *Journal of Peasant Studies* 39 (3–4): 873–98.

Sawyer, Donald. 2009. "Fluxos de Carbono na Amazônia e no Cerrado: Um Olhar Socioecossistêmico." *Sociedade e Estado* 24 (1): 149–71.

Schlosser, Janne Bandeira de Almeida Souza. 2014. "Características Históricas e da Gestão de Políticas Públicas de Cultura do Município de Luís Eduardo Magalhães." PhD diss., Universidade Federal da Bahia.

Scott, Parry, and Dayse Amâncio dos Santos. 2014. "Flexibilidade, Liberdade e Direitos: Políticas e Práticas de Trabalho de Mulheres Migrantes no Polo de Fruticultura do Rio São Francisco–PE." *Vivência: Revista de Antropologia* 1 (43): 29–46.

Sexsmith, Kathleen. 2019. "Decoding Worker 'Reliability': Modern Agrarian Values and Immigrant Labor on New York Dairy Farms." *Rural Sociology* 84 (4): 706–35.

Shirley, Robert W. 1971. *The End of a Tradition: Culture Change and Development in the Município of Cunha, São Paulo, Brazil.* New York: Columbia University Press.

Silva, Camilla de Almeida, Marilda Aparecida de Menezes, and Roberto Véras de Oliveira. 2018. "Às Margens do Desenvolvimento: O Trabalho das Mulheres e a Luta por Direitos no Polo de Fruticultura de Petrolina/PE–Juazeiro/BA." *Cadernos Pagu* 52:e185208.

Silva, Claiton Márcio da. 2012. "De um Dust Bowl Paulista à Busca de Fertilidade no Cerrado: A Trajetória do IRI Research Institute e as Pesquisas em Ciências do Solo no Brasil (1951–1963)." *Revista Brasileira de História da Ciência* 5 (1): 146–55.

———. 2019. "The Barren Side of Brazil: Science, Water Resources, and the Debate on the (In)Fertile Soils of the Brazilian Cerrado, 1892–1942." *História, Ciências, Saúde-Manguinhos* 26 (2): 483–500.

Silva Coutinho, Elen da, Guiomar Inez Germani, and Gilca Garcia de Oliveira. 2013. "Expansão da Fronteira Agrícola e Suas Relaçõs com o Trabalho Análogo a de Escravo no Oeste da Bahia." *Brasiliana: Journal for Brazilian Studies* 2 (2): 236–63.

Silva, Queina Lima da. 2018. "Educação do Campo e Luta pela Terra no Contexto MATOPIBA: Um Estudo de Caso sobre o Acampamento Zequinha Barreto, no Oeste Baiano." PhD diss., Universidade Federal da Brasilia.

Smythe, William Ellsworth. 1905. *The Conquest of Arid America.* New York: Macmillan.

Soares-Filho, Britaldo, Raoni Rajão, Marcia Macedo, Arnaldo Carneiro, William Costa, Michael Coe, Hermann Rodrigues, and Ane Alencar. 2014. "Cracking Brazil's Forest Code." *Science* 344 (6182): 363–64.

Sobrinho, Sousa, and José de. 2012. "O Camponês Geraizeiro no Oeste da Bahia: As Terras de Uso Comum e a Propriedade Capitalista da Terra." PhD thesis, Universidade de São Paulo.

Sodikoff, Genese Marie. 2012. *Forest and Labor in Madagascar: From Colonial Concession to Global Biosphere.* Bloomington: Indiana University Press.

Soruco, Ximena, Wilfredo Plata, and Gustavo Medeiros. 2008. *Los Barones del Oriente: El Poder en Santa Cruz Ayer y Hoy.* Santa Cruz, Bolivia: Fundacion Tierra.

Stein, Serena, and Jessie Luna. 2021. "Toxic Sensorium: Agrochemicals in the African Anthropocene." *Environment and Society* 12 (1): 87–107.

Stein, Stanley J. 1986. *Vassouras: A Brazilian Coffee County, 1850–1900; The Roles of Planter and Slave in a Plantation Society.* Reprint edition. Princeton, NJ: Princeton University Press.

Stengers, Isabelle. 2010. *Cosmopolitics II.* Minneapolis: University of Minnesota Press.

Styles, Megan. 2019. *Roses from Kenya: Labor, Environment, and the Global Trade in Cut Flowers.* Seattle: University of Washington Press.

Summerville, Melanie, and André Magnan. 2015. "'Pinstripes on the Prairies': Examining the Financialization of Farming Systems in the Canadian Prairie Provinces." *Journal of Peasant Studies* 42 (1): 119–44.

Suzuki, Taku. 2006. "Becoming 'Japanese' in Bolivia: Okinawan-Bolivian Trans(National) Formations in Colonial Okinawa." *Identities: Global Studies in Culture and Power* 13 (3): 455–81.

Tanaka, Akihiko. 2016. Foreword to *Development for Sustainable Agriculture: The Brazilian Cerrado*, edited by Akio Hosono, Carlos Magno Campos da Rocha, and Yutaka Hongo, x–xi. New York: Palgrave Macmillan.

Thompson, James. 2014. "Secrets of the Brazilian Mega-Farmers: Management Tips from Your Toughest Competitors." *Farm Futures*, 2014.

Togni, Pedro H. B., Madelaine Venzon, Lucas M. Souza, João P. C. R. Santos, and Edison R. Sujii. 2019. "Biodiversity Provides Whitefly Biological Control Based on Farm Management." *Journal of Pest Science* 92 (2): 393–403.

Top'Tiro, Hiparidi. 2009. "My Cerrado." *Cultural Survival Quarterly* (September 2009). https://www.culturalsurvival.org/publications/cultural-survival-quarterly/my-cerrado.

Tsing, Anna Lowenhaupt. 2011. *Friction: An Ethnography of Global Connection*. Princeton, NJ: Princeton University Press.

——. 2015. *The Mushroom at the End of the World: On the Possibility of Life in Capitalist Ruins*. Princeton, NJ: Princeton University Press.

Tsing, Anna Lowenhaupt, Andrew S. Mathews, and Nils Bubandt. 2019. "Patchy Anthropocene: Landscape Structure, Multispecies History, and the Retooling of Anthropology; An Introduction to Supplement 20." *Current Anthropology* 60 (S20).

Tsing, Anna, Heather Swanson, Elaine Gan, and Nils Bubandt. 2017. *Arts of Living on a Damaged Planet*. Minneapolis: University of Minnesota Press.

Turner, Frederick Jackson. 1893. "The Significance of the Frontier in American History." In *Annual Report of the American Historical Association*, 197–227. Chicago: American Historical Association. https://nationalhumanitiescenter.org/pds/gilded/empire/text1/turner.pdf.

Turner, Victor. 2017. *The Ritual Process: Structure and Anti-Structure*. New York: Routledge.

Valdivia, Gabriela. 2010. "Agrarian Capitalism and Struggles over Hegemony in the Bolivian Lowlands." *Latin American Perspectives* 37 (4): 67–87.

——. 2015. "The Sacrificial Zones of 'Progressive' Extraction in Andean Latin America." *Latin American Research Review* 50 (3): 245–53.

Vale, Mariana M., Erika Berenguer, Marcio Argollo de Menezes, Ernesto B. Viveiros de Castro, Ludmila Pugliese de Siqueira, and Rita de Cássia Q. Portela. 2021. "The COVID-19 Pandemic as an Opportunity to Weaken Environmental Protection in Brazil." *Biological Conservation* 255 (March): 108994.

VanWinkle, Tony N. 2018. "Weeds, Herbicides, and Bodies: Emerging Entanglements in Toxic Agricultural Landscapes." *Engagements* (blog). March 8, 2018. https://aesengagement.wordpress.com/2018/03/08/weeds-herbicides-and-bodies-emerging-entanglements-in-toxic-agricultural-landscapes/.

VanWinkle, Tony N., and Jack R. Friedman. 2017. "What's Good for the Soil Is Good for the Soul: Scientific Farming, Environmental Subjectivities, and the Ethics of Stewardship in Southwestern Oklahoma." *Agriculture and Human Values* 34 (3): 607–18.

Vennet, Bert Vander, Sergio Schneider, and Joost Dessein. 2016. "Different Farming Styles behind the Homogenous Soy Production in Southern Brazil." *Journal of Peasant Studies* 43 (2): 396–418.

Voyles, Traci. 2015. *Wastelanding: Legacies of Uranium Mining in Navajo Country*. Minneapolis: University of Minnesota Press.

Waltz, Amber. 2016. "The Women Who Feed Us: Gender Empowerment (or Lack Thereof) in Rural Southern Brazil." *Journal of Rural Studies* 47 (October): 31–40.

Warrior, Carol Edelman. 2017. "Indigenous Collectives: A Meditation on Fixity and Flexibility." *American Indian Quarterly* 41 (4): 368–92.

Welch, James R. 2014. "Xavante Ritual Hunting: Anthropogenic Fire, Reciprocity, and Collective Landscape Management in the Brazilian Cerrado." *Human Ecology* 42 (1): 47–59.

Welch, James R., Eduardo S. Brondízio, Scott S. Hetrick, and Carlos E. A. Coimbra Jr. 2013. "Indigenous Burning as Conservation Practice: Neotropical Savanna Recovery amid Agribusiness Deforestation in Central Brazil." *PLOS ONE* 8 (12): e81226.

Westermeyer, William H. 2019. *Back to America: Identity, Political Culture, and the Tea Party Movement*. Lincoln: University of Nebraska Press.

Wesz Junior, Valdemar João. 2016. "Strategies and Hybrid Dynamics of Soy Transnational Companies in the Southern Cone." *Journal of Peasant Studies* 43 (2): 286–312.

Willems, Emilio. 1946. *A Aculturação dos Alemães no Brasil: Estudo Antropológico dos Emigrantes Alemães e Seus Descendentes no Brasil*. São Paolo: Companhia Editora Nacional.

Wolford, Wendy. 2010. *This Land Is Ours Now: Social Mobilization and the Meanings of Land in Brazil*. Durham, NC: Duke University Press.

——. 2021. "The Plantationocene: A Lusotropical Contribution to the Theory." *Annals of the American Association of Geographers* 111 (6): 1622–39.

Wolford, Wendy, and Ryan Nehring. 2015. "Constructing Parallels: Brazilian Expertise and the Commodification of Land, Labour and Money in Mozambique." *Canadian Journal of Development Studies/Revue Canadienne d'études du développement* 36 (2): 208–23.

Wright, Angus Lindsay, and Wendy Wolford. 2003. *To Inherit the Earth: The Landless Movement and the Struggle for a New Brazil*. Oakland, CA: Food First Books.

Yanagisako, Sylvia Junko. 2002. *Producing Culture and Capital: Family Firms in Italy*. Princeton, NJ: Princeton University Press.

Yeh, Emily T. 2013. *Taming Tibet: Landscape Transformation and the Gift of Chinese Development*. Ithaca, NY: Cornell University Press.

Zippay, Andrea. 2003. "Wallbrowns Pioneer Farming Abroad in Brazilian Countryside." *Farm and Dairy* (blog). July 24, 2003. http://www.farmanddairy. com/news/wallbrowns-pioneer-farming-abroad-in-brazilian-countryside/1057. html.

Zorzoli, Facundo. 2022. "Tierras Cansadas: Agronegocios, Acumulación y Naturaleza en el Sudoeste del Gran Chaco." PhD thesis, Universidad de Buenos Aires.

Index

www.ingramcontent.com/pod-product-compliance
Lightning Source LLC
Chambersburg PA
CBHW032348280326
41935CB00008B/496